Shakespeare Plays the Classroom

—☙

Edited by Stuart E. Omans and Maurice J. O'Sullivan

Pineapple Press, Inc.
Sarasota, Florida

Inquiries should be addressed to:

Pineapple Press, Inc.
P.O. Box 3889
Sarasota, Florida 34230

www.pineapplepress.com

Library of Congress Cataloging-in-Publication Data

Shakespeare plays the classroom / edited by Stuart E. Omans and Maurice J. O'Sullivan.–1st ed.
    p.   cm.
ISBN 1-56164-277-0 (alk. paper)
1. Shakespeare, William, 1564–1616–Study and teaching. I. O'Sullivan, Maurice, 1944–   . II. Omans, Stuart E., 1940–   .

PR2987 .S486 2003
822.3'3–dc21   2003001168

First Edition
10 9 8 7 6 5 4 3 2 1

Design by Shé Sicks
Printed in the United States of America

Front cover photo: Rehearsal of *A Midsummer Night's Dream* from *William Shakespeare: The Extraordinary Life of the Most Successful Writer of All Time* by Andrew Gurr. Photographs by Dominic Clemence. Copyright 1995 by HarperCollins Publishers Ltd. Reprinted by permission of HarperCollins Publishers, Inc.

Contents

Introduction

On Play and Plays

Maurice J. O'Sullivan and Stuart E. Omans

Maurice O'Sullivan is Kenneth Curry Professor of English at Rollins College and a cofounder of the Drey Shakespeare Institutes.

Stuart Omans is a professor at the University of Central Florida and codirector of the Drey Shakespeare Institutes. He was a founding director of the Orlando Shakespeare Festival.

IN 1997 CHARLOTTE GEYER AND DONNA MILLER of the Central Florida Branch of the English-Speaking Union talked with us about developing a summer program for teachers. After decades of providing scholarships that allowed Florida teachers to study in the United Kingdom and brought British teachers to Central Florida, the ESU wanted to use a generous bequest from Jessie and Eugene Drey to expand its support of education.

As a result of these discussions, we developed the English-Speaking Union Drey Summer Shakespeare Institute at Rollins College, a series of annual two-week, multidisciplinary workshops focusing on teaching Shakespeare through performance and based on our idea that at the heart of the plays lies the idea of play. Most contemporary American high school students look on studying *Romeo and Juliet*, *Julius Caesar*, or *A Midsummer Night's Dream* as work. The plays' language, conventions, and complexity seem like the products of an alien, archaic, frustrating parallel universe. But offered a chance to interpret and perform scenes from those plays, these same students realize that they are engaged in a playfulness of extraordinary importance and come to understand the power of play to change lives.

The English and social science teachers we knew had a wonderful understanding of the plays as texts but few had extensive experience with theater. Our goal became to establish a series of dialogues between teachers and theater professionals and to turn teachers back into students who would perform scenes from the plays. During the two weeks of each Drey Institute, teachers experience the same terrors and exhilaration, frustrations and victories as their own students do in convincing an audience to suspend its disbelief and imagine itself in Caesar's Senate, Juliet's bedroom, or Puck's woods. To explore the full potential of those scenes, we have the teachers interact with a wide range of experts—actors, directors, costumers, set designers, artists, musicians, and even a certified fight choreographer.

As the program evolved, our alumni recommended colleagues who brought to the institutes their energy and creativity. What they asked from us was information and direction, ideas and resources. Our consultants developed workshops to provide historical contexts and to allow teachers to experience the challenge of embodying a character, choreographing a duel, and building an ensemble. The performance-based pedagogy that participants have adopted for their classrooms has touched thousands of students and resulted in an explosion of theatrical productions, Renaissance fairs, student acting, and cross-disciplinary teaching. As teachers have brought back to us new ideas from their classroom experience, we have added them to the institutes. This constant reciprocity has kept the programs fresh and vital.

Shakespeare Plays the Classroom is an attempt to distill some of that experience by bringing practical, pedagogical, and historical information together with personal accounts. Our ultimate goal is to help teachers understand the many ways to make classical theater immediate and compelling for their students. To that end we have gathered essays from internationally known actors and scholars, from theater professionals who have worked with the English-Speaking Union Drey Institutes, and from teachers who have integrated these ideas into their classrooms.

These essays blend practical advice with personal stories to show how the ideas and techniques discussed here demonstrate the ways they have transformed the classroom experience for both teachers and students. A unique dimension of the book comes from the contributing professional artists who ordinarily restrict their insights to the private confines of a rehearsal space or behind-the-scenes technical working spaces. By offering an opportunity to eavesdrop on the backstage thoughts of a Royal Shakespeare Company actor, a Broadway actor, and one of England's most highly regarded designers and costumers, this collection can share with a far wider audience some of the experiences the Drey programs have made possible.

We have organized the essays into five sections or acts, all of which emphasize the importance of play. The first, *Playing with Shakespeare*, introduces some of the preliminary issues of transforming students into performers. For the second section, *Playing with Language and Character*, a distinguished group of actors discuss ways of helping modern students speak and feel the language of the Renaissance. The third section, *Playing with Productions*, focuses on such technical aspects of production as music, costume, and duels. The fourth one, *Playing with Texts*, explores ways of editing and reimagining the texts. Finally, *Playing with Challenges* discusses the challenges of teaching Shakespeare in the complex, diverse cultural environment that Florida has become.

To extend the ideas *Shakespeare Plays the Classroom* explores, we have created a complementary web site, www.shakespeareplaysthe-classroom.com. It includes lists of educational programs available through Florida theaters, adapted versions of Shakespeare's plays, exercises created by Florida teachers, an annotated filmography, and announcements of additional programs.

Acknowledgments

We would like to thank our wives, Jan and Sue, for their continuing patience and support; our mothers, Bess Omans and Agnes O'Sullivan, for fostering our love of literature and the arts; our colleagues, the staff, and administrators at Rollins for encouraging us to pursue our interests in connections among all teachers and students; our board of advisors from the Florida Center for Shakespeare Studies; and the extraordinary group of teachers who have passed through the ESU Drey Summer Institutes and shown us again and again what is best about our schools. In particular, we would like to thank Karen Slater and her staff for their continuing work on the institutes; Alicia Stevens for her editing skills; Brianne Bergeron for her genius in indexing; President Rita Bornstein of Rollins for her constant enthusiasm and encouragement for our programs; Steve Briggs and Roger Casey for their steady support; and Charlotte Geyer, Donna Miller, Trudy McNair, Joan Leslie, and Bob Pittman of the Central Florida English Speaking Union for their advice and guidance.

Above all, however, we thank Jessie and Eugene Drey for their legacy and commitment to education and the Central Florida Branch of the English-Speaking Union for holding fast to its belief in the power and importance of language and education. To them we dedicate *Shakespeare Plays the Classroom*.

–Maurice O'Sullivan, Rollins College
–Stuart E. Omans, University of Central Florida

Foreword

Play's the Thing

—ᘐ

John F. Andrews

John Andrews, a former editor of the Shakespeare Quarterly, *founder and CEO of the
Shakespeare Guild, and Executive Director of the Washington, D.C. Branch of the
English-Speaking Union, has worked with all the major Shakespeareans and presides each
year over the international gathering that has presented the Sir John Gielgud Award to
such distinguished figures as Sir Ian McKellen, Dame Judith Densch, and Sir Derek
Jacobi. Here he recalls his experiences with the legendary Jonathan Miller as he went
about the task of producing Shakespeare for the BBC.*

—ᘐ

WHEN STUART OMANS AND MAURICE O'SULLIVAN told me about
Shakespeare Plays the Classroom, and invited me to contribute a foreword to
the volume, I immediately thought back to earlier occasions when I've
had the good fortune to take part in, or provide a consultant's perspective on, their artistic and educational endeavors. I've always been
impressed by how imaginative, well planned, and edifying they are, and
I've invariably found them stimulating.

Several of the programs Stu supervised in the late 1980s and early
1990s were made possible by grants from the National Endowment for
the Humanities. This was an agency with which I'd been associated
both as a project director and as a division administrator, and I knew it
as one that sought to invest its resources in exemplary initiatives whose
benefits could be extended to multiple settings. Stu's programs have
always met that criterion, and many of them have drawn supplemental
funding from the Orlando Shakespeare Festival, which he established,
and from the University of Central Florida, whose English department
he'd headed prior to his bold decision to take on new challenges as a
theater producer.

As a former editor of *The Shakespeare Quarterly,* I have also been
aware of Socky O'Sullivan's books, especially his award-winning works
on popular culture and his *Shakespeare's Other Lives.* With extensive experience in organizing workshops and programs with teachers and as a
teaching consultant and department and division chair at Rollins, Socky

brings a wide range of talents to the Drey programs.

As I've observed the activities these inspiring and dedicated educators have overseen since the mid-'90s, I've become increasingly aware of another key partner in their ventures, a branch of the English-Speaking Union whose philanthropy has made a significant difference in one of America's most dynamic metropolitan areas. By happy coincidence I now devote a good deal of my own time to an ESU constituency that serves the National Capital region, and it pleases me enormously to commend the generosity of my associates in the Sunshine State and extol the impact their wise disbursements have had upon the teaching, performance, and appreciation of drama and literature, not only in their own locale, but in dozens of others that have been touched by the kind of energy that animates this anthology.

Its pleasures are rich and multifaceted, and I'm pleased to note that many of them derive from such unexpected juxtapositions as an essay on Shakespeare's concept of neighborhood by the inimitable Fred Rogers. That, for me, is a wonderful treat. And that is why I'm persuaded that *play* is so aptly singled out as the theme for this collection. After all, it focuses upon the writings of an author for whom *recreation* appears to have retained its primal link with *re-creation*. That link echoes through virtually all of the essays in this collection, as Ben Gunter shows ways to play with physical space, Ian Borden suggests how to stage safe fights with teenage actors, and the remarkable Tony Church, the longest tenured actor with the Royal Shakespeare Company, reflects on his life in theater.

A couple of decades ago, in late July and early August of 1981, I had the good fortune to look in on what an extraordinary polymath was accomplishing as producer of a *Troilus and Cressida* which would soon take its place as one of the highlights of a series that was being telecast over PBS as *The Shakespeare Plays*. During that London sojourn I made three visits to the BBC Television Centre on Wood Lane, and I spent most of my time there in a sound-equipped booth watching Jonathan Miller and several of his colleagues while they in turn were fixed upon a bank of video monitors that enabled them to manage traffic in a studio two floors down. Miller wore a microphone as he worked. This allowed him to communicate with cameramen, technicians, and actors, and it permitted me to eavesdrop not only upon what was taking place below but upon what a fascinating intellectual was thinking and saying and doing as he instigated and reacted to it. While Miller moved about the monitor area and occasionally descended to the set to interact more immediately with the personnel involved in rehearsals and taping, I had an opportunity to observe him rearranging the composition of a particular shot, or making changes in the lighting or in the sound pickup, or suggesting that a different set of gestures, expressions, or vocal emphases be used by the perfomers in a given scene. Every once in a while he'd step into the producer's booth or invite me to walk around the set with him, commenting as he did so on what he was trying to accomplish and eliciting my opinions about how well his intentions were coming across. By the time I emerged from my privileged catbird seat, I felt that I'd learned a great deal about some of the problems a director faces in attempting to realize Shakespeare on television. And I came away reinforced in my view that Jonathan Miller is one of the true Renaissance men of our era, a genius whose creativity, intelligence, and sensitive wit are a continual source of astonishment for those who are lucky enough to spend some time in his presence.

In some ways Miller's orientation to the BBC Shakespeare series—at least for a maverick of the type he'd been in the past—seemed remarkably conservative. He'd spent a good deal of time doing archaeological spadework—endeavoring to discover, for example, what a Renaissance portrait artist contemporaneous with Shakespeare would have considered an appropriate way of costuming Mark Antony, or what a European painter would have represented as the ambience of a domestic interior for such settings as the ones we encounter in *The Taming of the Shrew*. Even more importantly, Miller had extended himself to become acquainted with what he called the "mental furniture" of those who attended, and whose sensibilities are thus reflected in, Shakespeare's plays at the Globe. As he'd pointed out during an interview several months earlier, a director "has to have at his disposal readings in the philosophy and history of the period which can all be brought to bear upon the unlocking of the themes that a complex imagination like Shakespeare's is working with. To assume that you can unlock that imagination merely by intuition," he'd gone on to say, "is to bring down Shakespeare to the level of a television hack writer. Here was a writer who was immersed in the themes and notions of his time. The only way in which you can unlock that imagination is to immerse yourself in the themes in which he was immersed."

In *Troilus and Cressida*, as in the earlier plays he had produced for the BBC sequence, Miller had given careful thought to every detail of setting, costume, and thematic emphasis. As usual, he'd drawn heavily on materials with which Shakespeare might have been familiar. His Greeks and Trojans were attired, for the most part, in ways that would have made them at home in Elizabethan or Jacobean England. His rooms were based on a perspective exercise book from Renaissance Italy. Amusingly, in keeping with the line sketches he admired in this tome, Miller had had his construction crew do everything possible to make the walls and edges of the set seem as unfinished and rough as they could be brought to look. His Grecian camp featured tents, weaponry, and other military paraphernalia of the sort that one would find depicted in such contemporary sources as German artillery manuals and English guide-books on battlefield tactics. In most respects, then, one found in the visual aspects of Miller's *Troilus and Cressida* the same kind of attention to historical nuance that had characterized his earlier experiments in the series.

Upon closer inspection, however, one saw in this production a degree of inventiveness that was new to *The Shakesepare Plays*. Over to one side in the Greek camp, for example—and never shown on camera so overtly as to make it more than a tongue-in-cheek footnote—was a bit of carpentry that would eventually become the Trojan Horse, at this point in its early stages of execution as the undergirding for a giant hoof. In the tent of Ajax was a pinup, wittily supplied from an art-book reproduction of Lucas Cranach's portrayal of Eve. On the breast-pockets of a few suggestively modern-looking olive-drab uniforms one saw hints of a name-tag of the sort that viewers would associate with the soldiers who appeared in the American television series *M*A*S*H*. Could it be, I asked, that Jonathan Miller really wanted us to think of that popular sit-com when we watched his *Troilus and Cressida*? Yes, indeed. He perceived a strong affinity between the lassitude and purposelessness of the Trojan War as depicted by Shakespeare and the boredom and cynicism with which the sensitive men and women in *M*A*S*H* approached their daily routines during a Korean Conflict that was clearly meant to suggest analogies with the Viet Nam War. What we got, in short, was a multi-layered vision, superimposing images and ideals from antecedents as diverse as Homeric epic, Chaucerian romance, Shakespearean coterie drama, and 20th-century political and military satire.

To my mind, the recipe that Jonathan Miller had concocted for his production of a seventeenth-century problem play was a delicious blend of whimsy and high-seriousness. And what it taught me was that we should never get so caught up in solemnity about the world's most influential dramatist as to forget that, as successful as they became, he and his fellow thespians never ceased to think of themselves as "merely players." That is the central motif of this volume, and it is a message that would have received wholehearted endorsement from the "sweet Swan of Avon."

Prologue

At Play in the Neighborhood

Fred Rogers

One of America's cultural icons, Fred Rogers, creator of Mr. Roger's
Neighborhood, *visits Mr. Shakespeare's neighborhood to reflect on the timeless
and crucial value of play and its ability to transform lives. The piece has been edited from a conversation Mr. Rogers had with Stuart Omans and Alan Nordstrom,
which turned out to be his last interview and thus perhaps his last words on play.*

Speak what we feel, not what we ought to say.
—*King Lear* V.iii.324

SHAKESPEARE CERTAINLY KNEW THE UNPARALLELED VALUE of authenticity. Personally, I think that the greatest teacher in the world is the person who can be authentic in front of his or her students . . . in front of
anybody! I remember when I worked at the Family and Children's
Center of the University of Pittsburgh. The director of that child development center was Dr. Margaret McFarland and she once invited a
well-known sculptor from the faculty of Carnegie Institute of
Technology (now Carnegie Mellon University) to come to our nursery
school. Dr. McFarland said to him, "I don't want you to teach sculpt-
ing. All I want you to do is to love clay in front of the children." And
that's what he did. He came once a week for a whole term, sat with the
four and five year olds as they played, and he "loved" his clay in front
of them. The adults who have worked at that center for many years
have said that not before nor since have the children in that school used
clay so imaginatively as when they had those visits from that sculptor
who obviously delighted in his medium. Yes, he loved it, and the children caught his enthusiasm for it, and that's what mattered. So, like
most good things, "teaching" has to do with honesty. In fact, I think the
greatest gift (the only unique gift) we can give anybody is the gift of our
honest self, be it in teaching or in any other relationship.

All children are creative; nevertheless, some are damaged from the moment they're born by being told or shown (or both) that they're not wanted. That can destroy much of their ego and creativity. On the other hand, there are those who have been devastatingly hurt yet have used their innate creativity to survive. If we are willing to search for it, all of us can find a spark that longs to be nurtured. Life is remarkable and the human spirit absolutely wonderful to behold.

Both the title and first sentence of our book *Playtime* (Philadelphia: Running Press, 2001) focus on the importance of play. "Child's play" is sometimes considered a phrase that means "trivial," but of course it's just the opposite. There's a great deal of work that goes into a child's play. For children to know that "what comes naturally" is something to be respected by those who happen to be their whole world—yes, their parents are their whole world—and to be able to look into their parents' faces and recognize that they're loved exactly as they are will make the greatest difference for good in any child's life.

As someone who has communicated with the very young through-out my life, I find that sometimes it can be hard for children to differ-entiate between what's real and what's pretend. There are two univer-sal things that a child of any age brings to any activity (any "produc-tion"): that particular child's personal history as well as that child's developmental tasks! Reading Erik Erikson's *Childhood and Society* (rev. ed. 1993) could be very helpful for anyone considering the different stages of a human being's development. How wonderful it would be if people who are exploring "performance" for students could work more closely with child-development programs. How enriching for everyone it could be to encourage—through drama—some kind of dialogue or tri-alogue among people in the disciplines of English literature, child devel-opment, and education!

When I started work in television, I was blessed to be able to study with Margaret McFarland and Ben Spock as well as with visiting pro-fessors Erik Erikson and Helen Ross and others. Margaret developed the university's "family and children's center" where we all worked. It was invaluable for me to have an ongoing conversation with these peo-ple so I could hear what the young people they had in school or in ther-apy were going through.

I remember one time I wanted to produce a Neighborhood program about fire. I took my ideas to Margaret (as I did with most Neighborhood themes). We met about three times a month reviewing my ideas for upcoming scripts, lyrics, props . . . everything. This particular time I said, "Margaret, I'd like to do something on the air about fire." She helped me to realize that it was essential to deal with control of fluids before even introducing anything about fire. I learned, for instance, that most children's dreams about fire center around their control of their own body fluids! That's how personal a "fire" can seem to a child.

So we produced films of children damming up streams and looking at waterfalls. We showed all kinds of things with the bathtub. And then, finally . . . a tiny fire—and I mean tiny—in the Neighborhood of Make-Believe. We didn't show flames, just some smoke; and the fire was put out in half a minute by the make-believe fire people.

When that Neighborhood week of programs aired (dealing with control of fluids on Monday, Tuesday, and Wednesday and a little fire quickly being put out on Thursday and talked about on Thursday and Friday), we still had seven calls of "complaint." I took every call that came in. Each parent told me that their child was very frightened by the fire in make believe. As gently as I could, I "interviewed" these parents on the phone. It turned out that every one of them had children with urinary difficulties. I was fascinated. If I hadn't had the developmental insight, I wouldn't have been able to begin to understand the obvious tie between what was presented on our program and the children's personal developmental concerns dealing with anything related to fire. Some of the stories I heard from those parents who called revealed that when their children went to the doctor for urinary examinations, the examinations themselves felt like "burning." All that reconfirmed my belief that it is absolutely essential to talk with professionals who are in touch with children regularly before planning a production that's meant to be of help.

During my university child development training, I worked with one boy in "play interviews" who really "stretched" me. We called our private sessions with children "play interviews" because Margaret told us, "You all are not trained therapists; you are trained observers and listeners." The things that children would play about in our "safe presence" were exceedingly helpful to our own professional development. Usually what they were playing about (with puppets or blocks or costumes) had to do with what was going on in their own lives. At any rate there was this one little boy who did everything he could to turn every man he met into an abusive father. Because of his home situation, that's all that he knew from men so that's what he had learned to expect. That boy was a master at being able to get me just to the edge of being very angry. Then I would remember, thanks to my supervision, that this is exactly what he was trying to do, and I must never give in, because one of the best things I could do for that boy was to let him know that all men are not abusive. He and I did a lot of puppet play together. That happened to be one of my mediums. After a while, he was able to use those puppets to talk through his hands. (Just that little bit of distance helped him to work things through.) That boy has since grown up to be a healthy man. He certainly taught me a lot. We helped each other grow. How fortunate we both were to have had such a nursery school and kindergarten with professionals who understood his personal developmental needs and my continuing educational needs.

Even though I had been accepted at Pittsburgh Theological Seminary right out of Rollins College, I decided to go to NBC in New York instead, because I had looked at television for the first time and thought, "This medium could be used for so much good. I'd like to learn how to work with it." Since I had a music degree from Rollins, the people at NBC assigned me the *NBC Opera Theater*, the *Voice of Firestone*, and the *Kate Smith Hour*. Eventually I became a floor manager for all three. I learned production from "behind" the camera. Two years later when I heard that educational television was starting in Pittsburgh, I applied. My friends at NBC thought I was crazy. They said, "That educational station isn't even on the air yet; and here you are in line to be a network producer, director, anything you want." But something (Someone) kept encouraging me to make the move.

So when I was hired in Pittsburgh to help start that educational television station, the general manager said, "Fred, you'll be the program manager for all the programs." So I said, "Fine, and we must be sure to do something for the children." Well, you know, fools rush in! We decided to do an hour a day five days a week. Imagine—five hours a week live for children! It was not *Mister Rogers' Neighborhood* then, it was *The Children's Corner*. I voiced and manipulated the puppets and played the organ for the hostess, Josie Carey.

During those eight years of *The Children's Corner* I decided to take some courses at Pittsburgh Seminary on my lunch hour. With only one course a semester, little by little I was able to study systematic theology, Greek and Hebrew, church history, homiletics, everything. I never expected that I'd be able to complete the Master of Divinity course; but finally, after eight years, I did. And with some encouragement from our presbytery I thought I might be able to produce a series for the Presbyterian Church. But at the last minute the media department of the national church discovered it didn't have enough money to do any programs at all. I was convinced, though, that I'd be used in some way; and sure enough the very next day after I heard the Presbyterian news, I got a call from the head of children's programming at the CBC in Canada asking if I would consider producing a daily program for their network—in Toronto! So Joanne and our two young sons and I moved to Toronto and lived there for over a year. In fact, it was there that I was encouraged to be seen on the air. "I've watched you talk with children, Fred," the supervising producer said. "I'd like to translate that kind of care to the television screen. Let's call this program "MisteRogers!" And we did! What a big change for me!

When we came back home from Canada, I wanted to know more about children, so that's when I signed up for the masters course in child development at the University of Pittsburgh and started working with Dr. McFarland and the rest of the Family and Children's Center staff.

When people ask me what I believe to be the most important contribution *Mister Rogers' Neighborhood* has made, I think it may be dealing as creatively as we know how with the developmental tasks of childhood. Such common things as grief or separation and return. These are enormously important challenges for people of all ages. After all, feelings from childhood (the pleasant and the tough) never go away. They may get hidden, but they're always part of who we are.

Several years ago, I happened to be watching a television cartoon program with some children. The animation was simple yet clear. There was a deep sea diver who dove to the bottom of a lake where he found a huge plug (like a bathtub drain plug!). The diver pulled the plug loose and water started surging down the hole at the bottom of the lake. Finally everything in the lake: the fish, the plants, the boats, the diver, EVERYTHING was sucked down the hole. Now I don't think that the creators and animators and producers of such a cartoon set out to frighten children with their work; nevertheless, any child who had any concern about being sucked down a bathroom drain (and most very young children do!) would certainly have found that cartoon horrifying. Those who created it were probably operating out of their own unresolved childhood fears; however, that is not the place from which to operate in order to create healthy productions for children. If those people (adult producers) had been well versed in the developmental themes and needs of childhood, they would have never produced such a cartoon for preschoolers. And what's more, there wasn't even an adult on the screen at the end of the cartoon saying, "That's just pretend. Something like that could never happen . . . except in pretending. Nobody could ever get sucked down a bathroom drain."

Responsible programming for children grows out of an understanding of what children are dealing with in their own lives . . . in other words, a deep respect for childhood.

I remember when we produced a special program for families after Robert Kennedy was killed. His assassination was the third in a row and the country was in deep grief. It felt very much like the September 11th events. After Kennedy's death, I said, "We've got to do something on the air." And so we went into the studio and produced a half-hour program. In it, little cars became one metaphor for "loss." As you watch children play in the film, cars go away and come back. We wanted to help with a wide range of separation themes: moving away, going to school, divorce, death. We knew the atmosphere of the country and we knew the kinds of concerns children had in their inside growing. Both were indispensable for producing responsible programming. That special was also a plea for parents to include their children in their own ways of handling sadness: some might take a walk in the woods, others might pray, others might make up stories or read books. Whatever was helpful in the family could become the beginning of a child's tradition of dealing with grief.

Early this year, I was talking about our book *Playtime* on the *Today Show* and said that I felt it was important for parents and caregivers of young children first to discover what children know about tragic events such as assassinations and the terrorism of the World Trade Center. From the children that we've talked with, there seem to be many exaggerated fantasies associated with September 11th. It's much more important to find out what they really "know" and go from there, because naturally they're going to bring their own life history to any current event. Some will say ten thousand daddies were killed, or a hundred little children flew out the windows.

After the *Today Show* time, one of the hosts came up to me and said she'd like to talk with me a little about September 11th. She said, "I found that it was very helpful with my kids to let them know about heaven." She said that those children whose parents were killed will not be separated from them forever, that they have some of them already inside. And she said, "I just wanted to share that with you." Isn't that interesting: a newscaster delivering terrible news each day, holding Heaven in her heart! My hunch is that her own parents helped her with that belief early in her life. Now she's helping her child.

On the Neighborhood we continue to talk about separation and return. There are many other concerns. And that's why play and playing, teachers and drama are essential. We all need to learn to be gentle, especially in working with children. Some people have a gentle core but haven't learned to express it in a gentle way.

Another exceedingly important subject for children is honesty about the future. Children love to be told what to expect. One of our Neighborhood songs says:

I like to be told
When you're going away,
When you're going to come back,
And how long you will stay.
How long you will stay.
I like to be told.

I like to be told
If it's going to hurt.
If it's going to be hard,
If it's not going to hurt.
I like to be told.
I like to be told.

It helps me to get ready for all those things,
All those things that are new.
I trust you more and more
Each time that I'm
Finding those things to be true, true.

I like to be told
'Cause I'm trying to grow,
And I'm trying to learn,
And I'm trying to know.
I like to be told.
I like to be told.

This is a song for a child to sing to an adult. Again: authenticity! Helping people deal with their feelings is one of the greatest contributions any of us could ever make. We at Family Communications, Inc., now have a project of workshops throughout the country called, "What Do You Do with the Mad that You Feel?" In our world there are many people who seem to be enraged. Shakespeare certainly knows rage. Look at (and listen to) Othello and Iago and Richard III! What a theme to base some creative work on with children! Children know about being small and scared and wanting to lash out. How "easy" it would be for them to learn about those in history and/or literature who had some of those same feelings!

Although many people believe that the kind of open or even dis-guised fury that Shakespeare so often portrays is more widespread today, I don't think so. Most of us know more people today, and some of them are angry because they don't have the kinds of material things that others seem to "have." If you don't have enough to feed your family, that would certainly enrage you. And one of the most difficult things is that people don't feel appreciated. The less anyone feels appreciated, the angrier that person can become. (Of course, if you're a person who is not going to allow yourself to be appreciated, you're going to be naturally miserable.)

When we learn to operate from "a gentle place" in relation to others, we can experience a wonderful mystery. In fact, I feel that's what God does. After all, God is the Creator of all and delights in being able to find whatever there is to "appreciate" about each one of us. I think the most important way children get to grow is to be in touch with that kind of appreciation. When Henry James's nephew was about to go off to school for the first time, he came to his uncle and asked, "Do you have any advice for me?" Henry James answered, "I have three pieces of advice. The first is to be kind. The second is to be kind. The third is to be kind." What memorable advice! Especially coming from somebody like Henry James!

Although the educational system seems to be shifting to a philosophy that focuses on test test test, our little nonprofit company, Family Communications, Inc., has concentrated on developing creative training materials to help in interpersonal and developmental areas. A new project which people have asked us to create is called *One Kind Word*. This is an intervention program that is starting with a Pittsburgh grocery store chain with 35,000 employees. The employees sometimes see adults hurting children in the stores, and some of those employees want to try to do something about it. What we've discovered is that someone can often defuse such a potentially volatile situation just by offering one kind word or sentence such as, "It's really tough some days, isn't it?" It's amazing what can happen when an angry person feels "understood" and "appreciated."

Another FCI project is the *Safe Havens* project. These materials are for people who might be in the classroom when a child would say something like, "My mommy shot my dad last night." And that happens! The first phase of the project is completed, and we're filming the second phase of it, which features policemen and policewomen who are often seen in neighborhoods as surrogate parents. It's wonderful to witness how opposite such relationships are to the stereotype. I've seen some of the raw footage. It's astounding to witness how certain police officers might see a kid or a group of kids starting a fire in a vacant lot, and take that as a hint to visit those children at home. The officers don't arrest the children, they just go to the home and talk as gently as they can with the families. They're trying to reach—early on—young people who might be particularly susceptible to crime.

I went to a session in which members of our staff were training some of the trainers. There was one woman practically in tears because she felt so deeply for the children in her classes. She has them in the daytime, but she said, "I know what they go to at home." She added, "All I can do is to let them know that I love them all the time, and that I'll be there for them the next day." I wonder how many teachers there are who would like to gather some of their students and take them home . . . and allow them to "speak what they feel" and love them into being more than they ever dreamed possible.

Here we are, all on this boat together . . . this floating planet . . . together. I feel so blessed even in times of trouble. I wonder how human beings get that feeling? I guess it comes from a long line of people in our life who have, in one way or another, "sung" that song:

> It's you I like
> It's not the things you wear.
> It's not the way you do your hair,
> But it's you I like.
>
> The way you are right now,
> The way down deep inside you,
> Not the things that hide you
> Not your toys—they're just beside you.
>
> But it's you I like.
> Every part of you—
> Your skin, your eyes, your feelings
> Whether old or new.
>
> I hope that you'll remember
> Even when you're feeling blue
> That it's you I like, it's you yourself
> It's you. It's you I like.

And I think all of us long to hear that we are accepted as we are. That kind of message can draw the world together.

Act 1

Playing with Shakespeare

Though This Be Madness, Yet There Is Method in It

Common Questions and Answers about Shakespeare in the Classroom

—☙

Betty Donald

Betty Donald, a teacher at Hunter's Creek Middle School, outlines a dozen common questions and answers about Shakespeare in the classroom.

—☙

1) MOST OF MY STUDENTS COME TO SHAKESPEARE with the idea that his plays are difficult and irrelevant. How do I inspire some interest and make his work less threatening?

Shakespeare contributed thousands of words and phrases to our everyday language. As English/Language Arts and social science teachers, most of us are familiar with these words, idioms, and expressions. However, many of our students are not. One means of acquainting students with Shakespeare's language might be to assign a vocabulary list of words coined by the Bard. Most students will be surprised to learn how many of the words they use regularly stem from Shakespeare: hint, gloomy, green-eyed, obscene, assassination, frugal, leapfrog, laughable, hurry, courtship, dwindle, excellent, lonely, rely, premeditated, auspicious, barefaced, critic, exposure, suspicious, pedant, hot-blooded, acceptance, eventful.

Shakespeare also originated many phrases that have become part of our everyday speech, phrases which your students may find even more familiar. Examples to play with and discuss include: "brevity is the soul of wit," "the beginning of the end," "beat it," "the world is my oyster," "a blinking idiot," "it's all Greek to me," "love is blind," "elbow room," "not so hot," "he left, bag and baggage," "it's neither here nor there," "don't fall for it," "to catch a cold," "a method in his madness," "loved not wisely but too well," "the seamy side," "flaming youth," "star-crossed lovers," "out of the question," "a spotless reputation," and "in the mind's eye." A book of quotations will provide you with more wise words from the Bard and plenty of opportunities to acquaint your students with Shakespeare.

Finally, a more fun way of getting students acquainted with Shakespeare's language might be through his insults. After getting a book of Shakespeare's insults (widely available) or finding some of the Bard's biting rhetoric on the Internet (there are pages devoted to this), try putting one insult on the overhead projector or blackboard each day, and asking your students to paraphrase it (using dictionaries). This useful class starter will make your students' insults more creative as well as increase their familiarity with Shakespeare's language.

2) How do I involve my entire class in a production of Shakespeare?

Before you begin a production, you will have to decide what your focus or objectives should be. For example, you may decide that your priorities are (A) best possible performance, (B) learning the language of Shakespeare, and (C) interpretation of the text. But in order to involve your entire class, one of your goals should be for every student in your class to become actively involved in the production via a speaking role or a presence onstage requiring some justifiable and convincing stage action. By ensuring that each of your students fills a valid role in the production, a sense of collective ownership and control will evolve. The text and students' personal interpretations after reading (and rereading) should be the threads out of which the final production is woven.

3) How do I turn a class of students into an acting ensemble?

The largest reason for a reluctance to perform is anxiety. You will be able to help students through any initial fears of performing by building an environment of trust, safety, and community within the company. Build up to the performance slowly with classroom activities that develop movement, speaking, and communication skills and establish an atmosphere of trust and respect. Many theatrical warm-ups are an effective way to accomplish this; some of the warm-ups include:

> 1) trust games—name games, human bingo, word association, faith falls
> 2) short, protected, and non-threatening performance activities
> 3) experiential performance activities
> 4) reader's theater

Examples of these are included in the workbook *Dramathemes: A Practical Guide for Classroom Teachers* by Larry Swartz (Ontario: Pembroke, 1995). *Dramathemes* contains many activities and useful assessments, as well as a bibliography of books that incorporates drama activities into the language arts classroom.

---

4) How do I get this show on the road?

First, you must determine the level and attention span of your students. A comedy is a good place to start with younger students. Be realistic. You may wish to consider a shortened version of your play, or edit it yourself. If you choose to edit the play, do it collaboratively with your students as you read and explore the play together. As you involve and guide them, students will soon begin to get a feel for the parts they prefer. Encourage students to examine the text closely and experiment with different ways of delivering the lines, using pauses, facial expressions, and body language to enhance the meanings in the lines.

5) What about auditions/assigning parts?

It is best to let each student select the character he/she wishes to play if possible. As you explore the play through class discussion—stopping when necessary to discuss such issues as character, motivation and actions—students will gain the understanding needed to decide on a part that is attractive to them and their abilities. Be careful not to give way to typecasting. That heavyset girl who is so quiet may have a wonderful Juliet buried inside but dying to emerge.

6) What if there are too many or too few parts in relation to the size of my class?

Editing, double casting, or splitting roles will solve the problem. You could also consider breaking up the class into smaller acting ensembles which are assigned a scene from the play. Finally, you might try dividing the play among your classes by scene, and then having each class/ensemble perform their scene in order.

7) Sounds great, except that the students I teach are frequently absent with excuses ranging from the serious to the ridiculous. How do I handle these problems?

Create a contract that addresses the issues of attendance, minimal grades for participation, cooperation, respect and trust, memorization of lines, and any other criteria you feel necessary to make assessment more objective. A letter sent home to parents explaining your participation contract and schedule/time line that requires both student and parent signatures will significantly reduce problems down the road—as they say, "An ounce of prevention is worth a pound of cure."

8) How do I decide whether to do a modern version, a Renaissance version, or a period piece?

Let the students come to that conclusion, with some subtle guidance on your part. They will have a vested interest in the production only if it results from what they have discovered, rather than your vision of the play. This decision should grow out of your students' interpretations of the recurrent metaphors/images/references in the play. Keep in mind that high concept (trendy, avant-garde) productions can be difficult to produce and that, whatever the decision, the play should not get lost in its attendant trappings. However, if your students choose to ignore your advice, remember that the most valuable lessons are often a result of failure, rather than success.

9) Rehearsals will be time consuming and scheduling tricky. How do I plan for this?

If you plan to perform in a space outside of your own classroom, reserve that first. You will have to work backwards from that point, planning for dress rehearsals in that space, if possible. The time you allow is the time you have available. If you prepare your students well, you should be able to do a scene from a play in a week or so. If you're planning a full-length, elaborately costumed play in an auditorium, you will obviously need more time. You may wish to start small and simple and work your way up to a bigger production, but try it. You'll be amazed at the growth of your students' enthusiasm as the production progresses.

10) How can I avoid the chaos that I envision during rehearsal time?

Again, planning is important. Students who are not working directly with you can be rehearsing smaller segments of the larger scene(s). If they have trouble staying on task, you can plan other activities that tie into the play and help the students to understand their characters. Writing activities, for example, such as journals about the experience, journals written from a character's point of view, character sketches, monologues, original songs and dances, and poems will help you and the student to use time productively. Further, art activities like collages, paintings, drawings, or masks can help students to discover their characters, or even combine writing and art to give your students' imaginations fuller license. Finally, you can have your students construct scenery or make costumes if all else fails.

11) I am concerned about complying with the new Sunshine State Standards and County Benchmarks. What can I do to integrate that required content?

If you weave in the suggested writing activities (see #10), you should be easily able to incorporate all the strands—reading, writing, listening and speaking, viewing, language, and literature—into your lesson plans. Those activities will also cover a number of the benchmarks.

12) It sounds like assessment could be difficult.

   If you establish criteria for the grade in a performance contract (see #7), this should not be a problem. The writing and art activities can also constitute part of your assessment. Thus, by keeping the activities varied, every student can excel at some facet of the production. There are some handy assessment, self-assessment, observation, and reflection rubrics for the more subjective areas of interpretation and participation in Larry Swartz's *Dramathemes.*

Stand up, Listen, Whisper, Whistle, and Shout Your Way to Shakespeare
An Approach to a Three-Dimensional Read-Through

Stuart E. Omans

Stu Omans, a professor at the University of Central Florida and codirector of the Drey Shakespeare Institutes, uses his experience as the founding director of the Orlando Shakespeare Festival to show how young student/actors and teacher/ directors might approach a first reading of the plays.

THIS ESSAY DESCRIBES A PROCESS APPROACH to teaching Shakespeare that allows students who are not "actors" to explore their imaginations as actors do and then create the plays as the three-dimensional works of art they were originally written to be. The process can be called a "stand up, listen, whisper, whistle, and shout your way to Shakespeare: an approach to a three-dimensional read-through"—just so we don't get too pontifically serious about ourselves as our discussion proceeds. In reality, if we keep a spirit of play central, the entire process allows students to become increasingly, imaginatively specific as they discover they can create a vivid Shakespearean world through the filter of themselves. By three-dimensional I mean that our primary goal from the beginning is to move away from the idea that the plays are words, evenly, metrically spaced on the page to the idea that the plays are, instead, a remarkably rich orchestration of sounds, often words and often not words, sometimes evenly spaced, often not, and metrically more like a rubber band than a steel ruler, accompanied by an equally rich orchestration of movements and that together—in space—these create the dynamic world called the play.

The key ideas governing our approach must be (1) a spirit of play, (2) excitement, (3) continuing revelation, and (4) emphasis on the moment. I should add before we begin that I have used this approach with college students, high school students, and with high school and middle school teachers cajoled into playing the roles of their students and even, in modified ways, with middle schoolers. Its main virtues: it works, and it is true to the art and spirit of the play.

So, to begin, realize that you'll not be starting with the play text, but rather with students and their sense of themselves occupying and recreating space. The ideal situation is to be in a classroom where the student desks (or chairs) can be arranged in a large circle with as much empty classroom space inside the circle as possible. This inside space will quickly become your place for experimenting and discovery.

Our approach is unlike that of professional actors in the first meeting of their company for a read-through of the play they are about to rehearse. These actors would almost never move out of their chairs. Our method will include leaving our chairs early in this process and periodically thereafter, with more and more ease and fluidity so long as our read-through continues. Further, while a professional company (12–20 people) aims to get through the entire play in about three to three and one half hours, our process will continue over several days, with little expectation that our 30–40 students will ever get through the whole play. Maybe we would be as well off calling this a read-true because that's what we're really trying to create in our students' attitude. But, although we do not expect to get through the play, we will have every expectation that each student will have many different opportunities to give voice, physical expression, and meaning to one of the play's characters and to "sound off" as they journey toward creating the world of the play.

From the first moment of our process our emphasis must be on the playfulness and the excitement of discovering a script that begins with one unique moment of text filtered through one unique human being. Our emphasis must be that we are about to enter a dramatic world designed with thousands of possible moments, inhabited by sounds and movements that express emotions and thoughts, in combinations never experienced before because for the first time in history it is being filtered through this unique collection of individuals who make up this about-to-be created acting company.

Therefore, our goal from the outset is not to get through the play, nor to confirm anyone's predisposition about what the play means. Rather, our primary goal is to find the delight of how its art will reveal itself to our individual personalities.

In the fullest sense, our process begins not with the play (this will come later), but with our selves as the central filters beginning in a game of sounds that will reward us first with apparently useless old-fashioned giggles. Yes, just giggles! And later on, our rewards will deepen as we realize our capacity to create living images.

To start this, the teacher must be brave enough to participate, really participate in the game. Most likely, he or she will be its first vocal player. Without the teacher's willingness to play, to experiment, and to abandon the authority of knowing the right answers about each play, the method will not work. The teacher must also recognize the possible need to condense some features of the process, given the realities of time constraints in his/her school. Using all of the process would be ideal; using some of it will be better than using none.

Here, then, is our opening scene. Thirty-plus of us are sitting in a large circle (the larger, the better) with plenty of space inside. Everybody must be in the circle, including, especially including, those students who always feel separated from the group. Additionally, it is important that all are randomly placed so that the usual cliques are abandoned and so that there is no first person and no last. The teacher is seated like everybody else, and copies of the play are distributed. It is best, too, that there are not enough playtexts to go around, so that two people who might not ordinarily work together or even associate much are required to share a text. (Later in the process when we get to actually reading and moving, the necessity of sharing and/or exchanging copies will unconsciously help create a feeling of camaraderie through ensemble that we're trying to achieve.)

But for now we're at a different place. To get to Shakespeare, we're going to begin with our selves—the filters. The teacher asks everyone to put their playtexts down and to simply stand in front of their chairs inside the circle. Some students will be reluctant to do so, but if the teacher leads, everyone will follow. With this first movement, just this one alteration in physical movement, we have begun to explore space, to create a new world, and every student, either consciously or subconsciously, will understand this. The sense of discovery has started. At this point students should be encouraged to express their experience of how moving from sitting to standing in the circle has affected them.

Emphasize that so long as their response is sincere, it is virtually impossible to give a wrong answer. Indeed, this is true, since each individual's unique personality will experience the movement differently, but if my past experience is a reliable indication, all will somehow describe how their sense of self and relationship to the others has changed, just by this one movement. Answers in the past have been: "I feel stronger, standing up." "I feel less separated from everybody else." "Yes, but also less protected, not as safe." "There's nothing to hold on to now." "I'm so obviously the shortest girl in the group." "I want to move now that I'm standing."

A variety of answers and voices is what you can expect and what you should encourage. From here, encourage students to talk about the differences in their voices as well. But do so without value judgments. No distinct voice is better than another. Whose is high-pitched? low? loudest? shy? most forceful? even melodic? The emphasis here as the discussion unfolds is that each one of them is a vocal sculpture in space: a sculpture in proportion and size, of pitch, of volume, tone, pronunciation, accent. Each is a living, three-dimensional demonstration of what Shakespeare may have meant when Hamlet said, "What a piece of work is man. . . . How infinite in faculty." At this point in the process, each student should be discovering that his/her uniqueness is capable of altering the environment and making it newly real. If the game works as it has in the past, each participant will discover that there is more to each of them than they imagined.

The teacher's function at this starting point in the read-true is to be sure that each participant recognizes the richness of variety in his presence. They constitute a fascinating world if each of their 'vocal moments' is given the *attention it deserves* to receive. The discoveries made here during this opening movement will be similar to those we'll explore once we are ready to formally enter the play. So, if possible, the teacher should give this plenty of time. At this point in our preliminaries, the teacher asks each person in the circle (we are still standing) to say his/her name. The most common response here is a mixture of giggles, laughs, raised eyebrows. "What's the point?" seems to be the undercurrent of the group's embarrassed response. Everyone knows his name. This obvious truth will not be as obvious as it first appears as we are each asked to say our name a second time, but exploring it this time, really pronouncing and listening to its sounds—sounds that most of us have been unconsciously ignoring for a long time—perhaps simply because we've lived with them for so long.

Our emphasis here is to honestly try to give full voice to all these old and familiar sounds. The teacher's function here is to encourage and emphasize sincere play with the sounds. Students should whisper, should shout, should sing (if they are brave enough) the sounds of their names. They should draw out the most apparent of the sounds or in some cases, the least apparent of them. I, for example, am Stuart O-maenz as I continue my vocalizations. And it is the O that intrigues me, and that I choose to draw out.

Eventually, after three or four tries, participants should choose a version of his/her name that somehow has the most personal appeal. What is there about this one version that demands attention? Can each student express a reason for the version's power? You will be startled by the responses. If nothing else, this not-so-apparent name game will make students begin to wonder about the unique collection of sounds they associate with their identity and about why one version of the sound's pronunciation is the one they've chosen to represent them. For me, the writer, as mentioned above, it's that heavily emphasized O sound, not as a moan, but as the fullest bodied sound in my identity. I like its sense of surprise, its openness, its assertion that for me, Stuart Omaenz, the world is continuously astonishing! Each of the students needs to go through this exercise. It is important that nobody rushes—or fakes—or dismisses it. The teacher must stress that through sincere play will come discovery.

Add a next step by asking each of them to listen as carefully as they can to the chosen version of the name voiced by the person next to them. And then ask the listener to try to repeat exactly, to echo, the name and its voice. Then ask the originator to evaluate the echo, trying to explain where, why, and how the echo succeeded or missed the mark. What we are trying to accomplish through this game is a rediscovery of our selves through the unique collection of sounds we have lived with so long (15 to 58 years) and that they may have become sort of tarnished. The surprise exhilaration of rediscovery will sensitize us to discovering how carefully Shakespeare uses (and suggests) sounds in his scripts and how those sounds take on added reverberations in his characters, giving voice to his own, but mostly to others' names, once we've sensitized ourselves to listening to our own names. Romeo is identified differently by each character who gives his name a voice. Mercutio, Romeo's irreverent, teasing friend, emphasizes the sighing 'Ohs' in Romeo, the smitten lover; Tybalt taunts Romeo, his enemy, by tossing back 'the meow' in Romeow that others have used to tease Tybalt calling him Prince of Cats, and Juliet repeatedly experiments coyly, lovingly, playfully, longingly, or angrily with every possible dimension of her beloved's name. Similarly, Miranda in *The Tempest*, hears her name pronounced very differently by her sometimes stern father than by her husband-to-be, Prince Ferdinand. Her father has used her name many times, but Ferdinand hears it for the first time and repeats it to himself, rolling its sounds around in his mouth and imagination. For him, she emerges as "Ad/mi/red Miranda" i.e. perfectly herself (as the Latin derivative of her name insists): she who ought to be wondered at, fully admired. Every dimension of her name's sound is new and exciting to him, including how her beautifully formed lips have just pronounced it and his have echoed it. Every nuance contained in her name possesses magical meaning for him. Especially, the caressed 'm'.

Our name game brings us a little closer to being ready to explore sounds as we prepare to meet Shakespeare. "Listen! Listen! Listen!" is our lesson here. Discovering the exquisite possibilities locked away in the sounds of our and others' names will lead us to those sounds awaiting in Shakespeare's script. All the nuances are there if we will only learn to listen.

We are now ready for the second part of our game. It's time to add one physical gesture to the version of the name we've now chosen to represent us. This gesture is to be chosen because to the name's owner it seems most appropriate. The gesture I choose is a long, sweeping extension of my arm and hand, palm up and out in front of my body. I have chosen it to invite everyone into my open 'O' astonishment. "Be part of the Oh" I am gesturing. Join me. Each member of our circle needs to make his/her personal decision about the appropriate gesture here.

By the conclusion of our experience, we will have a rich new mixture of sounds and gestures that has never existed before anywhere in the universe. And, of course, we will have the beginning of an imaginable world.

If time allows, we could take our game one increment further by seeing how many of the names and gestures each of us can remember and repeat. This step is both simpler and more fascinating in its implications than it first appears. Start anywhere in the circle and ask that person to be first, saying his or her chosen version name with a gesture. Have the person to the right 'echo' the name and gesture and then add his/her own. The third person to the right does the first two and then adds theirs and so on. By the time we've reached number ten or eleven, memories are getting stretched and virtually everyone on the circle will be in rapt attention. The remarkable thing, and this I can promise from past experience, is how brilliantly *everyone* will do, and how, when one member of the group is struggling to recall a name or gesture or both, others in the group will be moved to private prompting, often unconsciously mouthing the name silently. The whole group progressively becomes protective and proprietary of everyone else. Each member of the group is concentrating intensely on the other's succeeding. And when this happens, and it will happen, we have succeeded in creating an acting ensemble, which is ready emotionally and imaginatively to encounter the play proper.

They are ready to listen, to watch, to experiment and concentrate to help one another, without judging. They are prepared to link their unique gifts as they move forward from moment to moment in the play.

Since we used this process with *The Tempest* in a Drey Shaespeare Summer Institute, I shall apply the method here, trying to document our exploration during this play's first few moments. Though my description here is limited to only the first moments of the play, this same method should be used as you explore longer sections or the entirety of any of the plays.

The scene opens during a sea storm with the Master of a foundering ship calling to his second-in-command. "Boatswain!" he calls. And the Boatswain replies, "Here, Master." Before moving beyond these opening moments, these three words, choose any two members of the ensemble to come into the center space and experiment with the volume and pitch of the call and response. Ask the rest of company, one by one, to imagine the sound of a large wooden ship under the most severe physical strains. As each student imaginatively responds, "wood planks would be straining and rubbing against one another, creaking, almost like screams," "the sails will all be snapping in the winds," "there will be canvas ripping," "waves will crash against the ship," ask each inventor to create the sound he/she's imagined. The more they help one another, adding suggestions, the better. Once the ensemble has agreed on the sound—at least for now—challenge several of the ensemble to make one distinct ship-in-storm sound, progressively adding another and then another one by one to the mix. In a relatively short span of time, you will have a remarkably rich, choreographed sound of a ship caught on the seas in a storm. And virtually everyone will be involved in the invention of the collective sound imagery they've raised off the page.

Now, again try the Master's call and the Boatswain's response, but this time over the ensemble's ship-in-storm sounds, asking all the participants to experiment with adjusting their volumes and intensities so that the storm becomes increasingly believable. This means that the Master and Boatswain must shout over the storm sounds, but, also, that the sounds be adjusted just enough that the Master and Boatswain can be heard. Someone may suggest that the only way to accomplish this is to rehearse those opening few moments a number of times before trying to go on. Keep asking for suggestions about how else to create the 'reality' of the scene as it unfolds moment to moment. I guarantee that one of the ensemble, most likely the Boatswain or Master, will want to experiment with finding his/her physical position on the ship, "the where" those opening lines are delivered. Pretty quickly this will lead to an animated discussion of how much of the inner circle space makes up the ship and whether it would make theatrical sense to have one of them, maybe the Master, begin the scene vertically above–standing on a chair and shouting, while the Boatswain is at the opposite end of the space standing on the ship's deck.

Other suggestions will follow. "Maybe the wind is so strong and the rain is so heavy that they are close to one another and just don't know it." Another might suggest that the Master may be standing at an imaginary steering wheel, trying to keep the ship on course, as it twists through the seas. The point here is that all the suggestions, in active experimentation, accepted or rejected, are valid and playable, and once choices among them are made, they begin to add up to an exciting, imaginable world. Howling winds, snapping sails, lightning strikes, thunder explosions, and bashing waves, all have been created by the company, under the opening shouts of the first two characters. The company has also recognized the need to accurately record and be able to repeat their choices. Our collective lesson? If we listen carefully to what the page is telling us and then use our gifts as sound and image makers playing in ensemble, together we will discover the moment Shakespeare has given us.

By the time you've reached this point (and it may take several periods), most everyone will be excited about adding to their collective discoveries. Now is the appropriate time to read through the remainder of the scene, focusing on finding any other particular sounds specifically mentioned or suggested in the text. Every scene in Shakespeare will provide these. Here there is the repeated reference to a whistle. "Tend to the Master's whistle!" shouts the Boatswain as he goes about his tasks to keep the ship and its passengers safe. And so another specific sound is uncovered and required as part of the emerging image. But there are whistles and there are whistles, and here as with the other discoveries, the company must recreate the sound that works. The Boatswain is telling the other sailors to "tend to" [pay attention to] the Master's whistle, a signaling device–probably with a variety of set sounds that instruct movement and cut through the chaos of the storm. Who amongst the ensemble is a whistler? Where does the whistle happen? What does it sound like from occurrence to occurrence? Does it cease at a given moment and if it does, what does that moment mean in the collection of all the sounds and moments that we've been discovering?

As with our opening name/gesture exercises, it is important here to not make decisions too quickly. When we return to playing with the scene moment to moment and adding discovered sounds to our already beautifully rich world, we will want ensemble agreement about which combination of whistle sounds they feel to be the best.

Having established a strong auditory and physical sense of the opening moments, our challenge as a group is to continue, adding discovered moment after discovered moment.

And part of our delight will be to discover how the sounds we've introduced suggest imagined physical objects and gestures as the scene unfolds. Clearly, the storm we've created is moving the ship violently and erratically. This too can be discovered through the collective talent of our subhuman sound machine.

The students not yet physically inside the space, i.e. those who are making the sounds of the storm, join together as a single entity (the storm sounds made physical) by laying their arms over the shoulders of one another. Now this outer circle begins to sway slowly left to right, right to left, creating the motion of the waves and wind, gradually increasing until discovering the momentum of the storm. If the wind shifts direction at a certain moment in the scene, then so will the wind machine. Those inside the circle space (now the Master, the Boatswain, and the Mariners who are attending to the whistle) will physically catch the rhythms of our wind machine as the ship and its deck begin shifting under their feet. As together we discover the tossing rhythms of the ship, we'll also together discover multiple other dimensions of the scene. As the storm grows in intensity, the ship founders as it is carried closer and closer to a reef.

The Boatswain shouts, "Down with the topmast!" and, of course, the ensemble members who are on the ship, must agree to where the topmast is located in the space, how tall it is, how thick, and how it is to be taken down. By imagined ropes? Where are they located? How thick are they? Who is tending them? Do they lurch away and burn the hands of the mariners? All are dimensions to be discovered and given imaginative reality by the company in the context of the scene. "Yare!" shouts the Boatswain. It's a moment of readiness that he wants from his mariners, and so a tensional pause seems to be called for as the mariners create before our eyes the ropes and the topmast. The company together imagines as they see it, hear it, do it—and so does all the audience. "Lower, lower!" he shouts. And then "Bring her [the ship] to try with the main course."

Each command must be realized as a discrete theatrical moment, matching each storm sound to the created physicality of the ship. At each discovery and invention, the script reveals more. The more attentive we are, the more we will come to invent. And what do our ensemble students discover through this full participation, full concentration experiment? They discover as they journey, moment to moment, that through the filter of their imaginative selves paying attention to Shakespeare's script, they are creating every detail of the storm, the ship, and those who people it. They also discover that they are the spirits who create the play's world.

As the "mariners" lay hold the ropes, they will metamorphose from "mariners" to individual human beings that emerge through the distinct person of each student. There will be no abstractions here as each frightened sailor desperately works to change the direction of the ship by taking down the topmast and then the topsail and then "bringing [the ship] to try with main course" (trying to hold the ship close to the wind) and away from the reef under only the mainsail until finally the ship smashes against the reef. "Set her two courses. Off to sea again! Lay her off [the reef]. Lay her off!"

"All lost. All lost. . . . We split. We split . . . we split. We split . . . we split."

During this incarnation of the first few moments of the scene, our student ensemble will discover together how one imaginatively created sound will point to one exacting movement and to a correspondent moment of personality.

The beautiful truth is that all of the above will take place organically. As they become the wind and waves in orchestration, as they invent to give voice to the thunder claps and place them in the action, as they embody the lightning strikes and the creaking boards under the shouts and calls of the desperate sailors trying to guide the foundering ship, the students, as actors, will discover the play as an invented, three-dimensional imaginal creation. And it will be, as we want it to be, and as it should be, all theirs.

Oh, Had I but Space Enough and Time
Rethinking Space

Ben Gunter

Ben Gunter, an actor, director, and former artistic director of the Southern Shakespeare Festival, explores ways to transform an average classroom into a magical space.

THE TIME HAS COME TO TALK ABOUT SPACE. Where are you going to find a place to rehearse, explore, and perform your Shakespeare play? And what will the play find in your space, in terms of possibilities for expressiveness, collaboration, and discovery? This three-stage set of experiments, field-tested at places like the Drey Summer Shakespeare Institute, can launch you on a trek towards answers for these questions. The experiments will be presented in a sequence, a kind of space-time continuum, but feel free to rearrange their order and modify them to suit the demands of your own particular journey. In our kind of space science, the more unique, even unreplicable, your results are, the better. Your voyage of discovery lifts off from two ideas:

    1) Space is dynamic—not a cold, impersonal thing to conquer, but an active, responsive participant in the process of making theater.

    2) You are not alone. The quest for space is an organic part of Shakespeare's playmaking, and undertaking it collaboratively, as a process shared by your whole production team, will pay off in every part of your performance.

C.S. Lewis captured these ideas eloquently in *Out of the Silent Planet* when Dr. Ransom, the astronaut, suddenly realizes that though he once imagined space as a dark, cold and utterly barren vacuum that separated worlds, he now sees it as the womb of worlds, an empyrean ocean of radiance in which all life swims.

Stage One: The Womb of Worlds
Experiments in Configuring Ground-Zero Space for Zero-Budget Theater

> There's a place for us,
> Somewhere a place for us.
> Peace and quiet and room and air
> Wait for us
> Somewhere.
>
> *West Side Story*

Questions: What shapes can theater take? How do you make an empty room into a theater? What should the playing space look like for your play?

Space: Any open, empty area (e.g., a gym floor, a parking lot, a classroom, a cafeteria, a quadrangle, a football field, even a stage)

Time: 30 minutes (minimum); can be repeated or spread over several days

Equipment: Scripts, folding chairs (or blocks or blankets or blank floor space—anything that lets folks swiftly reconfigure their arrangement)

Actors: 1 or 2

Auditors: 10 or more

Optional: Boombox, music, hand props

Exercise: Choose a speech from the play of some 10 to 16 lines. Arrange your auditors in different configurations to hear actors read the speech. Discuss how spatial arrangement influenced your actors' and auditors' experience of the speech.

The first stage in your voyage is experiencing the theater-building power of space. With these experiments, you can try out five different theater configurations—proscenium, thrust, arena, traverse, and environmental—in the same empty room, then compare their communicative impact.

Start by choosing a speech from your play, a brief, pithy passage that's captured the imagination of your production team. Actors at the Drey Summer Institute at Rollins College clamored to try out Antony's famous funeral oration ("Friends, Romans, countrymen, lend me your ears!") when we were working with *Julius Caesar*, Orsino's opening ("If music be the food of love, play on.") that sets the tone for *Twelfth Night*, and Romeo and Juliet's first-date sonnet: "If I profane with my unworthiest hand/This holy shrine . . ." We've gotten grand results with all three speeches. What matters is that the speech you look at make a difference in how you and your collaborators look at the physical context. Letting folks nominate candidates for the play's greatest speech and then choosing the speech you'll use by democratic ballot can be a great way to launch this experiment.

After choosing the speech, recruit volunteers to read it. Then get the audience to face the actors, seating themselves in orderly rows. This creates a *proscenium* theater configuration, the kind of formal, unidirectional, single-focus arrangement used in most movie theaters, courtrooms, civic auditoria, and churches. Have the actors read the speech to their auditors while everyone watches intently.

Now make the audience move, folding the ends of their rows so the seating arrangement morphs into a U. Stand the actors in the mouth of the U, with auditors on both sides and in front of them. This creates a *thrust* arrangement (often called a three-quarter thrust, since the audience surrounds the action on three sides). Have the actors read the speech again. Encourage everyone to observe energetically everything they see, hear, and experience.

Ask the actors to step forward and the audience to complete a circle around them. This creates *theater in the round*, also known as an arena configuration, the familiar shape of a football stadium, racetrack, or boxing rink. Get the actors to read again, again exhorting the audience to absorb every detail, every aspect of the experience extremely actively. You can keep the audience on its toes by reversing roles. Have folks sitting in the circle read the speech while the actors listen in the middle to create a reverse arena arrangement.

Now split the sitting circle, bisecting it with an aisle. Let the actors inhabit the aisle, like a high-fashion runway between facing rows of audience members, as the auditors take a lively interest in the sights, sounds, and dramatic experiences offered by a *traverse* theater configuration. Read the speech yet again.

Finally, invent an *environmental* setting for the speech. Ask your collaborators where the situation that inspires the speech would turn up. Participants in the Drey decided that "Friends, Romans, countrymen" would be heard in a funeral home; "If music be the food of love" in a ritzy nightclub; and "If I profane with my unworthiest hand" at a rowdy party. Get your group to make suggestions, adopt one (a quick vote can settle where you'll start), then turn every single person loose to create the cutting-edge, contemporary setting you've selected. Music and hand props can come in handy; we used silly hats and noisemakers to enhance the frat party, a boombox with Ella Fitzgerald crooning "The Man I Love" to set the aural scene for the nightclub, and a black velvet throw and organ at full tremolo for the funeral home. But what really counts here is involvement. Everybody gets to play; and when the atmosphere is ripe, the actors read the speech.

Now you're ready for discussion. While the experience is still raw, pull the cast and crew together to wrestle with what they've just learned. Consider the readings one by one, trying to figure out the differences that different configurations of space made for each of you as you experienced the play. Focus on specifics: what the space made you see, hear, or understand.

Probe deeper than first reactions, down to how the space constructed conditions of awkwardness, intimacy, or festivity. Go beyond the literal to investigate who the space invested with power, focus, or responsibility. Listen for variations in how the space acted on actors, and on members of the audience.

Discussions at the Drey have tended to appreciate the environmental configurations for their ability to lure audiences into active involvement (sometimes at the price of paying attention to the play), traverse arrangements for their dynamic impact on actors (who seem impelled to move when they set foot on that runway traversing the audience), arena spaces for their democracy and individuality (giving every member of the audience equal access to the scene but making every member of the audience see it at a slightly different angle), thrust theaters for their malleability (combining the intimate possibilities of an audience on three sides of you with the confrontational potential of a platform across the top of the U), and proscenium spaces for their power to communicate formality (rigidly dividing actors from audience), privilege (clearly defining center stage), and univocality (featuring one unified frontal focus).

But the more deeply discussion-sparked experimentation takes us into space, the more surprises we find. Playing with "Friends, Romans, countrymen," for example, we discovered that dramatic pressure could convert a proscenium arrangement's univocal formality into a powerful tool for multivocal intimacy. It happened this way. Antony was onstage, throwing his heart into the coffin there with Caesar. Since Shakespeare had scripted lines for street people to throw in—heckling, encouragement, and asides—we let anyone seated in the audience who wanted a voice to stand up and claim a street-people speech. A thoroughly magical moment happened when not one, but five readers from all over the "auditorium," leapt to their feet to yell, "We'll hear the will! Let's hear it!" Every person there—actors, auditors, supervisors, skeptics, oldtimers, and newcomers—felt the electricity of that moment. By happy accident, we had found a way to use the expectation of formal distance that proscenium seating creates as a tool for engineering a surprise breakthrough into hair-raising intimacy.

Similarly, debating the freewheeling frat party we'd thrown to stage Juliet's debut led us to a deeper appreciation of environmental theater's possibilities. Audience members had become so engrossed in the life of the party (especially their own singing, dancing, drinking, and flirting) that they overshadowed Juliet meeting Romeo. Indeed, some of our space travelers were ready to discard environmental settings as too unfocused and out of control, until the actors playing Romeo and Juliet told us that they'd felt more relaxed and "real" reading the sonnet to each other here than in any other performance configuration we'd tried. That gave us pause. Maybe, we thought, environmental settings held promise for rehearsal. And maybe, we found as we re-staged the experiment in our minds, the multi-focal elements of party music, rave lights, and spontaneous social interaction could actually work to create focus in the scene, in a dramatic, zero-budget way. If the music came from a boombox whose carrier faded the swing band under the sonnet; if the lights came from partygoers with glowsticks in their mouths and flashlights in their hands, and the flashlights all converged on Juliet as she met Romeo; if the whole party shifted into slow motion when the sonnet started, perhaps a *Romeo and Juliet* rave could feel real and tell the story of the play at the same time.

Critiquing settings for "If music be the food of love" led us to another discovery: configurations can be blended, sending a scene into hyper-drive through setting it in a hybrid space. We first tried the speech in a traverse setting and found the Duke and his retinue crossing the room from side to side, as traverse settings seem to inspire actors to do and audiences to expect. Then we transformed the traverse configuration's single austere aisleway into a deliciously sophisticated cabaret environment, with auditors clustered around what our imaginations insisted were chic little supper tables, listening to Ella Feste-Gerald carry a torch for "The Man I Love." In the middle of the song, Orsino entered (with entourage). He proceeded quite unpremeditatedly to cross the room, traversing a striking wall-to-wall diagonal before landing at a table of his own and singing along with Ella's grand finale. Mixing spatial elements—introducing the traverse configuration's strong diagonal into our cabaret configuration's fragmented environment—seemed to reveal a rich mixture of dramatic elements in the performance. In discussion afterwards, folks repeatedly remarked on how this rendition of Orsino's speech combined unconsciously comic pretension with touchingly romantic desire and unsettling socio-sexual insecurity, tremendously fertile ground for a staging of *Twelfth Night*. This surprise encounter with multiplicity inspired us to imagine productions with multiple settings, where different arrangements of actors and auditors foreground different subtexts in different acts or scenes.

Experimenting with theater configuration can help your students set a broad spatial agenda for imagining productions. These ground-zero exercises can also give you and them tools for adjusting very finely calibrated performance problems. Try them early; repeat them often. Space speaks. Putting the play into different spatial configurations and listening intently to what your whole team hears can open new worlds for you and your audiences.

Stage Two: Found Ground
Experiments in Surveying the Playing Field

> There's a place for us,
> A time and place for us.
> Hold my hand and we're halfway there.
> Hold my hand and I'll take you there
> Someday,
> Somehow,
> Somewhere!
>
> *West Side Story*

Each group of performers, as they develop a unique vision of the play, must discover the space most appropriate to that vision.

Questions: What free, "found" spaces might be used for our play? How can location enrich the play's production and reception? How can we interview specific spaces for a role in the play?

Space: A "home base" to explore; space to which you and your team of collaborators can have safe, free, regular access (e.g., a campus, a school building and its grounds, a playing field and its fieldhouses, an art gallery, a museum, a city park, a shopping mall, a church, a synagogue garden, a cemetery, a courthouse, or a parking garage)

Time: 30 minutes (minimum); the time can be spread over a weekend or longer

Equipment: Scripts, survey questions, a stopwatch, and a whistle

Exercise: Make a list of important places in the play. Choose teams to prospect for several of those places. Commission teams to interview each other about spaces they find.

Zero-budget Shakespeare doesn't have to be spatially poor. Even Shakespeare, the George Lucas of his day, who made a fortune building special-effects emporia like The Globe, knew what it was to have to go out and hunt for space to put on a play. For command performances at court, during periods when the theaters were closed, and in aggressively exporting their culture abroad, Elizabethan actors and producers learned how to make do with found space.

Finding ready-made places to put on your play can be an adventure that will bring you and your collaborators closer together as a team and mature your version of the play. Get ready to go where many have blindly gone before by reading the script with an eye to space, jotting down references to prominent physical places that turn up in the dialogue. If you're working on *Romeo and Juliet*, for example, your list will include the streets of Verona, Capulet's house, a walled orchard, Friar Lawrence's cell, Juliet's bedroom, the apothecary's shop, and the Capulet's mausoleum. Focus on the play's biggest spatial challenges—places like Juliet's balcony, or the Duke's Oak where the rude mechanicals meet to rehearse in *A Midsummer Night's Dream*, the box tree that lets a party of practical jokers in *Twelfth Night* see Malvolio find a love letter without being seen themselves, *The Tempest*'s boisterous storm at sea, the royal residence blessed at the end of *The Merry Wives of Windsor*, and the Senatorial statuary overlooking the assassination of Julius Caesar.

With your place-list in the back of your mind, get clearance for your production team to explore a well-defined area in your community. This could be public space (like a playground, civic center, or a public school campus), private space (like a churchyard, office complex, or residential park), or a mixture of the two. Ideally, it will be space where you could eventually stage a performance of your play, should that prove desirable. But all you'll need to start with is permission to explore for half an hour or so. Clearances and place-list in hand (but not necessarily visible), initiate this experiment with a full cast and crew discussion about places in the play that stand out to your collaborators. Encourage folks to defend their suggestions passionately, with specific evidence from the script about what happens in the space they've named and why that's vital to the plot, theme, or symbolism of the play. Allow the debate (ten minutes should suffice) quickly to identify a handful of core spaces, enough to split your group into teams of explorers with at least three members on each team. Once the teams are formed, have them huddle for mission command.

Each team's mission is a time-limited quest (i.e., fifteen minutes or so) to find within the search area an actual, architectural, physical space that corresponds to the imaginary, fictive space they see as pivotal to the play. Their method of navigation may be intuitive ("Follow the Force, Luke, follow the Force!"), empirical (We know this campus, let's head for the football field!), or exploratory (Go where no man has gone before!), but each team has to locate one space and come back with answers to seven survey questions:

- Entrance/Exit: Where are the entrances and exits for actors and for audience members?
- Levels/Sightlines: What playing levels does it offer actors; how many points of view does it offer auditors?
- Sound/Light: How do its walls, plantings, ceilings, and floors direct and reflect sound; where are light sources, and how do they change with the time of day?
- Movement: What natural pathways cross the space; what gets revealed and what gets hidden as people move from place to place?
- Power Points: What focal points dominate the space visually and acoustically; who "owns" this space?
- Architectural Features: How do plantings, paintings, carvings, statuary, arches, columns, balustrades, banisters, staircases, doorways, canopies, fountains, facades, overhangs, archways, cloisters, colonnades, clerestories, windows, grillwork, railings, fences, sidewalks, terraces, and signage organize the space?
- Creature Comforts: How long could an audience comfortably visit here or actors act in this space?

You can maximize the effectiveness of the quest by dividing your search area into sectors, then sending each team out in a different direction. When the time for searching has elapsed, blow the whistle and reassemble the teams for debriefing. When students from the Drey searched Rollins College campus for settings from *Romeo and Juliet*, debriefing was a riot, crammed with new insights into the world of the play and the world around us. Teams had identified Capulet's monument, the streets of Verona, and Friar Lawrence's cell as places pivotal to the play. Team Lawrence found a quiet ramp hedged by boxwoods that led up to a doorway set into a rounded, gable-roofed arch. The placement of the door—unobtrusively perpendicular to an imposing administrative façade—reflected the friar's marginality. The space's mixture of sylvan and urban elements (trees, cement, shade, and sidewalk) set the friar in a world between city and country. And the architectural timbre of the scene, its simple square door complicated by a shadowy set of columns on either side, hinted at this very public friar's secret involvement in private affairs.

Team Verona found a network of terraces skirting the college's student union. These terraces offered a richly provocative field for airing animosities and breezily observing the results: framed by open lawn on one side and huge picture windows on the other; visible from all sides and accessible from a multitude of angles through doorways and short flights of steps; built of flagstone and furnished with classic wooden lawn furniture (sturdy enough to stand on, light enough to move); complete with a smattering of colorful table umbrellas (retractable, mobile, festive) and interlinking three levels of action.

Team Monument unearthed a lakefront basketball court hedged by a chain link fence. Cut into the basement level of a dormitory, the court's cracked asphalt surface was bisected by a bedraggled tennis net and faced the lake's unmowed shore on the downhill side. Uphill stood an archway tunneling into the rear of the dormitory, truncated by a padlocked door. The setting's atmosphere had a funereal neglect, its torturous approach (we had to wind our way in through switchback double gates), and the stimulating possibilities of the chainlink fence (space for Romeo and Paris to duel through, even space for the audience to watch through) powerfully attracted the team.

Our most stimulating discovery, however, was not a playing space, but an insight into space's potential for enriching play. Reassembled as a group, we were rereading the sonnet that inaugurates Romeo and Juliet's romance. We suddenly realized that our readers, "poor blushing pilgrims" preparing to pray with kisses, were powerfully supported by the wall behind them. They were standing on the hearth of a huge, house-warming fireplace. Directly above them hung the icon of a virgin, her right hand lifted in ecstatic prayer. This found space was eminently economical. It was already constructed, ready, and waiting for us, free for the simple price of seeing its potential. Even better, it was profoundly theatrical, enriching the scene we played in it by the dialogue it started between the performance and the performing space, opening space for our imaginations to work in.

Opening space for imaginations to work in is one of creative staging's most potent effects. Its value is immense, but its price tag can be miniscule. When the Southern Shakespeare Festival staged free public showings of *The Merry Wives of Windsor* in Tallahassee's Kleman Plaza, for example, we wanted folks to experience the intersection of political power, civic promise, and community example that the play's original audience associated with Windsor Castle. That way, the blessing of the castle at the end of the play would make sense. As we surveyed Kleman Plaza, we realized that our performances would take place within easy eyeshot of Florida's Capitol tower. It cost very little money to copy the Capitol's silhouette into the backdrop of our simple indoor set, but it paid off enormously. Windsor's blessing resounded with immediate, accessible, Tallahassee overtones.

Other low-cost, high-imagination Shakespeare stagings have used the tailgate of a village firetruck for Juliet's balcony, city-hall steps for the assassination of Julius Caesar, an active county courthouse for the *Merchant of Venice*'s climactic trial, state parkland for the fairies' *Midsummer Night*'s wood, federal marshals for the officers called to keep order in *The Taming of the Shrew*, and World-Wide Wrestling Federation arenas for the wrestling match that treacherously opens *As You Like It*.

"Found" space's capacity for setting up provocative resonances between the play and the place where it's played is only part of the picture. No-budget, brainy approaches to space can powerfully motivate your actors, instruct your audience members, and pace your production by personifying your sets, marking plot parallels, engineering character transitions, projecting themes, and explicating the text with context. Which brings us to stage three.

Stage Three: Mindspace
Experiments in Stimulating Imagination through Creative Spacing

> Somewhere
> We'll find a new way of living,
> We'll find a way of forgiving
> Somewhere,
> Somewhere . . .
>
> *West Side Story*

Questions: How can the space create zero-budget settings for specific scenes? How do we build no-budget social orbits in the performance? How can the space (rather than the budget) be exploited to mark important parallels, levels, turning points, and progressions in the play's production? What low-budget contexts can enrich the world of the play?

Space: An area you have permission to perform in (i.e., "found" space, a classroom, or a formal rehearsal room)

Time: 15 minutes per voyage (minimum); several days of sequential experimentations would not be wasted

Actors: Full cast

Equipment: Scripts (full texts or selected scenes), all the furnishings native to the space (tables, chairs, boxes, desks, stools, planters, tree stumps, decks, dumpsters, fencing, blackboards, et al.)

Exercise: Select staging challenges from the play (i.e., set pieces you'd love to have appear, elements of the plot you'd like to make clear, symbols you want to ring in people's mind, archaic jokes and outdated customs in need of cultural CPR). Then experiment with turning actors into set pieces. Exploit parallels and levels and repetitions in the playing space to mark parallels and levels and repetitions in the action.

Let's say you've found a place, absolutely free, to perform the play. You're aware of your "found" space's potential to enrich the performance at no additional charge whatsoever. You've explored your options and decided how to configure your playing space, setting your actors and your auditors in the most productive, provocative, and engaging set of relationships (possibly even changing the performance space's configuration as the production proceeds). Trek complete? Home free? Not quite.

Locations in Shakespeare's plays—orbits within the playing space—can be deliciously fluid and nonspecific, turning a street into an orchard or a bedroom into a battlefield with the turn of a phrase. That's why the Chorus of *Henry V*, needing "a Muse of fire" to bring the world of the play to life, calls on the audience to use their "imaginary forces" to Think, when we talk of horses, that we see them

> Printing their proud hoof i' the receiving earth;
> For 'tis your thoughts that now must deck our kings,
> Carry them here and there; jumping o'er times,
> Turning the accomplishment of many years
> Into an hour-glass. . . .

Imagination—free for the tickling—can manufacture most of Shakespeare's locations. But some Shakespearean plots call for specific settings that your dramatic instincts (not to mention centuries of stage tradition) hanker to see realized in real space and time. So even when you've found a place for your production and a shape to perform it in, the prospect of constructing specific spaces within the orbit of the play may fill you with dismay. Say you want to build a balcony for Juliet, for example, or plant a box tree for Malvolio, or raise a Duke's Oak for Peter Quice & Company. How do you do that on no budget, with maximum dramatic impact?

Experiments at the Drey suggest that actors can become stage spaces, articulating places the play needs with their own bodies. We happened to attack the problem of *Midsummer*'s towering oak in a room inhabited by (in addition to our troupe of twenty-odd actors) a handful of well-worn wooden chairs. We pulled a sturdy, wide-bottomed armchair to the head of the room, right below a staircase. Then we started building a tree out of people—two actors standing on the seat; five more on the floor, bracing and branching out from the actors on the chair; three more on a table they'd dragged into the picture; and two on the staircase, topping the construction. The tree that emerged was tall, imposing, and dynamically dramatic. It could whisper, it could sway, it could cue the actors in playwright Quince's rehearsal, it could watch their play, and when Puck slid down the banister to crown Bottom with donkey ears (two fingers held behind the actor's head, like middle schoolers mugging for a class picture), this living tree could dissolve quite startlingly into a horde of attacking fairies.

Twelfth Night's box tree came to us, appropriately enough, in a black box, an empty playing space in a nearly empty room. We were brainstorming approaches to a double-edged problem: how to make a space that beguiles Malvolio into discovering Maria's letter, and how to create places for Toby, Fabian, and Aguecheek to oversee Malvolio's discovery without being discovered themselves. A double stroke of genius later, we had a dramatically exciting, scenically fluid, zero-budget solution. Malvolio found the letter in a colonnade—a living colonnade, created by two rows of actors arching their arms and touching fingertips. This colonnade actively seduced the steward into taking delivery of the letter, first by sycophantically echoing phrases from his soliloquy, then by sloping its ceiling to force Malvolio to stoop directly over the envelope, and finally by placing the epistle directly in his hand. Delivery accomplished, the colonnade morphed into a box tree—a square column of actors standing back to back, all facing outwards. We added height to the column by putting Sir Andrew, Fabian, and Sir Toby on milk crates in the middle of the tree, literally blending them into the scenery. Malvolio's reaction to the box tree's back-talk was hilarious. Without the use of a single nail, without the expense of one red cent, actors had created spaces that enlarged our dramatic world.

Other experiments at the Drey have shown that simple, generic props can become powerful tools for specifying playing spaces and unifying the play. Using the same sack of leftover tulle, for example, we built a veil for Olivia that later transformed into Malvolio's prison, an orchard wall for Romeo that rose in the world to become the balustrade to Juliet's balcony, a wrestling rink for *As You Like It* that dissolved into the Forest of Arden, and the central fixtures of *The Tempest*'s first three scenes. Our tulle came to us in strips approximately six feet long and three feet wide, the remnants of a white-wedding extravaganza.

For *Twelfth Night*, we had tulle handlers (two to a strip) surround the duchess in mourning, processing with her as visible embodiments of her grief. Dismissed when Olivia unveils for Cesario, the handlers reappeared to swaddle Malvolio with their strips when he's officially declared insane. Wrapping the madman in tulle, we found, made a jail-space that was simple, mobile, economical, and (most importantly) dramatically meaningful, since it physically linked Malvolio's imprisoning self-conceit to the self-indulgent grief that had paralyzed Olivia earlier in the play.

Two actors holding strips of tulle like jump-ropes gave our experimental Romeo a real but very inexpensive orchard wall to leap. The same tulle, lifted to arm's length and allowed to unfurl towards the ground, became the guardrail of Juliet's balcony (a rail instantly adjustable to Juliet's arm, chin and cheek).

We staged *As You Like It*'s scenic shift from the cutthroat competitiveness of court to the playful ambiguities of Arden by building a wrestling rink—a square of actors holding tulle ropes—that transformed into a bucolic bivouac (each actor pitching a tent, spreading a picnic basket, or tooling a tulle lean-to where the spirit moved her).

The Tempest's breathtaking sequence of shipwreck, followed by Prospero's conversation with Miranda, segueing into Prospero's conference with Ariel, inspired our actors to hoist a mainsail (tulle anchored to globe of a lamppost) that could dissolve into a hermit's cell (tulle draped between table umbrellas) and then gloriously take flight as Ariel's wings (tulle stretched by handlers to the full width of the terrace from the hands of our smallest actor, perched on our tallest actor's shoulders).

This experiment with *The Tempest* took place on the grounds around Rollins College's student union, where the fluidity of the space—one seamless sweep rolling from lawn to spacious steps to curving terraces—eloquently expressed the dramatic structure of the play's opening, flowing seamlessly from ship to cell to spirit world. Another place on Rollins campus—a courtyard where a circular fountain punctuates the intersection of two sidewalks—helped us find spatial expression for the psychological scenery of another play.

It had struck us in discussing *Twelfth Night*'s love triangles that a strong spiritual kinship linked Viola, Olivia, and Orsino. All three characters were survivors of shipwrecks that had violently split them from their better selves: Viola from her twin, Olivia from her brother, Orsino from the hope of a balanced, satisfying love. For protective coloration in the alien world they're cast adrift in, all three assume the semblance of the thing they've lost: Viola the spitting image of Sebastian, Olivia the ghost of her brother (a walking corpse complete with shroud), Orsino the embodiment of insatiable, impossible desire. We wanted to know if the space could communicate this kinship as subtly as the text does, so we tried staging parallel processions to introduce these characters.

We divided our actors into three teams of seven or eight people each. Each team took a character, a stretch of sidewalk leading up to the fountain, and a grab-bag of toys recycled from children's birthday parties. (The bags held a random mix of noisemakers, balloons, silly hats, hula hoops, flyswatters, animal noses, music boxes, beach balls, and miniature confetti canons which the procession teams could use or ignore as they saw fit.) With ten minutes to rehearse, the teams staged a sequence of three processional entrances—a crew of seamen rushing a sodden Viola to the fountain's edge to perform CPR, accept her thanks, then disguise her with /in/ an ensign's hat; a solemn procession of mourners supporting Olivia (impersonated here by a distinguished male professor of English in dark glasses, pillbox hat, and veil) as s/he sinks to the fountain's lip, dragging her fair hand through the water and sobbing; and a gaggle of high-society playboys sweeping Orsino toward the waterfront to ring in the New Year, smothering giggles as he waxes sentimental, then setting off their confetti canons with a bang.

Watching these processions, we found that the space clarified the play's connections. In giving us a common shape for the central characters' entrances, in marking the place where three worlds meet, the space mapped out *Twelfth Night*'s psychological terrain.

Other experiments in mindspace have shown how levels, repeated use of locations, and progressions in the playing space can articulate themes in Shakespeare's plays. Surveying for playing levels, we found two staircases in the same building that were mirror images of each other (one interior, one exterior). When we used these two staircases to stage *The Tempest*'s successive labors of Caliban and Frederick forced to carry firewood (one compulsively cursing his taskmaster, the other patiently toiling to prove himself noble), the contrast between the man-beast's devolution and the rational lover's rise above the level of brute instinct popped into the foreground, strikingly inscribed into the performance by the space.

Physical levels in our set—we tried Caliban descending the outside staircase curse by curse while Frederick ascended the inner one, then (to experience a subversive post-colonial inversion of the paradigm) reversed directions—made symbolic dimensionality visible. Repeatedly using another set of levels, colonized from the margins of a café courtyard, helped us perform a symbol central to *Romeo and Juliet*. The image of fertile promises proving fatal (i.e., of Romeo's extended hand of fellowship guiding Tybalt's sword through Mercutio's guard, for example) struck us as the heart of the star-crossed lovers' tragedy. We were awestruck by Capulet's speech during Juliet's apparent death on the morning of her wedding day:

> All things that we ordained festival
> Turn from their office to black funeral;
> Our instruments to melancholy bells,
> Our wedding cheer to a sad burial feast;
> Our solemn hymns to sullen dirges change,
> Our bridal flowers serve for a buried corpse,
> And all things change them to the contrary.

Delivered bedside, this speech set us looking for a location we could re-use both as Romeo and Juliet's wedding-bed and as their deathbed. We found a freestanding garden bench framed by a low wall near the entrance to a café courtyard. Sitting in the café chairs, we could look up at the bench, and make it the heart of a honeymoon suite. Standing up, standing on the wall, or even standing on chairs, we could look down on the bench, making it the center of a mausoleum. (In fact, we found that simply having an actor playing the Nurse or Paris or Peter or Balthasar approach the bench from below or above could create this illusion of shifting levels for the audience.) When Romeo and Juliet re-used this location, creating the same spatial relationships to wake up after their wedding-night and to die with a kiss, the dramatic impact was shattering. (We had similar if less dramatic results by using the same location for both Friar Lawrence's herb garden and the Apothecary's shop, another example of cordial potential proving poisonous.)

In another exercise, progressions in the playing space helped us map the thematic anatomy of *Twelfth Night*. Orsino punctuates his opening scene with a recipe for fully-grounded love:

> When liver, brain, and heart,
> These sovereign thrones, are all supplied and filled,
> . . . with one self king.

We read the gathering of these ingredients—kindred feelings, compatible thoughts, and consensual desires—as a guide through the progress of the plot's romances. Orsino, for example, starts the play with his physical appetite fully aroused ("If music be the food of love,

..." 1.1), then attaches his passion to Cesario through debate ("Make no compare / between that love a woman can bear me/And that I owe Olivia" 2.4), and finally finds satisfaction when he sees the passion is mutual ("Boy, thou has said to me a thousand times/Thou never shouldst love woman like to me" 5.1).

Olivia, Viola, and even Sebastian follow similar progressions through admiring their intended partner's appearance, intelligence, and fidelity. As literary critics, we saw clear connections. But how could we make our love-pilgrims' progress performable? Space naturally came to our rescue, especially since we had access to the student lounge of a classroom building, furnished with vending machines, bookbag cubicles, and a couch. When we placed the "liver" stage of each romance at the vending machines, the "brain" stages at the bookbag cubicles, and the "heart" stages at the couch, the spaces clearly and effectively mapped out our production concept.

Space can powerfully express the mind of your play. Imagine the cumulative impact of Julius Caesar's suicides staged on the site of Caesar's assassination, or Prospero recanting revenge precisely where he first called up the tempest, or Desdemona strangled with her handkerchief upon the very spot where Iago found it. Moreover, space can powerfully prepare audience and students to think about the plays, by framing action in accessible, entertaining contexts.

Consider the Apollo Mission undertaken by the rude mechanicals of *A Midsummer Night's Dream*. As Peter Quince, the harassed author-producer of their "Most Lamentable Comedy of Pyramus and Thisby," puts it: "There is two hard things; that is, to bring the moonlight into a chamber: for you know, Pyramus and Thisby meet by moonlight. . . . Then there is another thing. We must have a wall in the great chamber; for Pyramus and Thisby, says the story, did talk through the chink of a wall" (III.i.42-56).

Shakespeare recognized that such seemingly insuperable problems can eventually inspire brilliant, breakthrough solutions as they do in Bottom. "Some man or other must present Wall; and let him have some plaster, or some loam, or some rough-cast about him, to signify wall; or let him hold his fingers thus, and through that cranny shall Pyramus and Thisby whisper!" (59-62) As for moonlight, "One must come in with a bush of thorns and a lantern, and say he comes to disfigure or to present the person of Moonshine!" (51-53) In an intensely playful, extraordinarily imaginative epiphany, Shakespeare has his players reconceive the significance of space, and their play takes flight.

The same mental aerodynamics can work for all of us. Stop

thinking of space as a thing. Instead, start thinking of it as a person, a collaborator who can help us and our students tell a story, rouse an audience, project a point, raise a question, problematize a relationship, highlight a scene, make lovers meet by moonlight, and bring in a wall between our nonexistent production budgets and our sky's-the-limit performance goals. In staging Shakespeare, space acts like *Midsummer*'s Puck. Finding "a play toward," he never can just sit still. He must get involved, both as "auditor" and "actor, too, perhaps, if I see cause." And the result can be pure magic.

Happy space trekking!

What's Reality Anyhow?
Puppets and A Midsummer Night's Dream

—☙

Ellie Conde, Lindsay Hunter, Heather Williams,
and Lauren Yarborough

Four graduate students from the University of Central Florida suggest ways of integrating puppets into performance by describing ways to use them in a fanciful exploration of A Midsummer Night's Dream.

—☙

We are such stuff as dreams are made on ...
The Tempest IV.i.157

LONG BEFORE JIM HENSON, THE MUPPETS, AND *SESAME STREET*, puppets and marionettes had an impressive theatrical history. Socrates discusses them in the *Symposium*, and their use seems to have been common in the Renaissance, as Ben Jonson's *Bartholomew Fair* (1614) suggests. Recent theatrical productions have explored a variety of ways of incorporating this tradition into performances of Shakespeare. Julie Taynor, for example, whose Broadway interpretation of *The Lion King* revolutionized theatrical spectacle, opens her film version of *Titus* with a young child creating a puppet theater battle.

College productions, like ones at the University of Maryland and Gustavus Adolphus College, have mixed live actors with puppets, while the Genesis Repertory began its version of *Richard III* with miniature marionettes summarizing the action of all Shakespeare's earlier history plays. Perhaps the most intercultural, intercontinental experiment in this tradition is the Czechoslovakian-American Marionette Theater's *Hamlet*, in which the puppeteers appear as actors alongside their antique Czech puppets.

Using puppets clearly offers an enormous range of possibilities in classroom productions. To explore some of those possibilities, we chose the fifth act of *A Midsummer Night's Dream*, a play that offers its characters opportunities to discover alternative worlds. Our production had to fit within the confines of an ordinary classroom, had to experiment with crossing the boundaries between audience and players, and could cost no more than about twenty dollars.

After reading the play over and over, we found ourselves starting at what we thought was a very unusual place in the text, one that occurs far before the fifth act. As with most experiments, this exercise revealed that what at first seem to be unrelated scenes begin to reveal startling connections. As teachers, it is essential to follow such connections without losing track of the main purpose of the exercise.

For us, the line that jumped out at us occurs in the fight between Helena and Hermia that centers on the differences in height and stature between the two girls. Helena in her rage calls Hermia a "puppet" and a "counterfeit": "Fie,fie! You counterfeit, you puppet you!" And Hermia, stung by the insult, responds:

> *Puppet?* Why so? Ay, that way goes the game.
> Now I *perceive* that she hath made compare
> Between our *statures*; she hath urged her height
> And with her . . . tall personage,
> Her height . . . she hath prevailed with him.
> (III.ii.289-293)

Like most readers, we were first attracted to the escalating cat fight because it seems so contrary to Helena's first appearance. But since we were also looking to a central concept for our prodution and had decided on the questions raised in the play about the nature of reality, we became intrigued with the idea of stature and the emergence of a Helena who has more to her, or less to her, than first meets the eye. This apparent change in personality, combined with the references to physical stature and the concrete imagery of puppets, started us thinking about how the possibilities of "puppet" and perception might help us explore both perception and reality. Reality continues to shift throughout the play. After all, at the very moment the fairies appear as full size actors, Shakespeare's words convince us that they are tiny, almost miniscule. In *A Midsummer Night's Dream*, what is real often seems impossible and the impossible invariably appears.

The fight also reminded us of a Punch and Judy show, part of the historic tradition of puppet theater. Characters frantically run, fight, scramble, tear hair, and scream, but they do so in a world in which no one is ever hurt. When we asked students if humans ever behave like this, they realized how human all of this seems. Of course, in the play they are all caught under the magical spell of Puck, somewhere between two worlds, manipulated and maneuvered like puppets. Perhaps when Helena calls Hermia a little puppet, she speaks with more truth than she realizes. And this insight became a central concept for our *Dream*.

In our production, all human beings, especially the most apparently rational ones, would have puppet equivalents, created and manipulated through the imagination of a full-sized Puck, who would function as instigator or creator of the play's mortals. This fairy master of chaos suspends ordinary reality as he controls the magic of the night.

Our Puck appears in act V as a full-sized invisible human actor holding a puppet Peter Quince and delivering his Prologue to Pyramus and Thisbe sometimes from an offstage voice and sometimes with his own onstage voice. But Puck always and clearly manipulates the actions. Hearing Puck's voice in the Prologue opens the text to entirely new possibilities:

> If we offend, it is with our good will
> That you should think, we come not to offend
> But with good will. To show our *simple skill,*
> That is the true beginning of our end. . . .
> The actors are *at hand*; and by their *show*
> You shall know all that you are like to know."
> (V.i.108-117)

Here our audience had a new sense of what it means to have the actors at hand, squinting to see who was real and who was not. The audience also experiences what Hermia had in IV.i.190-191: "Methinks I see these things with parted eye/When everything seems double."

For our production, the puppet Quince, manipulated by Puck, also got all the punctuation wrong. At cued moments, Quince turned on his master's hand to see what was going wrong in his carefully rehearsed speech. The audience loved the confusion. Quince as Puck. Puck as Quince. All of this made even more sense when we staged Puck's last speech to emphasize the ways its rhythms, structure, and repetition, along with its promise to make all things right, echo Quince's Prologue:

> If we shadows have offended,
> Think but this and all is mended:
> That you have but slumbered here,
> While these visions did appear.
> And this weak and idle theme,
> No more yielding but a dream,
> Gentles do not reprehend.
> If you pardon we will mend. (V.i.422-429)

Is the Epilogue Prologue and the Prologue Epilogue?

In his Prologue, Quince introduces all the characters from *Pyramus and Thisbe*, who, in our production, make their entrances as puppets. Puck, of course, remains central as the whole scene unfolds in his theater, his playground. He calls up music at every opportunity, with the musical references emphasizing the comic dimensions of all human behavior, especially human sexual behavior: "Lords, what fools these mortals be!" (III.ii.115)

As our audience settled into this perception, the puppeteer and his puppets once again changed direction and transformed reality. Puck suddenly sprinkles fairy dust on each of the puppets and they all disappear. But the rude mechanicals reappear moments later as full-sized human beings, dressed exactly like their puppet counterparts. The audience must once again shift reality gears as the humans act out their play, only to be interrupted by Puck, this time holding puppets of the aristocrats. Our new puppets begin to comment on the play within the play's action.

We complicated the confusion even more by having the aristocratic puppets identify themselves with name tags for people in our audience, with those audience members giving lines for Demetrius, Lysander, Hermia, and Helena on cue. As auditor and actor, fiction and reality became more obscured, audience members tried, without being prompted, to imitate the puppets' voices. Throughout the performance, we attempted to keep the audience off balance, continually confronting a newly emerging world. After all, the play constantly seems to be ending only to be revived in a new direction. With an alternately sarcastic and suggestive Puck pushing the audience to lighthearted confusion, we wanted everyone to realize that we are the stuff dreams are made on.

By comically challenging the audience to look and look and look again at what constitutes certainty, our characters helped blur the distinction between dream and reality, night and day, puppet and human. The music for the production helped convey the mixture of comedy and seriousness, dream and reality, with a recognition of the play's emphasis on courting rituals, romance, and marriage. Thisbe's first entrance is accompanied by Marvin Gaye's *Let's Get It On* and the Bergomask is danced to *Baby Got Back* by Sir Mix A Lot.

The key to experimenting with puppets is in the experiment. Students need to be encouraged to explore any possibilities that open up, recognizing the need, finally, for a coherent production that they can actually perform. Giant marionettes in a small space will lose their effect as much as miniature puppets on a massive stage. As in all productions, the teacher's role is to reorient continually, to question assumptions, and to help students find ways to realize their visions. Since using puppets requires making puppets, we developed the following list of materials and simple pattern for construction. Felt, our primary material, is very inexpensive.

Supplies:
Felt
12 pieces of peach-colored felt for the puppet bodies
2 sheets of red felt
2 sheets of black felt
1 sheet of cranberry-colored felt
1 sheet of white felt
2 sheets of pink felt
4 sheets of gray felt (Wall and Pyramus' Armor)
1 sheet of green felt
3 sheets of yellow felt (Lion and hair)
2 sheets of brown felt
One package of medium sized googlie eyes
Craft glue

Basic Body Pattern

The following pattern, much reduced, of course, assumes no creative or sewing skill or experience. If you have skill, experience, or both, be creative. The books below offer a wide range of ideas. The pattern we used works for all puppet characters except Wall, who—or which—can be made from two pieces of felt sewn together. Be sure to cut a front and back for each character. Use a basic pattern like the one below and then individualize each puppet so that the audience can distinguish Hermia from Helena and Snug from Bottom. If you plan to have human doubles, you will find it easier to make the puppets first and then replicate their costumes in full size.

Once you cut out the puppets, glue on the pieces of their costumes. Be sure to glue on the hair, mouth, and nose before you sew the puppets. Attach the googlie eyes, too, before sewing. Once all of the small feature parts are on, sew the puppets together with a simple hand stitch.

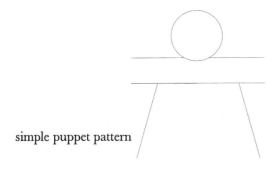

simple puppet pattern

Resources

Allison, Drew and Donald Devet. *The Foam Book: An Easy Guide to Building Polyfoam Puppets*. Charlotte, NC: Grey Seal Puppets, 1997.

Buetter, Barbara MacDonald. *Simple Puppets from Everyday Material*. New York: Sterling, 1996.

Currell, David. *Puppets and Puppet Theater*. Wiltshire, England: Crowood, 1999.

Engler, Larry. *Making Puppets Come Alive: How To Learn and Teach Hand Puppetry*. Mineola, NY: Dover, 1997.

Fling, Helen. *Marionettes: How To Make and Work Them*. New York: Dover, 1973.

Flower, Cedric. *Puppets: Methods and Materials*. Worcester, MA: Davis, 1983.

Lade, Roger. *The Most Excellent Book of How To Be a Puppeteer*. Brookfield, CT: Copper Beech, 1996.

Latshaw, George. *The Complete Book of Puppetry*. Mineola, NY: Dover, 2000.

Ross, Laura. *Hand Puppets: How To Make and Use Them*. New York: Dover, 1989.

Speaight, George. *The History of the English Puppet Theater*. Carbondale, IL: Southern Illinois University, 1990.

Playing Games with People
Fifteen Steps Towards Ensemble

—Ꮬ

Judith Rubinger

Judith Rubinger, a Central Florida drama therapist, offers fifteen games to build a class into an ensemble.

—Ꮬ

TO ACT AS AN ENSEMBLE, STUDENTS MUST THINK of themselves as an ensemble. The following fifteen building games, improvisations, and opening exercises have proven especially effective with high school students. Both practical and fun, they help students realize the challenge, joy, and energy of working in a community.

1. Introducing Ourselves

In this deceptively simple game, the group forms a circle and, after a brief warm-up/stretch session, is told that we will go around the circle with each person saying her name, while playing with the sounds of the letters and the "feel" of their combined resonance in her mouth. Also, and in conjunction with exploring the sound of the name, each of the participants is to spontaneously produce a movement that "feels" like a fit to the name and to oneself; after each person has pronounced her name and expressed along with it some kind of movement, the entire circle reproduces the name, attempting to recreate both the verbal and physical movement pattern and emotion that has accompanied the name. The important premise here is that there is no wrong sound or movement. Once the realization registers that there are no "rights" and "wrongs" in this stage of creative work—that we are here for genuine exploration without preconceptions about what we are to produce—there tends to be an incredible sense of relief and freedom. Along with this shared sensation of relief and freedom emerge feelings of joyfulness, self confidence and the newly found recognition that we are all unique individuals who are safely allowed to explore ourselves in the group setting. In reality, being allowed or, even more precisely, encouraged to experiment with the knowledge that no judgments will be made against

---

us is a gift which is all too seldom offered in our schools or other educational settings.

Admittedly, among any newly formed group of this nature, there will inevitably be a certain amount of embarrassment and trepidation: these exercises in form and objective may well feel uncomfortably foreign at first to those who are unfamiliar with this type of creative process. In our ensemble, this feeling was alleviated by the participation of seasoned alumni role models who had experienced these "games" and by staff who modeled childlike playfulness in the presence of the new ensemble members.

One of the most critical aspects of this "game" is that the players not pre-plan their actions. This is a difficult task for most, particularly because so many young people are accustomed to hearing the command to "think before acting" from adults and other authority figures. In the "game" described above, the opposite is the case: the more spontaneously the participants can express their actions, the better. Unlike many of the day-to-day goings-on of the young people, the goal here is to move away from the regimen imposed daily by their "rational" minds and to summon up an entirely different part of their being. After the first person creates her name/movement, and the others repeat it, the process continues around the circle.

2. Truth or Lie

Seated in a circle, each ensemble member makes one true statement about himself, as the others carefully observe the member's voice and body language. Then each member proceeds to make one false statement. Again, the other ensemble members should watch and listen carefully. On the third round, the player states a truth or a lie, attempting in either case, to convince the others that his statement is true. Through careful observation and listening, the ensemble members try to determine the truth or falsehood of his statement. Not only does this game have the obvious advantage of forcing the participants to zero in on and truly take note of the body language, voice tones, and other characteristics of their peers, but it results in a great deal of laughter, self disclosure, and discovery about one another, and ultimately, brings about a wonderful sense of camaraderie.

3. Interview

The group is divided into couples—ideally members should be paired up with someone they do not know well. Each person gets four to five minutes to interview her partner; after the eight to ten minutes during which both partners have interviewed one another, each member will introduce her partner to the group. A variation on this exercise is to ask the partner who is doing the introducing to slip three lies about the interviewee into the introduction with the objective of passing these lies off as truth. The lies must not be pre-agreed on by the partners, but are to be created spontaneously. In order to "deceive" the group, both partners must behave as if the lies were completely true. The rest of the ensemble members try to identify the three lies.

This game has several benefits. First, it provides a safe structure whereby each member of the ensemble is afforded the opportunity to get to know one other member more closely. Building on this, the remaining members of the ensemble are introduced to one another in a more creative, focused manner. Also, the added twist of the three "slipped in" lies will initiate an immediate bond between the partners who are working together to "fool" the audience. The audience is, in turn, more tuned in to each member because of the challenge of picking up on all three of the lies, thereby exercising their listening and observation skills, and more truly observing their fellow players.

4. The Healing Gift

The ensemble is divided into two equal lines—one stands at one end of the space; the other faces them at the opposite end of the room. One of the groups is told that they are to play the "healers": in other words, each of them is to imagine that he possesses a special, magical ability to "heal." The others are each asked to imagine being in need of some form of "healing" and to attempt to convey this silently to one of the healers so as to attract him to come to his assistance. The "healers" are asked to "study" the members on the other side of the room and to decide, each on his own, who is most in need of his healing and precisely what is needed. It may be a gentle shoulder massage, a handshake, a pat on the back, a listening ear, a few words of encouragement, or even a funny story or a joke. Or it may be something entirely different from any of these. The important thing is for the "healer" to completely tune in to the person needing his healing, so that the appropriate "healing" act can be accomplished.

When the leader gives the signal, each "healer" makes his way across the room to the person upon whom he has chosen to bestow his "healing" gift. Two "healers" cannot "heal" the same individual: if one person has been selected by a particular "healer," the other healers must choose partners who have not yet been selected.

This exercise is one of my favorites for many reasons. Perhaps most significantly, just as all good acting is grounded in truthful human emotions and real actions, the notion of "pretending" in this case is immediately superseded by reality. The objective of "healing" here becomes a true driving force because ultimately it is a real aspect of our human nature. Just as substantial is the very real human need to be "healed" or touched in some way by another. The players, then, through this exercise, come to realize personally that good acting springs from a truthful core intention. The act of giving and receiving— of real human contact—lies at the core of the ensemble experience. Indeed, this is the very heart of theater. By drawing the players imme- diately into this powerful experience, this "game" provides one of the most compelling entries into the work that will be further developed through the human connections forged among them. Moreover, this "game" is one of the most nearly perfect demonstrations of the fact that belief in oneself—confidence in one's own inner strength and ability to touch others—is the first step in the transformation of the intangible to the tangible. Miraculously, while belief in oneself may begin as a mere game of pretend, the exercise tends to draw the player into actually believing in, discovering and then assuming the person power that he has imagined. From here, it is only a matter of time and repetition until the player comes to view himself differently and in a more competent and effective light than ever before. Like so much of the magic of the- ater, this "game" must be experienced in order to be truly appreciated.

5. Walk, Freeze; Walk, Hi; Walk, Name; Walk, Hug; Walk, Compliment

This game is a simple exercise serving to get people up, moving, and making physical connections with one another. There is no anxiety or stress because there are no judgments; the completion of simple phys- ical tasks is both easy and enjoyable.

The players are first asked to walk around comfortably and ran- domly, but at an energetic pace. At the command "freeze," they are to stop all movement, holding their precise physical posture. This is repeat- ed several times. They then commence walking once again, but on the command to stop, each person lets out an energetic whooping "hi" to whoever is physically nearest. By the third section, the command "name" is the signal to make eye contact with another player and say one's name. This is repeated several times until the players are instruct- ed once again to walk. On the command "hug," each player gently hugs whoever happens to be closest. (This can be varied by announcing a specific number of people who must be hugged when the command "hug" is given.) As with the other segments of the exercise, this is also repeated several times. The players are finally asked to walk energetically, but then to stop and pay a sincere personal compliment to whomever they find themselves closest. (It may be as simple as complimenting one's outfit or as deep as complimenting one's character.) The person complimented is to receive the compliment with a simple "thank you."

In addition to getting people moving energetically but safely, this exercise provides practice in learning to listen and respond spontaneously without judging or second guessing. Moreover, it is an important bonding activity, particularly as each participant is asked to touch, hug, make eye contact with and ultimately truthfully compliment another member of the ensemble. Finally, as is true of each of the games we are proposing, this activity provides a shared, pleasurable experience, reinforcing the newly forged bonds emerging among the members of the ensemble.

6. Patterns

The group is asked to merely walk around the space in no particular pattern or manner. As the members are walking, they are asked to try to sense the pattern being created by the group and to attempt to allow themselves to become part of the group's pattern. Once a pattern has been created, the players are asked to break out of the pattern, walk in a random fashion once again, sense the pattern that is now the will of the group, and gradually allow themselves to become a part of it once again. This exercise teaches the players something of what is involved in working as an ensemble—each player must learn to tune in to the will of the group. One learns both to merge one's personal intent in the collective enterprise, as well as to break out of the collective when necessary.

It is important to bear in mind that this exercise can appear as a complete failure when first attempted. The director must be prepared to accept that the young ensemble may not be able to master this one in the early stages of the work without regarding the effort as a failure; if one approaches this with a sense of humor and an honest readiness to observe the group dynamics as they develop and change over the course of the rehearsal period, however, it can be an effective and fun means of assessing the group cohesiveness of the ensemble. Remember to keep your sense of humor!

7. The People Knot

Players form a tight circle of fifteen or so and, with everyone's eyes closed, all reach their arms straight out in front of them so as to clasp a hand with each of their hands. No one can hold both hands of the same person or the hand of someone right next to themselves in the circle. Everyone now opens their eyes and, climbing through and around one another, without letting go of anyone's hand, all try to untangle the knot so as to form a ring of people holding hands (or possibly two interconnected circles of hands) side by side. The participants may pivot their grasp, but may not let go of any hands.

This exercise is a wonderfully structured and safe way to allow the players to become physically comfortable with one another while working on a common goal—the untangling of the knot and restitution of the perfect circle. The effort to solve the problem of the knot as a group requires cooperation, team work, effort, perseverance, creativity, and flexibility—all of which are important ensemble skills.

8. Freeze Tag

This is another popular improvisational warm-up. In this version, one player begins in the center of the circle of players. He does not know who, where or what he is doing here. Anyone from the circle may come up with an idea for a scene and then enter the space, interacting with the person in the center accordingly. It is the responsibility of the person in the center to pick up cues as to what his relationship with the other player is supposed to be and to play along accordingly. The scene may be as realistic or as fantastic as its conceiver determines. The player who enters may determine, for example, that he is watering his droopy flower, so that the person in the center ends up becoming the flower. By the same token, the "flower" may end up speaking, complaining, dancing or doing any other sort of "unrealistic" activity in connection with the person who is watering it. The main thing, however, is to go along with (i.e. accept the offer) the concept or frame presented by whoever is determining the scene. When someone else in the circle spontaneously spots an opportunity for a new altered scene (through closely watching the body positions of the two players), he calls out "freeze" and the players in the center freeze their positions at that moment. The person who has called for a "freeze" then enters the circle, taps the player he wishes to leave the center space, and proceeds to play whatever idea he has brought to the playing center. Once again, the person in the center plays along with the idea.

This favorite warm-up teaches several important ensemble skills. Perhaps the most crucial skill is to open oneself up without judgment so as to accept the scenario created by the other no matter how ridiculous the opening setup may at first appear. Of equal import is the willingness to "let go" or to allow the improvisation to go wherever the players jointly take it, without either player feeling compelled to force or determine the course and outcome of the scene. This improvisation demands trust—in oneself, in the other, and, ultimately, in the players as a team constituting a newly formed entity with its own will. The thrill of participating in and allowing the scene to emerge, is akin to the thrill of ensemble creation. At the same time, the common awareness that the scene may be completely altered at any moment enhances the exciting nature of the endeavor. As in life, one can never be certain of what the next moment will offer; nevertheless, the players must attempt to greet each moment with openness and enthusiasm, allowing themselves to follow their intuitive impulses as they arise, while still playing within the structure of the game.

9. The Trust Circle

The trust circle is another favorite among ensemble exercises. The players form a circle (6-8 is about the optimum number of people per circle; if necessary, more than one circle may be simultaneously formed), standing closely together facing forward with their shoulders nearly touching. There should be no gaps in the circle. One player steps into the center of the circle, closes her eyes and places her crossed arms over her chest. The players around her take a firm stance. I suggest that each one lean into the circle with front knee bent and solidly reinforced by the back leg a couple of feet behind and firmly planted. All then put their hands up, palms open and face the person in the center. They are informed that it is all of their responsibility to see to it that the person in the center does not fall—therefore, they must give total concentration to the exercise and not cause distractions through talking or joking.

The person in the center stands relaxed, but with her feet rigidly in place, and begins to fall backward until supported by the other players. The players carefully push the person in the center back and forth, and *gently* around so that she falls softly around the circle. The pushing should be light and easy at first, but then with greater force and firmness as the person in the center becomes more comfortable and trusting of the group. After a few minutes, the group leader stops and steadies the person who has been inside the circle; she opens her eyes and rejoins the circle. The exercise proceeds with each player taking a turn at being in the center

This activity is great fun, tending to bring out the child in each player. Players repeatedly report experiencing tremendous pleasure in being gently tossed around the circle while gradually increasing their trust and confidence that the group will not let them fall. Yielding control to a reliable, trustworthy community can elicit a wondrous sense of freedom and joy for the player in the center, who, precisely because he knows and trusts that the community will be there for him, can take advantage of the opportunity to let go of some of his own self-controls, and the need to be there at every instant—focused and attentive so as to take care of one another and prevent any possible injury—offers the ensemble players an incomparable exercise in communal responsibility.

10. Whose Hand

Players are instructed to remove all jewelry, watches, Band-Aids, etc. from their right hands. All then stand silently within the playing area and close their eyes, stretching out their right hands. The leader then helps guide each one to another, so that every person is holding the right hand of another, then asks the players to remain silent but to carefully explore tactilely the hand they are now holding. They are coached to ask themselves (without responding verbally) the following questions: Is this person a male or a female? Is this a "hard" person or a "soft" person? Is this someone I would trust? Is this person loyal? Would he make a good friend? Does this person have a sense of humor? Would I enjoy spending time with this person? Is this a shy or an outgoing person? Is this a confident person? Is this an intellectual person? An artistic person? An athletic person? A wise person? What else can I surmise about this person based on his hand? The leader then asks the players to release the hands of their partners, and, with all the players' eyes still closed, she separates the pairs, leading them to distant parts of the playing space. All are told that they may now open their eyes. Their task is, through their sense of sight, to now find the person whose hand they have been exploring, walk over, and test the hand to make sure it is indeed the right person.

This exercise is ideally suited to developing personal and group awareness of stereotypical assumptions and conclusions, with an eye toward destroying these stereotypical associations. The group can quickly appreciate that by using their sense of touch, rather than sight, the individual players can come to "see" a whole new set of qualities in another individual, and to negate much of what they have previously surmised based on stereotypical assumptions conditioned by media or visual messages.

Often, new and surprising discoveries are made. I remember one occasion, for example, when one of the female players was amazed to finally discover that the hand she had been examining belonged to a male, rather than a female, player. In keeping with certain male/female stereotypes, she had not allowed for the possibility that a male's hand could contain the kind and degree of sensitivity that she had experienced in that hand.

It is also quite telling to observe players who are surprised when they learn that the color of the hand is not at all what they had assumed. A secondary, but still significant, outcome of this exercise is that an important recognition is suddenly restored by our frequently neglected sense of touch. Thus, through personal rediscovery, we are reminded of the insight that is possible to attain through an alternative, underused sense.

11. Leading the Blind

Players pair up once again. One player is the "blind" one and the other is the "guide." The leader then explains that each guide is responsible for leading the "blind" partner safely, so as to give the "blind" partner as whole and as extensive an experience of the world as possible. The leader then specifies a particular time, by which all players are to be brought back to the rehearsal space. The "blind" partner must close his eyes and keep them closed during the duration of the exercise. A half-hour is a good amount of time for the exercise. Change roles to "return" the experience.

12. Transforming Objects

The members stand in a circle. One person finds an imaginary object and proceeds to use the object in some way. She then passes it to the player next to her, who also handles it until it gradually transforms itself into something else. She then uses this new object and passes it on to the player next to her who handles it until it once again transforms into a new object. This continues all around the circle until each player has had a turn to handle and transform an object. The important stipulation here is that the players "allow" the object to transform itself, not that they impose a transformation upon it.

13. Ball

Players form a circle. One player picks up an imaginary basketball and throws it to another player across the circle. The imaginary ball must be handled (thrown as well as caught) as if it had absolute reality—a task which requires complete cooperation and focus. The ball must remain the same size, shape, and weight for everyone. After some practice with one size of ball, the players may change the size, shape, and weight of the ball. The group leader may call out the changes, or the changes can be initiated by the players themselves. Eventually, different objects may be substituted for balls (i.e., hand grenades, eggs, or crystal wine glasses).

14. Different Walks

The players are asked to walk randomly about the space. Then, after a few moments of natural walking, they are asked to "test out" walking in different ways. The idea is to experiment with how a physical change effects their mood and/or persona. They are to test the following ways to walk: with their spines stiffened; with their necks pulled forward; with their chins lifted up in the air; with their heads dropped forward; with their left shoulders up; with their shoulders pulled back; with their shoulders rounded forward; with their arms stiff; with their hips, knees, and toes turned inward; with their hips, knees, and toes turned outward; bouncing from foot to foot; shuffling from foot to foot; with their weight on their heels; with their upper bodies bent forward; with their weight shifting from side to side.

15. Musicalizing the Poem

The ensemble is divided into groups, with four to five players to a group. Each group is given a poem or reading which has been selected by the director because of its connection to the play. The groups are then given drums and other assorted percussion instruments. They are asked to spend about 20 minutes reading the poem and setting it to a beat, using the drum and/or any other percussion instruments desired by the group. After the 20-minute preparation time is over, each group presents its work to the others.

Resources

I am deeply indebted to Gary Izzo's *Acting Interactive Theater* (Portsmouth, NH: Heinemann, 1998), and to Amiel Schotz's *Theater Games and Beyond* (Colorado Springs, CO: Meriwether, 1998), both of which provide excellent assortments of games and activities, and to nameless scores of other acting coaches and teachers from whose wisdom and techniques I have borrowed extensively in my work. To the director who would like to work with theater games, literally hundreds of books of theater games, improvisations, and exercises are readily available.

Act II

Playing with Language and Character

Speaking Shakespeare

—⟨⟩

Tony Church

*Tony Church, the longest-serving member of the Royal Shakespeare Company,
draws on his experiences of working with Peter Hall, Trevor Nunn, Ian McKellen,
and Derek Jacobi to describe how an actor learns to speak and feel Shakespeare's
language.*

—⟨⟩

BY THE TIME I REACHED CAMBRIDGE UNIVERSITY in 1950, I was main-
ly glad to have finished my military service. I knew, however, that
Cambridge was famous for theater, and I had a history of school
Shakespeare productions behind me—such parts as Petruchio, Polonius,
Falstaff (twice!), Othello, and Lorenzo (albeit only in the last act of *The
Merchant of Venice*). All I *knew* about Shakespeare was from playing him,
and seeing John Gielgud, Laurence Olivier, Ralph Richardson, Godfrey
Tuttle, Edith Evans, Anthony Quayle, and Peggy Ashcroft in famous
roles. Not a bad start, you may think. But I had no idea about how his
verse—or his prose—should be spoken, or even that there was any difference between verse and poetry or prose and the prosaic.

Salvation, however, was at hand—in the person of George Rylands,
a charming Fellow of King's College, who was in charge of the Marlowe
Society, a typically Cambridge institution in that it was devoted almost
exclusively to the works of Shakespeare. (Remember that May Week in
Cambridge lasts two weeks and takes place in June). This society produced a Shakespeare play every year in the professional Arts Theater and
had three rigorous traditions. One, that all scenes should flow straight
from one to the next with absolutely no break; two, that the scenery
should be minimal; and three, that the speaking should be swift, accurate,
and uninflated. The tuneful but laboured "singing" of Shakespeare still
common when I was young was utterly forbidden here.

Seven years later, Rylands was to begin directing the massive proj-
ect of putting *The Complete Works* on record in association with the British
Council and the Hugo Record Company (now combined with
Polygram). The process started in mono recording on the Amateur
Dramatic Club's small stage (heavily draped in curtains) but before long

transferred to the stereo studios in Abbey Road, later made famous by The Beatles. I played over twenty roles for the series, from Shylock and Macbeth to Christopher Sly and Ajax. A tremendous experience.

What did I or my colleagues—Peter Hall, Trevor Nunn, Ian McKellen, and Derek Jacobi—learn at the feet of this master, George Rylands, always, unaccountably, known as "Dadie"? First and foremost, that rhythm is more important than melody. This is, of course, just as important in prose as it is in verse. The only difference, of course, is that to detect and use the rhythms in prose is normally more difficult, and various. In the verse, the famous iambic pentameter rules—except on the many occasions when it *almost* doesn't. Shakespeare's actors heard the pentameter rhythm every day, so they noticed immediately when it was inverted or broken or shared between speakers.

Dadie also pointed out that as Shakespeare matured as a writer of dramatic language, he played about with the construction of the verse line, frequently inverting the "iamb" to a "trochee" (/ - instead of - /), and used the mid-line caesura or sentence break, not just to emphasize what came next but to initiate the thought process. None of this meant that the actor should ignore line endings, traditionally a stern guide to shaping the thought for the audience's benefit, but that the actor should find in these constructions added rhythm and urgency—springing the next thought forward in the abbreviated time left in the line, while still emphasizing the beginning of the next line. Rylands also drew our attention to the urgency of any line shared between two speakers, especially when the first speaker returns to complete the pentameter (or when a third speaker leaps in, although this is much rarer).

The uncompleted line is another device of great value, creating a dramatic pause, often indicating the length of pause required by the number of missing "feet." A classic example of this is *Hamlet's* first scene, on the battlements of Elsinor. An atmosphere of fear and questioning is created, then dropped, then created again, by leaving many feet out of the soldiers' lines—it is even possible that the length of the fearful silences is intended by the length of the gaps. When Horatio comes and is asked to explain the dangerous political situation, he speaks in much more regular patterns, a regularity everyone shares after the Ghost's second appearance and exit.

It is nowadays taken for granted by most scholars, and, I am glad to say, most theater directors, that Shakespeare was sending his actors—and the actors of the twenty-first century—clear signals of his "directing" intentions. Of course, he did not have directors in his time. But he was certainly concerned, I think, to make his text actable—even actor-proof!

I cannot say that he *has* made his plays director-proof, and certainly not designer-proof, but he tried.

All this seems rather mechanical to actors and students coming fresh to Shakespeare, until they understand that Shakespeare is like great jazz, absolutely dependent on a basic rhythm, and equally dependent on ingenious, thrilling ways of breaking it.

Is dramatic poetry mainly rhythm? Of course not. Like all poetry, it arises out of frustration, frustration that mundane language cannot express the extraordinary richness of human experience. Permit me a simple, real-life illustration. An old country woman was regaling friends with her air raid experiences in World War II: "A piece of shrapnel fell into the shelter and, well, it *ricocheted* all round the walls." She'd heard the word wrong, but she *needed* it. At moments of great happiness, great fear, great excitement, intensity of thought, frustration, love, hate, or simply youthful exuberance, we *need* extra powers of speech, and we *get* them. For these reasons, we use simile—but when the moment is at its most powerful, simile will not suffice, so we leap to metaphor, the direct substitution of a heightened image.

More and more I found, after Dadie Ryland's tutelage, but also working with directors like Peter Hall and Trevor Nunn—and, on one splendid occasion with Peter Brook on the Scofield *Lear*—that the most challenging task I had, when playing parts as various as Polonius, Henry IV (both parts in full), Don Armado, John of Gaunt, Friar Lawrence, and Pandarus, was first to locate the pressure in me that caused me to use an image at all. Then I needed to ask, "What are the constituent parts of my image, and why are they arranged in this particular way, and if the image is paradoxical, as so many of the Shakespearean images are, how can I relate to the opposite sides of the paradox, and what is the nature of my frustration that causes it?" Just consider *Troilus and Cressida*, when Pandarus hears of the inevitability of Cressida's separation from Troilus, and watches their despair in silence: "Where are my tears? Rain, to 'lay this wind—or my heart will be blown up by the root!" The scene has been passionate and bitter. Troilus accepts their fate—as a royal prince of Troy, he cannot go against arrangements made by his father—although he rails against it. Cressida still refuses to accept it. Troilus, mistakenly, pleads with Cressida to remain true to him, even though she cannot conceive of falsehood. Pandarus, knowing the world, sees the hopelessness of her position and the probable outcome; Troilus still does not realize the danger in what he says; Pandarus sees it all, but is utterly helpless. And so he needs rain because he is *beyond* tears, but the powerful wind of chance must somehow be governed—or his heart will be *uprooted*—not just broken—an image with which, although anatomically unlikely, we are familiar—but torn up from the mounting in the body and exploded. This phrase is so vivid that the actor must not overcolor it—that would be piling "Pelion on Ossa," in Hamlet's words—but somehow must experience its oddity, place the pitch of "root," perhaps, in an unexpected place. Significantly, when we next meet Pandarus, he is the victim of a "whoreson tisick," a rheum in his eyes, and an ache in his bones that he expects will kill him only weeks later in the time-compression of the play. The blowing up of his heart would have been a kinder fate.

Pandarus' role is written exclusively in prose (apart from two songs and two lines of verse in quotation), but his language is as rich as that of anyone in the play. Imagery can live anywhere and comes, as I have said, from *necessity*.

So, we must recognize the existence of the line in verse, and we must watch for inversions of stress, caesuras, short lines—and occasionally extra long ones—shared lines, the use of simile, metaphor, and basic devices such as alliteration and assonance. There is one other favorite device of Shakespeare's: antithesis, the setting up of one thought against or in contrast with another. And this the actor must *demonstrate*—a word anathema to drama teachers—by setting the *pitch* of one word or phrase *against* the pitch of the other. There is no other way to explicate this idea for oneself or probably for the audience. Hundreds of Shakespeare's speeches are constructed around antithesis, and without help from the actor the audience finds them hard, certainly in these days of poor public oratory.

These skills are not difficult to acquire. I am impressed by the speed with which good actors pick up the signals sent out by Peter Hall when he is directing and setting a text, even one as tough as *Troilus and Cressida*.

The most important discovery I have made in over fifty years of speaking Shakespeare is that if you follow the author's very straightforward instructions embedded in the character's text, you can gain a massive input of thought and passion combined. Far from restricting the emotional content of one's acting, it increases its emotional validity by leaps and bounds. There is no need to rant or declaim or, please God, sing. There is one final word of warning, and it is absolute: "Never act the paraphrase." Always act exactly what he wrote, with *all* its crankiness, oddity, contradiction or, when it comes, its sheer simplicity. Shakespeare looked after his actors, and he is still *our* best teacher.

Notes

There are two extraordinary books about acting Shakespeare which say everything I have said more specifically, but also more theatrically, and I recommend them to anyone appreciating the speaking of Shakespeare. One is John Barton's book of the scripts of his *Playing Shakespeare* video series (New York: Anchor, 2001). The book is more important than the videos because it contains, I think, five more scripts that were recorded but never edited—some never seen, and these chapters are very important. The other artful book is *The Actor and the Text* (New York: Applause Books, 1992) by Cicely Berry, voice director of the RSC. I think it is even clearer than the Barton book because it is not affected, as the TV scripts inevitably were, by individual actors' styles.

He's Alive!
Making Shakespeare Compelling in the Classroom

Bruce Miller

Bruce Miller, an award-winning professor and Director of the Acting Program at the University of Miami, describes a series of exercises which proved compelling in helping participants grapple with the plays' language during a workshop he conducted in Dade County.

IN 2001 I WAS GIVEN THE OPPORTUNITY to help develop a program intended for use with the Miami Dade County Public School System. The program, funded by a national education grant called Project Succeed, would use the resources of the University of Miami's College of Arts and Sciences and the School of Education to help develop more effective pedagogical programs and teaching excellence in secondary public schools. The program that a colleague from the English Department and I proposed was called *Making Shakespeare Compelling* and would be designed to bring high school English and drama teachers from the same school together and to offer them joint training in methods of how to more effectively teach Shakespeare, wherever possible as a team, in the classroom.

My colleague, an expert in Renaissance English Literature, and I thought that by offering his knowledge about Shakespeare from a literary point of view, and my knowledge and experience from a dramatic one, that our teacher/students would come away with useful material and strategies for the classroom. Initially, we thought that the drama teachers would get much more from what he had to offer and the English teachers would get more from what I had to offer, but all participants would profit.

The program would consist of six seven-hour sessions. The first three, held on consecutive days, would be run by my colleague. The focus for these sessions would be primarily literary. The plays we had selected were *Romeo and Juliet*, *A Midsummer Night's Dream*, and *Macbeth*, and would be covered in that order. The selection of plays was based on variety of genre, and the fact that these are the ones often used in high schools. The second three sessions would pick up after a three-week hiatus and would be held on consecutive Saturdays. I would lead these sessions, but they would be augmented by outside speakers, each an expert in a particular area of Shakespeare. Video clips from various productions of the plays we had read would also be used to demonstrate the range of interpretive choices available in acting, directing, and design. However, the main thrust of these sessions would be to immerse the class in actually acting portions of the plays studied, with a focus on how to use Shakespeare's language.

To be honest, I was intimidated by my colleague's reputation as a teacher and scholar. Momentary insecurities about possessing only an MFA rather than a doctorate kicked in, and I wondered if my practical knowledge about performing Shakespeare would prove laughable to a scholar of his caliber and to teachers trained in drama or English. Granted, I had had plenty of exposure to the Bard from my undergraduate days as an English major. And I had had a lot of practical experience and training in Shakespeare as an MFA acting student, as well as my years in the profession. But how could that practical stuff stack up to genuine, legitimate scholarship? How could a hands-on knowledge about performing Shakespeare prove profitable to an English teacher in an English classroom trying to meet the objective requirements of Shakespeare as literature? The answer turned out to be very surprising, and what I learned is what I'd like to share with you now.

The most important things we all learned about Making Shakespeare Compelling are related to the use of Shakespeare's language and dramatic structure. We discovered that the most important skill we could teach our students is the ability to say his words aloud in a way that makes them clearly understood by the listener. This easily learnable skill, we discovered, dwarfed all other educational objectives in importance, and made all other goals and objectives far easier to attain. Let me explain.

As a teacher of acting and script analysis, I am often required to remind my acting and directing students that their primary purpose is to tell the story of the play. That means that their focus should be on using the playwright's words to play actions, not character or emotions. Tell us the story! When actors use dialogue and actions to tell the story of the play, miraculously the play itself communicates character, symbol, and underlying meaning—by allowing the audience to get for themselves all those other elements of the play. Figurative language and great ideas are always better understood when connected to the story. Too often this essential truth is ignored by acting students and their teachers—and is never even considered in the English classroom.

This basic principle is particularly true when studying the works of Shakespeare. Many people assume that as we read one of his plays, we automatically absorb the developing plot elements and understand how new events, information, and discoveries affect character, relationship, and basic need. That is seldom the case. When Romeo finds out that Juliet is a Capulet, we practically take for granted the effect such information has on character, plot, and the resulting dialogue. Shakespeare gives very little dialogue to Romeo to express his thoughts and feelings when, at the Capulet masque, he finds out who this ravishing young woman is. But that knowledge profoundly affects his subsequent actions. When the freshly honored Macbeth returns home after being told by the witches that he is to be king, he has no intention of killing Duncan. Yet, in one brief scene, his wife manages to completely turn him around. How? The written dialogue offers some clues, but no answers. We usually just take for granted that it happens. But why? The question of "how it happens" is what makes the play most watchable. And the choices about how it is accomplished onstage give life to the words and actions that the audience sees and hears.

What we take for granted as readers and watchers often goes to the very core of what makes a play interesting to an audience, and, much of the time, to any reader. Remember how often as kids we resented the English teacher who tested us on plot items? Ironically, those teachers knew what they were doing. Without connecting the dialogue of the play to the essential elements of the play's action—the action that inspires the language—those words can remain as inaccessible and cold as a distant mountain peak, beautiful to look at perhaps, but hardly worth an expedition. As teachers, we must inspire the desire to make that climb. To do so, we must help them understand the connection between language and action.

Who's Reading?

During the first three days of our program, the drama teachers were more willing to read aloud than the English teachers—no doubt because the English teachers were intimidated by the assumption that drama teachers were "actors" and they, of course, were not. However, the drama teachers were not necessarily the better readers. True, the drama teachers generally emoted more and were more "dramatic." But that did not necessarily bring out the clarity of the language. I often tell my students, "Emotion without clarity is simply not effective in plays where language is the prime ingredient." Brilliant poetic language will speak for itself when permitted to.

Those who were able to shape the language and identify and give weight to the most important words were the ones that best held our attention and allowed us to follow along. It was they who provided the mechanism by which the poetry and ideas revealed themselves as part of the action and character, organic to the story rather than imposed on it. Their readings generally imposed less unfocused emotion on the words. Instead, the imagery created by the words themselves evoked the audience's emotions. As we continued to read through the plays, the best readers consistently proved to be the best actors.

Interest and focus ebbed and flowed during these seven-hour sessions in accordance with what was going on in the action of the play and on how effective any given set of readers were at a particular time. When everyone could read, the play jumped to life. When some could read while some could not, it was frustrating. When all the readers were weak, it was plain boring, and sometimes pure torture. Suddenly, I was transported back to my own high school days, as vivid memories of English class returned to me. Even back then, I could be either totally absorbed by a particular passage or scene, or gruesomely bored and put off by a particular class—totally as a result of who was reading.

For the first three seven-hour sessions, our group read the selected plays aloud—from beginning to end, much like the way I studied Shakespeare as a high school student. My colleague interrupted the dramatic flow regularly during these sessions to discuss points of literary interest, as did I, but far less often, with a point of dramatic import. Topics for discussion included the Elizabethan mind, social custom, and the great chain of being, and how these issues related to the language and meaning of the play. Discussion also included the structure of the language, its poetic motifs, repeated language themes, and the ways in which they all beautifully interconnected with each other and with the overall meaning of the play. My colleague knew his stuff, and it was fascinating. Most of the class was equally enthralled. It felt great to be a student again and to be learning for the pure joy of it.

The Obvious Is Not Obvious

During these readings many of the short dialogues were glossed over or ignored completely. As I saw this trend developing, I would interrupt to talk about how these passages contribute to the building of dramatic action, conflict, tension, and suspense onstage. My colleague and the teacher/students invariably seemed intrigued by what I said, yet on many occasions I felt that what I offered was little more than a statement of the obvious. It slowly dawned on me that the obvious is not so obvious to those not used to reading a play of Shakespeare as an actor and director does. As this insight became clearer, I remembered how it had taken me years to fully recircuit my brain to read a play from a dramatic point of view rather than a literary one. This change of focus was what I was demonstrating in my responses. More often than not, the oral reading of our teacher/students improved as a result of these comments, at least during the scene or passage being read. Over time, everyone else noted the difference.

In spite of my occasional dramatic contributions, by the end of the second session I was beginning to feel a little uneasy, and my uneasiness was reinforced because I had begun to overhear snippets of conversation here and there by members of the class. The essence of what I was feeling and hearing centered on a number of pragmatic questions: as fascinating and stimulating as this experience might be to our teacher/students, how would it enhance their teaching? Would their students really sit for this kind of literary analysis? Would this enhanced understanding by teachers in any way stimulate students to appreciate the plays of Shakespeare more than before? Would students be more likely to read a play by Shakespeare, or any other play, or any other piece of literature, as a result of what their teachers had learned? Would Shakespeare now be more compelling? Sadly, at least in my mind, the answer was "probably not."

During the break that followed the first three sessions, I did a lot of thinking. My original plan was to partner the English teacher from a particular school with the drama teacher and have each of them develop a scene from one of the three plays we had read in class. The idea was to have them actually perform a scene by the end of the third session. However, now that I had worked with the class, I realized that trying to get them to develop fully realized scenes was probably impractical and certainly unnecessary. It struck me that a basic analysis of the plays from a dramatic point of view would more than fill the plates of my teacher/students—if I focused on the goal of getting them able to read the plays aloud with clarity and with a dramatic understanding. What I decided to do was spend the time teaching my class how to read Shakespeare aloud, so they, in turn, could teach their students to do so. Fortunately, I had assigned sonnets to be read aloud on the first session back. I decided to see if the sonnets could serve my revised goal.

During the break between sessions, I discovered a new book. *Shakespeare Set Free* is a collection of essays and teaching strategies for the study of Shakespeare in high school published by the Folger Library. The book's editors had drawn many of the same conclusions about studying Shakespeare in a high school class that I had: that it should be taught actively through class participation by doing and saying the words of Shakespeare aloud. In fact, in the groundbreaking essay that sets the tone for the book, Michael Tolaydo, a teacher and member of the Library's Teaching Shakespeare Institute, makes a case for student immersion in a Shakespeare play by first doing a scene from that play as a class. As Tolayado points out, "learning in this way can also open up the play and provide the basis for further active exploration of plot, character, structure, language, genre, or What you Will."

Reading the Sonnets

And so, by the time my first all-day session was to begin, I had a revised strategy and game plan: use the assigned sonnets to introduce the basic principles for reading Shakespeare aloud. Since sonnets have no specific dramatic background to analyze and worry about, they provide a good starting point for teaching out-loud reading. Sonnets do, however, employ the same poetic devices and require the same basic reading rules and preparation necessary for a Shakespearean play. Once we discussed the skills in the first session, the class would move on to a dramatic monologue from one of the plays we had read, and then in the third session we would focus on two-person scenes. Monologues and scenes, of course, would require dramatic analysis as well as specific analysis of the language for reading. These activities would make the best use of our time.

Reading Shakespeare aloud requires three related but distinct types of analyses:
- a literal analysis of the meaning of the words individually and in context, including definitions, literary and historical allusions, and such poetic devices as metaphors and rhyme;
- an analysis of the words in their specific dramatic circumstances; and
- an analysis of all dramatic events leading up to a particular scene or section of dialogue so as to understand the speech in its overall dramatic context.

Antonio's opening line in *The Merchant of Venice*—"In sooth, I know not why I am so sad"—offers an excellent opportunity to examine how these three analytical tools might work on a piece of dialogue. I actually borrowed ideas for using this line from the television series and subsequent book called *Playing Shakespeare* that featured director John

Barton and members of the Royal Shakespeare Company. (This series of programs on how to do Shakespeare can be of enormous benefit to teachers and students. The tapes are expensive and somewhat difficult to find, but the book based on the programs is easy to come by and offers a wonderful opportunity to observe how expert actors think about and make their choices.)

Antonio's words are all monosyllabic and, except for the word "sooth," their literal meanings well known. Try this as an opening exercise with your class. It's a terrific icebreaker since many of your students will be reluctant to speak verse—especially Shakespeare's verse—aloud, certain that the words are too difficult. Ask each of your students to repeat Antonio's speech. Just let them have a shot. Everyone will be amazed at the variety of readings produced, a result of some emotional connotation supplied by the speaker and/or the word or words chosen to emphasize. Some of the readings will be more effective than others simply because they sound better to the ear, the result, as we shall see later, of respecting the meter of the line.

Discuss which readings the class liked best, and ask them to discuss why. Once your discussion is completed, have your students try reading the line aloud again, emphasizing a particular word. The italics below represent possible words that might be stressed.

> In *sooth*, I know not why I am so sad.
> In sooth, I *know* not why I am so sad.
> In sooth, I know not *why* I am so sad.
> In sooth, I know not why I *am* so sad.
> In sooth, I know not why I am so *sad*.

Each of the readings, with the exception perhaps of the line with the *know* emphasis, delivered a specific meaning and sounded right. By emphasizing *sooth*, the speaker seems to be confessing to not knowing why he is so sad. By emphasizing *why*, the speaker seems to be acknowledging that he has no explanation for his mood. By emphasizing *am* (a weak choice because verbs of being tend not to carry much meaning), the speaker seems to be agreeing that he is sad and confessing that he doesn't know the reason why he feels as he does. Finally, by emphasizing *sad*, the speaker seems to be discovering in the moment that he is sad.

All of the readings described above seem like good possibilities. In a dramatic vacuum, each would work nicely. But remember that the line is spoken in the context of the play. This is when dramatic analysis comes into action. Again, no one answer is correct, but the context clearly narrows the choices. For example, if Antonio had just been asked, "Why are you so sad?," his answer might very well emphasize *sooth* or *why* or both *sooth* and *why*.

Have your class read the line again after you ask them some improvised introductory question—in other words, after you provide a dramatic context. The responses that sound right will be the ones that acknowledge the question in their answer. Try asking several other lead-in questions. You will find that the emphasized words in the answer will change in accordance with the question you ask—if your students are really listening.

Now suppose that we know more about the dramatic context of the chosen line. To show students the importance of contexts, establish recognizable situations for them. For example, set up the following four scenarios with your class before allowing them to speak:

1. A party where everyone is underage and has been drinking

2. A private discussion with a family member who has done something wrong. (Be very specific about the wrongdoing.)

3. A private discussion with a lover who is cheating.

4. A conversation with a priest, teacher, therapist who is trying to provide support.

You get the idea. Each of these suggestions should affect the way a line is delivered and give it a specific color that might occur if no one thought about the specific and overall dramatic contexts. Eventually, your class will realize that all reading involves contexts. Every effective reading reflects a knowledge of situation.

For instance, consider what a reader must know to read clearly and effectively Juliet's address to the sun in *Romeo and Juliet* (III.ii.):

> Gallop apace, you fiery-footed steeds,
> Towards Phoebus' lodging; such a wagoner
> As Phaeton would whip you to the west,
> And bring in cloudy night immediately.

The reader of these lines must know the literal meaning of the words, the mythical references used to construct the poetic figurative language, the situation at hand, and the reason for Juliet's wanting the fiery-footed steeds to pull that sun-laden wagon. In short, the reader must consider how badly Juliet wants night to arrive so that the time of Romeo's arrival will be at hand. All of this is fairly obvious. But too often in their reading, students ignore the obvious. As a result, they miss the opportunities to bring the full measure of Juliet's impatience to her words. By understanding both language and context, they not only learn more about the play's poetic structure, they invariably pull their audience into the scene's pulsing drama. Is this not what we all want from the time spent in class with the plays of Shakespeare?

Now, let's return for just a moment to that earlier speech by Antonio. Here again is the opening line to *The Merchant of Venice* with some other stressed words that you might have heard during the earlier exercise:

In sooth, I know not why I am so sad.
In sooth, *I* know not why I am so sad.
In sooth, I know *not* why I am so sad.
In sooth, I know not why *I* am so sad.
In sooth, I know not why I am *so* sad.

Just why is it that when your students choose to emphasize these words, the lines sit poorly on the ear, and seem to provide less clarity to the meaning of the line? In the first place, stressing those particular words doesn't provide enough clarity. The ear tells us that. But suppose that some of your students still lack an ear sophisticated enough to hear what is missing? The answer lies in the natural stressing of this iambic pentameter line, with every second syllable stressed (e.g., the second, fourth, and so on). Most of Shakespeare's verse adheres to this pattern, and a simple reading for the stressed syllables, or *scansion*, can help the reader get clues as to what should or should not be emphasized. Of the four lines above, only the one with the *not* emphasis has a clear meaning. This particular violation of the natural rhythm works, because it emphasizes a possible meaning of the line. (The question of whether the violation works better than one of the earlier readings that follows the natural rhythm of the line is a fascinating one, but one that needs to be discussed at another time.)

This reference to scansion suggests that there are other rules and guidelines that can be taught to our students that will help them read Shakespeare more clearly and effectively. Actually there are several. None of them is difficult, and with a little practice and help all they can be mastered quickly. Once students realize that they need to pay attention to these ten tools, effective class readings will quickly become the rule rather than the exception:

•Punctuation—Obey the traffic signs.

•Operative Words—Circle and emphasize those words that best communicate the meaning of an idea, phrase, or sentence.

•Verbs—Because verbs lie at the heart of every clause, think about the relationship of all the other words to that central verb.

•Energy—Don't drop your energy at the end of a line unless it is also the end of an idea, phrase, or sentence.

•Phrasing—Remember that sentences are collections of idea units and should be read in groups.

•Caesura—In iambic pentameter lines, the pause that often occurs after the fourth, fifth, or sixth syllable often separates ideas and helps the line make sense.

•Breathing—Remember that your breathing should follow the punctuation.

•Transitions—Make a vocal shift when the idea shifts.

•Apposition and Antithesis—Opposites and repetitions offer an excellent opportunity for vocal shifts.

•Alliteration and Assonance—Develop a vocal strategy for presenting alliteration and assonance.

Adventuring Between the Lines

Sybil Lines

—ᔆ

Sybil Lines uses her extensive acting career on Broadway and in Shakespeare theaters throughout the United States and Britain to illustrate ways she worked her way through alternative choices in building her characterizations.

—ᔆ

WHEN A DRAMA CONSERVATORY ACCEPTED ME for three years, I knew I was enormously lucky to be trained to hone my natural acting abilities and to learn the technical skills of speech and movement for expressing them. The opportunity an actor is offered to journey into the psyche of another person—and another—and another—has always been to me the most exciting of adventures. The best luck, though, is that every show is so different from the last that the adventure is always new.

Where does the process of discovering an individual take place—in the heart or the mind? The process can vary considerably depending on the character you are invited to find and the production in which you are going to enact the circumstances of that life. A part may be offered to an actor after a general audition or by a producer who knows the actor's work, and most actors start exercising their imaginations about a character as soon as it is whispered they may play it. First, of course, the text is examined. Even if I already know that play, I always value my first reading of it after a role has been suggested to me. That play becomes a different experience when you know you're not only engaged by Rosalind's story, but that you are Rosalind. During that first stroll through the script you are as near to an audience's view of "your" Rosalind as you will ever be—the first chance to be afraid of the forest, the first awakening of interest in Orlando, and the first relief at finding out that all ends well.

However keen I may have been on another actress' portrayal of Rosalind, every word jumps off the page as a new and dazzling clue when I am going to play it myself. I may have been just as delighted by yet another actress's interpretation of Viola but there's rarely a temptation to copy a performance. After all, that actress has already achieved the best version of "her" Viola that there can ever be. Apart from the fact that I may be different in size and shape from the actresses I have admired, I will have a different sense of timing and comic delivery. Even more importantly, the adventure for me is to marry Shakespeare's witty observation with Sybil's sense of humor to find my own *Twelfth Night* heroine. Actors fervently hope that their efforts will complement a playwright's invention, so we believe we can make giant leaps forward with a characterization if we know about the author's life, his beliefs, aims, and the themes of his other writings. Investigation like this can produce wonderful signposts for character development. But it can also be a trap, especially if an actor starts producing a spokesperson for an idea instead of breathing a living identity into the script. So, although I am interested in the playwright's views, I try to keep homework concentrated on the specific character I am interpreting.

An actor's homework is done each evening after a day's rehearsal, but some of it is done before rehearsals even begin and can be as varied as the characters we play. As a British schoolgirl, I already knew a fair bit about British history and politics to inform plays by Shakespeare and Shaw. But a play like *Julius Caesar* sends me back to the history books again. However, not all of an actor's homework takes place in the library. If a drama is set in a mental institution, or a coal mine, or a police station, we will go to those sites to understand the day-to-day working of those lives.

However useful these outward details can be, the basic tools of an actor are ones we all use every day: empathy, memory, imagination and the various aspects of one's own personality. Everyone draws on memories, but most people are less aware that they also use emotional recall, substitution, and sense memory. Emotional recall is not only the memory of an incident but also exactly how one felt at the time. Although most people try to forget painful moments, it is a wise actor who retains exact memories of pain (physical and mental) and can draw on them when required. Empathy is obviously the wince you give when a friend hits her thumb with a hammer, but substitution occurs when you wince even if you've never had a similar accident. Why do you wince if you never experienced such a pain? Sympathy at the shock and agony in your friend's face? Yes. But feeling your friend's blow occurs because you instinctively measure her pain on your own Richter scale: you deduce it's probably not as bad as childbirth but worse than a pinprick. And by adding experience to imagination, you recall a pain you have never felt.

Sense-memory refers to a trigger for the memory: the smell of apples may equal contentment if they remind you of your grandmother's garden. An actor can invent a history for a prop that summons up one of the five senses and reminds him of a person or incident important to his character. This prop can then be incorporated into the production to help facilitate emotions. We all use our imagination plus experience daily. But actors learn to switch from one emotional memory to another very freely. I use the Richter scale metaphor because substituting a memory requires accuracy to prevent generalization. Let us presume an actress has become precise with her use of these recall tools and now is asked to play one of Shakespeare's exacting women. After she focuses on the most minor sense of injustice or revenge she has experienced in her own life and recalls that emotion exactly, she then works to magnify the feeling so that it envelopes her body language, her tone of voice, and her intellectual and emotional agendas. If her character kills, she can substitute a memory from her own life when she felt violent and, during rehearsals, deepen and darken that fury. Empathizing with these extremes can create the monstrous Tamara from *Titus Andronicus* or mad Queen Margaret in *Richard III*.

We all own Jekyl and Hyde personalities and we all make use of them. Most of us recognize that, at some time in our lives, we have played the benign neighbor, the efficient secretary, the adoring fan, the suave lover, the grouchy spouse, the bubbly friend, the irate customer, and the concerned parent. Some of us are adept at switching from one to the other because we have discovered that we get better service, closer friends and more obedient children by doing so. Still, however many Mr. Hydes we have available, most of us have vulnerabilities about showing certain sides of ourselves and the aspects of our personality we want to hide about ourselves can be surprising. The prude may be embarrassed to show his wild side, the organizer a reluctance to show laziness; the poet tries to shrug away his worries about security, and the cynic dare not confess her romantic daydreams. When actors resist mysterious quirks for the characters they are creating, they forget that illogic and paradox are what make people continually intriguing. In *Love's Labors Lost*, just as the princess of France declares her affection for the man she loves, she discovers that her father has died. We can see she is vulnerable with sorrow but at the same time strong in her resolve to assume her royal duties and, for a year, bid farewell to her prospective husband. We all live on many levels at the same time; when an actor is too linear in decisions, he takes away the depth from his characterizations.

Uncovering the many facets of their own personalities is the quickest way for actors to add more colors to their palate; therefore, they must overcome any inhibitions about revealing traits they may despise in themselves. Some actors, even after they have managed to discover and disclose such traits to their fellow actors in a rehearsal room, will sometimes shut them back in a box. By doing this, an actor denies himself one of his most useful tools. The other source of material is the myriad side of other people's personalities, which is why most actors are curious and self-conscious observers of everyone around them. I have the guilty trait of over-analyzing the behavior of others in my life, and I suspect I do it as a selfish greed for source material, attempting to follow a maze of convoluted agendas (confusing even to my friends themselves). Sometimes, when I feel connected to a role, the familiarity may not come from recognizing my own personality in the character but, instead, the reflection of someone close to me. Roles that fit like a glove, on the other hand, are a dream to rehearse because there is time and energy to spare on nuances. But discovering too many complex and, perhaps, conflicting agendas in a character can be risky. An actor must remember that although he can be spending weeks investigating a character, an audience will be absorbing a lot of information on one viewing. If actors overcomplicate their characters, audiences can get lost. This is one of the many instances where the guidance of a good director is so valuable.

When I have difficulty connecting to the essence of a character, I find that improvising scenes not written in the play is useful and gives everyone a chance of exploring their characters' histories with each other. I will discuss my choices for that history with my director, especially if I'm not sure which path to take. How was Lady Macbeth as a young girl—a spoiled brat or an overlooked sibling? Ultimately, I make the choice that will best feed the character's consuming needs. For Lady Macbeth, I decided on a woman trying to fill an internal emptiness by controlling world events. As her mind collapses in her last scene, she shows us that she has overestimated her own powers of resilience.

I have now mentioned two compelling aspects when building a characterization: need and choice. Never move without needing to and never speak a word without needing to utter it. Recently I watched an actor wrestle with a scene between Cassius and Brutus. The only need his Cassius seemed to exhibit emotionally would have been served perfectly by the one sentence, "Let's kill Julius Caesar." Of course, this is the general purpose of his conversation, but the scene contains over 150 lines, most of which belong to Cassius. The actor whizzed through his speeches in exhausting spurts because he didn't need all those words to communicate the generalized need he'd chosen for his character. Another actor, taking the same scene, would have analyzed not just

Cassius' ultimate desires but how Cassius perceives Brutus' psyche. Remember that Cassius is also an actor. What reaction must he elicit from the other characters in the scene? Whatever Brutus' needs are when the scene begins, Cassius must work to seduce him. The actor could have relished every word that trapped his prey. Instead, this Cassius ignored all the images the words could have conjured up, seeing them only as obstacles to get past. Shakespeare's Cassius actually raises a critical question about all characters. How much of what any of the characters say do they mean? If we all lie and half-lie, don't they?

Here we have another collection of choices about the text. What if your director wants you to move to the table and your character doesn't need to? The simple answer is that the actor is hired for his abilities, which should include an inventive imagination. Never go to the table because the director requires the move. Go to the table, which the director wants you to do, because you have discovered a need to go to the table.

Choices are the nearest the actor comes to creating and not merely interpreting. We cannot alter the circumstances into which we were born—the century, our physical structure, our parents. Perhaps we cannot even alter the incidents of our lives. But the way we choose to react to those incidents defines how we find a sense of ourselves and how we judge others. It's been said that maturity is the moment in life when we realize we cannot take all the roads available to us. The actor also has circumstances—the script, the set, the costumes, fellow cast members, and the director's vision—that are givens. The one delicious difference from real life is that I, as an actor, not only make decisions and experience reactions in a character's life, I also get to revise and try another choice tomorrow. If only real life could be like that! The less obvious the choice, the more chance an actor has of bringing a fresh perspective to an already well-known character.

The choice that propels a character to a momentous decision is where I particularly prefer to try to find the road less traveled. As in real life, our hopes or frustrations, our dreams and desires propel us. Finding that propelling factor is the oil that makes the character's engine run with ease. Often an extreme act of behavior occurs when we decide to go after our ideals, give them up, or run away from everything we have known in order to reinvent our lives.

Whatever work an actor does on a characterization, the fact remains that theater is a collaborative effort. The most perverse choices may work splendidly in one production and, in another, a rather conservative choice could seem to be outrageous. So, however innovative and viable a choice might be considered if it only had to stand by itself, the director must decide if it will work within the tone of the entire production. I once played Mistress Quickly with round circular plates of rouge on my cheeks, a tussle of orange matted hair, and an Alzheimer's moment in the middle of every speech. But since that production was a *Merry Wives of Windsor* based on British pantomime, the characterization fit the rest of the show. I have performed in three productions of *Merry Wives of Windsor*. The first, the pantomime version, had the furniture painted on backcloths and costumes straight from a children's storybook; the second was set in a circus with sword swallowers and jugglers with my Mistress Ford a white-faced harlequin clown; and the third took place in a rural English village with a coy Mistress Ford of 1870 replete with Victorian bustles and tea-set decorum. High concepts that remove a play far from its original setting are a director's choice, but the inner life of the characters should remain as true as in any traditional presentation.

Most actors light up when handed a meaty part. But along with the delight can come trepidation, because roles like King Lear, or Cleopatra, or Portia conjure up enough legends of the Great Interpretations to torture any actor's insecurities. Not only is there the fear that the director will sag with disappointment at your inadequacies during rehearsals but that your cast members will remember Paul Scofield, Janet Suzman or Dame Judi Densch and recoil in distaste from your choices. And let's not even think about the critics and future audiences demanding their money back!

For me, Juliet's Nurse was such a role. Initially, I was excited to think that I would get the chance to do it. But after immediately saying yes to the job, I was left to worry about the outcome. Edith Evans is just one of the famous names who has triumphed in the role, and physically there is a big, maternal size associated with the Nurse. I worried that the audience might crave an ancient, warm-hearted grandmother with high eccentric delivery, or long for a fleshy Tessie O'Shea full of wobbly congeniality. Having worn convincing fat suits in other roles, I wondered if I should immediately start phoning the costume designer. But before the queasy knees had more time to tremble, my director reassured me that he was setting the production in a Renaissance Italy with a traditional style of playing and felt that it was fine to make the Nurse my age and my build. As we discussed our immediate responses to the role, we felt she was a scrappy survivor. Thus, the scene where she complains of backache and tiredness did not have to focus on old age or great weight, it could just as easily be exhaustion from having just confronted the boisterous lads in the town.

Now I felt more relaxed to go back to the text and study it through my own eyes. I've seen the Nurse played like a kind old nanny from Victorian England, but historical research informed me that in fifteenth-century Verona the Nurse would have had nowhere near the status of such nannies. The first time the audience sees her, they learn that fourteen years earlier she had been employed by the Capulets because she had just given birth to a daughter of her own.

"God rest all Christian souls! . . . Susan is with God," she poignantly reminds herself. Producing milk for her own baby, she was hired for the vulgar task of feeding the newborn Juliet. For much of history few women of status performed this function themselves; instead, they hired "wet nurses" whose status would not even have been the equivalent to the lowest servant. Juliet and her mother seem, at best, to have a formal relationship, a reason that may explain why the Nurse was kept on in the household after Juliet was weaned. After all, the Capulets have no other children, so this woman might be out on her ear the moment Juliet gets married. Once I realized her situation, I read the script in a state of some anxiety. This was no longer the anxious actress but a conviction on my part that anxiety was my Nurse's uppermost emotion, an emotion that manifested itself in different ways: the incessant nattering in an effort to entertain, the sudden switches to cold hard practicality, the conniving and changing of agendas to stay on the winning side, and, at the terrible scenario at the end of the play, her plunge into despair.

The evidence from the text is that she is probably in a pretty precarious position. We do not hear of Juliet's friends, so we might assume that the girl would value the Nurse as one of her few sources of company. But she would have new companions in her husband's household. There's nothing in the text to indicate that either Lord or Lady Capulet have any great fondness for the Nurse; they never talk about her or confide any great secrets with her. Although we are introduced to the Nurse as a saucy character who toadies to Lady Capulet, she never receives encouragement from her employer. The Nurse tells us her merry husband is dead.

The text shows the Nurse championing Paris' courtship of Juliet, and in later scenes she disparages the Romeo link, perhaps because she decides that a Montague tryst will surely be doomed by the families' rivalry. This doesn't show the great loyalty to Juliet that a sentimental version of the Nurse would indicate, but it does show a healthy pragmatism.

The director of this *Romeo and Juliet* encouraged all the paths I was following but reminded me that the end result must include a lot of humor. He wanted me to make sure that the fears of displacement and certain resentments I felt as the Nurse would not overshadow her comic service to the play. Keeping in mind the resilient humor of London cockneys, I had confidence that my character has enough funny takes on the world that even under stress she would find plenty to tickle her. I have seen the Nurse interpreted as an easygoing slattern, but I felt her incessant chatter and attempt to entertain came out of a nervous desire to ingratiate. A realist, not afraid of a scrap, her words to Romeo as she starts their first scene are combative. Of course, she could be correct to be worried, not only about the family animosities but her responsibility for the consequences if any man led Juliet astray. Is she interested in hearing what this young man is like? Not at all. She interrupts him after just a few words.

I will tell her, sir, that you do protest
Which, as I take it, is a gentleman-like offer.

If there is sarcasm on the word "sir" and all of it is said with her world-weary knowledge of rogues, we can smile at her cynical view of romantic rhetoric. Then Romeo shows her money, and the Nurse responds, "No truly, sir, not a penny." If she lingers on the phrase and gives his coins a longing look he can keep at her, "Go on, I say you shall."

Realizing this Nurse is easy to corrupt, Romeo can now speak with confidence. Her short, snappy reply is even funnier in its 180-degree turn-around: "This afternoon, sir? Well, she shall be there." Given the money, she abruptly panders to Romeo, almost becomes Juliet's pimp, and, dismissing the audience's expectation for her to care for Juliet's honor, gabbles away and tries to curry favor with him: "O there's a nobleman in town, one Paris, but she good soul had as lieve see a toad … as see him. I anger her sometimes and tell her that Paris is the prop-erer man."

This is a typical street-smart thing to say. The audience knows she has praised Paris but now she covers her tracks by saying she has only praised Paris to tease Juliet. She then goes on to flatter Romeo, setting the groundwork for a new ally and, she hopes, future employer. When he asks the Nurse to "Commend me to thy lady," I decided, as the Nurse, to jingle the money in my hand while I enthused, "Ay, a thou-sand times."

The actress who was playing opposite me in this production was delightful in her perceptive portrayal of a Juliet who could wryly eye my sardonic Nurse and take any of my chatter with a pinch of salt. She knew that I was building a tough, self-serving character with no deep sympathy for the romantic notions of a little rich girl. This, of course, did not mean that her Juliet knew the extent of the Nurse's pragmatism. But as our characters got to live with each other I discovered I was giving a softer reading to some lines than I had originally planned and that, although my Nurse remained as canny as ever, she was warming to the personality of her young mistress. In one rehearsal, as my Nurse hobbled home under the exhausting Mediterranean sun, I found myself sincerely delighted that the man Juliet loved was serious in his affections. I really looked forward to having a joke with this young woman and decided to leave it to the very last moment (almost offstage) before I suddenly turned and told her the good news. Seeing her blush with pleasure elicited a genuine laugh from my Nurse because the tease had been successful and brought Juliet so much joy.

> Now comes the wanton blood up in your cheeks
> They'll be scarlet straight at any news.
> Hie you to church.

I found the last part of this speech suddenly became intense instructions, not only because the Nurse was a little nervous about crossing the Capulets but also because I found I wanted a successful outcome for Juliet. This is the way rehearsals really do become an adventurous journey; it's as if, at some point, the character takes over the actor's steering wheel. Studying alone, a scene can work itself out in our imaginations the way our homework dictates. But then suddenly, in rehearsal, everything goes up in smoke because a fellow actor has a look in her eye, a tone in her voice or a gesture that changes the carefully planned response. In the case of my Nurse, I blended, as most actors do, intellectual discoveries with the instinctive ones that save a character from being predictable and two-dimensional. Although my Nurse had surprised me by taking a turn toward sentimentality, her cynicism and fear came back with full strength after Romeo slew Tybalt.

"We are undone, lady, we are undone!" the Nurse hisses to Juliet. Terrified because that "we" shows she believes that she cannot escape punishment for the liaisons with Romeo, she suspects her punishment could be extreme and now curses Romeo for killing the worthy Tybalt. I suspect it was unlikely she was really friendly with Tybalt, but she needs to say anything to realign herself with the Capulets. As her anger swells into a bitter speech on men, I interrupted the belligerence with a cry of longing for her merry husband: "Ah, where's my man? Give me some aqua-vita."

I had already established that a little flask of liquor always hangs on her belt, and it is this "water of life" that she takes a swig of as she continues her lament. She is not at all dizzy in these later scenes, which was an early signpost to me that much of her rambling did not come from a silly brain but an overactive one. I felt she now has a sincere loathing for Romeo because it is his action that has put her in this precarious position. She does not want Juliet thinking of him ever again and would rather she join her parents in their mourning. When Juliet proclaims that she will kill herself, she jolts the Nurse into what was, for me, a surprisingly determined decision. I suddenly found myself seizing Juliet and firmly telling her:

...I'll find Romeo
To comfort you, I wot well where he is.

As my Juliet looked dazed with grief I shook her urgently:

Hark ye! Your Romeo will be here at night,
I'll to him; he is hid at Lawrence cell.

However bad things were, the Nurse's fate would be that much worse if Juliet commits suicide. Although the Nurse's hate for Romeo would continue until the play's conclusion, she is forced to fetch him to calm Juliet. During a rehearsal of the Friar's cell scene, I sneered, as usual, at the sight of Romeo:

...blubbering and weeping, weeping and blubbering.
Stand up, stand up, stand and you be a man.

As I knelt down to shove him, the actor wrapped his body around me like a baby and crying the one word given to Romeo, "Nurse," he rocked himself back and forward against me like a baby. I found myself slowly cradling him in my arms as he asked about Juliet. Again, my fellow actor's actions were not what I had expected and, although I could have pushed him aside to stay on my own track, I found the Nurse as taken-aback as I was and as grudgingly sympathetic. Of course, at this point it is difficult to say if the reaction is your own or your character's, and that is what actors will discuss after a scene. An actor's responses by this time have often started to meld with the character's anyway, and all that is left to decide is if that surprising reaction will serve, or not serve, the telling of the story. Although the way he had reacted to my entrance had also surprised the actor playing Romeo, the outcome worked for both of us. It also allows my Nurse to quieten down a little and made it easier for her to be impressed by the wisdom of the Friar's long soliloquy.

O Lord, I could have stay'd here all night
To hear good counsel. O, what learning is!

When we got into performance, this received an appreciative laugh from the audience as they realized the Nurse had been momentarily smitten by the Friar. By the next scene my Nurse had regained her balance and gotten back to her old pragmatic self. She briskly announces to Juliet that as Romeo is banished she should forget him and get married to Paris.

> O, he's a lovely gentleman!
> Romeo's a dishclouth to him.

I have seen this scene played with much sadness by the Nurse, assuming that she says these words with difficulty because she, too, is distressed at the lovers' parting. I did not take that tack. Fear had set in again with my Nurse; the tight worry in the stomach had returned and a desperation to make it through these events without losing her head. She had reverted to supporting her employer, Lady Capulet. Ardently believing what she says, she can say it with a determined smile. It is almost as if Juliet, with her willfulness, has become the Nurse's enemy. My Nurse encouraged Juliet to pretend she had never married Romeo, indicating that she'd been a silly, disobedient child, and I delivered the second half of the speech with a cold, tough, and dismissive tone.

> ...I think you happy in this second match,
> for it excels your first or if it did not,
> Your first is dead...

The Nurse cannot wait to assure Lord and Lady Capulet that Juliet is resigned to the match with Paris, and Juliet never trusts her again, hiding the fake-death plan from her.

We next see the Nurse full of good spirits and hopeful that the whole Romeo escapade will pass without anyone realizing she had anything to do with it. In this production Juliet had wrapped herself in sheets as she succumbed to her potion and was therefore hidden beneath the bedclothes when I entered to wake her for her marriage to Paris. I jumped on to the end of the bed to tell a lewd joke and slapped her with a little rag doll she kept in her bedroom. I had liked that this Juliet, emphasizing her youth and loneliness, hangs on to a childhood toy, but as I giggled and squeezed her body I suddenly realized something was wrong. In the instant panic anyone would feel at such a moment, I called for help but quickly returned to my own self-absorption: "O, weraday, that ever I was born!"

I did not deliver this line with sorrow but with utter fear that this death might be considered, somehow, my negligence. I called for water in the hope that God might let her live and tried to pour out the Nurse's ever-ready liquor on her lips, but by the time Lord Capulet entered the room I was in despair. The part of the scene that really surprised me was that while the other characters spoke I experienced a real loss. The shock of suddenly being without Juliet and the hopelessness of my situation left me too empty to think.

> O, woe! O woeful, woeful, woeful day!
> Most lamentable day, most woeful day
> That ever, ever, I did yet behold!
> O day, O day, O day, O hateful day!
> Never was seen so black a day as this.
> O woeful day. O woeful day!

Another surprise was that when I spoke those lines it was not a wailing and mourning passage as I had intended. As I spoke, my eyes fearfully on Lord Capulet, the repetition of the phrasing came from a nervous, handwringing lackey—it was as if I was begging him over and over not to blame me. Every "woe" was a frightened prayer to escape punishment as I trailed after the Capulets carrying Juliet off the stage.

As the first performance gets close, everyone becomes tense about the new member of the production—the audience. Actors consider the audience another character in the play and one that is added so late we all breathe a sigh of relief when a theater gives us at least a couple of previews to find out how this new addition will react to us. For weeks during rehearsal the director has been the witness and guide to our exploration of our roles. Now it is not only the director's sensibilities we will rely on but also those of the audience. We will discover that the audience might be confused by a scene we had considered perfectly clear, that they might give an unexpected laugh, or that a colleague's performance might distract them from what we had assumed was the focus of a scene. I mentioned that my Nurse's ogling of the Friar in *Romeo and Juliet* was rewarded by laughter and, although all three of us actors wanted to hang on to this laugh, we didn't want it at the cost of the serious aspects in the scene. We knew that if the response was too boisterous the Nurse would have to stop feeling gooey-eyed for the Friar. By tempering my Nurse's attraction, we got an amused response which didn't overwhelm the following speeches and the Nurse was allowed her romantic moment.

Although reactions can alter from audience to audience, sometimes drastically, from night to night, the actor must settle down to bring a fairly uniform characterization to the telling of the story. All those tools of memory, improvisation, text analysis, and the individual choices of different lives and different experiences have brought the detective work to an organic conclusion. I use that strange last phrase because discoveries do continue through the run of any play: actors invariably make adjustments in their own interaction. If an audience's reaction pulls a scene in a slightly different direction, our characters generally adjust slightly to accommodate the new circumstances. The audience invariably bring their own sensibilities to the journey of discovery. They join the actors in contributing their share of experience and imagination to explore the workings of other souls so that we can spend time together reflecting and informing the evolving adventure that is all our lives.

Speak the Speech
Trippingly on the Tongue
Reading Shakespeare Aloud

─────Ϛ

Bruce Miller

*Bruce Miller (see page 82) discusses exercises that help his students
learn to read Shakespeare's texts aloud.*

─────Ϛ

ARISTOTLE FIRST POINTED OUT THAT DRAMA is the imitation of an
action. As the finest examples of drama we have, Shakespeare's plays are,
above all, stories. Too often as teachers, however, we focus on the language
of his works at the expense of understanding them as stories. It is remarkable that when we guide our students to focus on the story of a play rather
than its literary merits, we can inspire a genuine appreciation for the language used to tell the story and reveal the play's artistry.

To focus successfully on the action of the plays, we need to teach
our students how to analyze and read aloud the words of the play. Until
they can do that effectively, the pleasure and deeper meaning of the
work is likely to remain behind a locked door. Yet the key for releasing
a successful unit of Shakespeare is not as difficult to achieve as it might
at first appear—once a few tools are mastered.

As my previous essay points out, these three tools should help students see the language as a means not an end:

Discuss the meaning of the words individually and in context,
including definitions, literary and historical allusions, and poetic language and imagery.

Focus on the overall dramatic context for what is spoken, determined by all dramatic events leading up to the scene or section of dialogue.

Determine the specific dramatic circumstances that result in these
words.

As a practical example of this process, let us take *Macbeth* Act I
Scene 5. This scene clearly demonstrates that the basic elements of
drama—plot, character, dialogue, and idea—which seem so obvious
when performed well onstage, appear far less so when our students read
the words in their texts.

Reading for the Story

Let's begin by reading the scene that follows just for meaning. I ask my own students to jot down any words or phrases that they are not sure about. It might be a good idea for you to do this exercise too. You are liable to be surprised at what you thought you knew but don't.

THE TRAGEDY OF MACBETH
Act 1 Scene 5

(Enter Lady Macbeth, with a letter)

Lady Macbeth: *(reading)* "They met me in the day of success, and I have learned by the perfect'st report they have more in them than mortal knowledge. When I burned in desire to question them further, they made themselves air, into which they vanished. Whiles I stood rapt in the wonder of it came missives from the King, who all-hailed me 'Thane of Cawdor,' by which title before these weird sisters saluted me, and referred me to the coming on of time with 'Hail, King that shalt be!' This have I thought good to deliver thee, my dearest partner of greatness, that thou mightst not lose the dues of rejoicing by being ignorant of what greatness is promised thee. Lay it to thy heart, and farewell."

Glamis thou art, and Cawdor, and shalt be
What thou art promised. Yet I do fear thy nature.
It is too full o' th' milk of human kindness
To catch the nearest way. Thou wouldst be great,
Art not without ambition, but without
The illness should attend it. What thou wouldst highly,
That wouldst thou holily; wouldst not play false,
And yet wouldst wrongly win. Thou'dst have, great
     Glamis,
That which cries "Thus thou must do" if thou have it,
And that which rather thou dost fear to do
Than wishest should be undone. Hie thee hither,
That I may pour my spirits in thine ear
And chastise with the valour of my tongue
All that impedes thee from the golden round
Which fate and metaphysical aid doth seem
To have thee crowned withal.

(Enter a Servant)
What is your tidings?

Servant: The King comes here tonight.
Lady Macbeth: Thou'rt mad to say it.
  Is not thy master with him, who, were't so,
  Would have informed for preparation?
Servant: So please you, it is true. Our thane is coming,
  One of my fellows had the speed of him,
  Who, almost dead for breath, had scarcely more
  Than would make up his message.
Lady Macbeth: Give him tending;
  He brings great news.

              (*Exit Servant*)
          The raven himself is hoarse
  That croaks the fatal entrance of Duncan
  Under my battlements. Come, you spirits
  That tend on mortal thoughts, unsex me here,
  And fill me from the crown to the toe top-full
  Of direst cruelty. Make thick my blood,
  Stop up th' access and passage to remorse,
  That no compunctious visitings of nature
  Shake my fell purpose, nor keep peace between
  Th' effect and it. Come to my woman's breasts,
  And take my milk for gall, you murd'ring ministers,
  Wherever in your sightless substances
  You wait on nature's mischief. Come, thick night,
  And pall thee in the dunnest smoke of hell,
  That my keen knife see not the wound it makes,
  Nor heaven peep through the blanket of the dark
  To cry "Hold, hold!"

              (*Enter Macbeth*)
         Great Glamis, worthy Cawdor,
  Greater than both by the all-hail hereafter,
  Thy letters have transported me beyond
  This ignorant present, and I feel now
  The future in the instant.
Macbeth: My dearest love,
  Duncan comes here tonight.
Lady Macbeth: And when goes hence?
Macbeth: Tomorrow, as he purposes.
Lady Macbeth: O never
  Shall sun that morrow see.

Your face, my thane, is as a book where men
May read strange matters. To beguile the time,
Look like the time; bear welcome in your eye,
Your hand, your tongue; look like the innocent flower,
But be the serpent under't. He that's coming
Must be provided for; and you shall put
This night's great business into my dispatch,
Which shall to all our nights and days to come
Give solely sovereign sway and masterdom.
Macbeth: We will speak further.
Lady Macbeth: Only look up clear.
To alter favour ever is to fear.
Leave all the rest to me.

(Exeunt)

I suspect that if you were to ask your students what happened in the scene above, the answers would be extremely interesting, but probably less than accurate. If your students had read the play up to this scene before taking on Act I Scene 5, they would probably do better than if you had assigned them the scene as a cold reading. But even had they read the scene in the context of the play up to that point, the language of the play would probably provide for many of them an insurmountable barrier to understanding, appreciation, and enjoyment.

The words in the context of the play and the context reflecting on the words intersect with each other to provide meaning. Without a specific understanding of that meaning, your students and your goals as teachers will founder. A dramatic understanding of the story, then, is the essential ingredient to making Shakespeare work in the classroom. Teachers often debate whether to start with a general discussion of the scene's dramatic progression or an examination of the language. But a discussion of the plot, when carried out effectively, invariably stimulates interest in a way that a discussion of the language without its context never can. For that reason, I always begin with the action, and then bring in the language once the groundwork of the scene has been established.

To discover the story, focus on the plot—the literal chronological action that is essentially a cause and effect process. The plot, which is so obvious when an audience sees it presented onstage, is far more deceptive lying quietly on a printed page. Dramatic points of interest that seem so absolutely clear when performed are often missed altogether when the play is read, especially if the language seems alien or difficult.

An effective way of getting to the heart of the action is to challenge your students to accurately list on paper the cause-and-effect chronology of a scene. They can be asked to do this on their own or in small groups. But they need to use the text to support any event they list. Once the chronological lists have been completed, a larger class discussion can distill the individual group conclusions into an agreed upon sequence. Surprising and impassioned discussions often arise as each group struggles to define its chain of events, and then debates its model with other groups. Students frequently have a great deal of difficulty isolating the action of a scene from its other elements. They want to mix character description, external circumstances, and personal interpretations all together. Their challenge will be to stick to cause-and-effect actions, the essentials of making the scene work actively.

Of course, any discussion should begin with the overall chronology of the play. But for our purposes we can jump right to the chronology of this scene. The actual cause-and-effect list of plot action that your class comes up with might look something like the following.

At the opening of the scene, Lady Macbeth is reading a letter from her husband. As the action begins, she reads of his encounter with the Weird Sisters, his description of their supernatural power to predict the future, and their sudden disappearance into thin air. Through implication, we conclude that Lady Macbeth already knows of her husband's victory and heroic action. ("They met me in the day of my success.") She then learns of the arrival of messengers who report on Macbeth's promotion.

After finishing the letter, Lady Macbeth declares that Macbeth will be king. However, she realizes his character is such that it may prevent him from doing what is necessary to get the crown. She wishes him home so that she might pour her courage into his ear and convince him to do what is necessary to become a king.

A messenger then enters and reports to her that the king will arrive that very night. Lady Macbeth suggests her murderous thoughts by declaring that the messenger is mad to have said such a thing. Quickly recovering, she praises the messenger for having brought great news and dismisses him. When alone, Lady Macbeth begins a soliloquy in which she hints that the king will soon be dead and conjures spirits of evil to stop up any weakness that being a woman might cause her to have. She enlists the help of the spirits to do what must be done with the murderous knife she will use.

At that moment Macbeth enters. They see each other. It is the wife who speaks first by flattering her husband with alluring titles old and new, and suggesting that greater titles await. Macbeth responds by saying the king comes there that night. Lady Macbeth asks when the king is to leave and her husband responds, "Tomorrow," but adds with great implication, "as he purposes." Lady Macbeth then reveals her heart by telling her husband that the king will not live until tomorrow. Macbeth's face betrays his doubts and fear, but his wife quickly instructs him to hide his feelings, lest they give him away. She further instructs him to leave the rest to her. Macbeth wants to speak further, but his wife silences him with a repeated warning that he must look innocent, and once again instructs him to leave all plans to her. They exit together.

Here is an even more concise version:

•Lady Macbeth reads her husband's letter.

•The contents of the letter cause her to declare that Macbeth will be king.

•The declaration causes her to realize that her husband has traits that will prevent his doing what he needs to.

•This realization causes her to beckon him home so that she can mold him into shape.

•A messenger interrupts with news that the king is coming.

•This news causes Lady Macbeth to blurt out an incriminating comment about her murderous intent.

•Having said the remark causes her to cover the moment so the servant doesn't catch on and further causes her to get rid of him as quickly as possible.

•Being alone again causes her to take the opportunity to conjure evil spirits to help her with her murderous plot.

•Macbeth's entrance causes her to be interrupted.

•Macbeth's arrival causes Lady Macbeth to face her husband for the first time. Seeing him causes her to start manipulating him, first using titles that will appeal to him.

•Hearing his wife's praise causes Macbeth to inform her that the king will come that night.

•Hearing this causes his wife to ask when the king will leave.

•Hearing his answer causes her to deny it and to begin to reveal her plan for murder.

•Hearing her suggested plan causes Macbeth to try to stop her.

•His attempt at stopping her causes her to take over and insist that he leave everything to her.

•Hearing her convincing stance, the couple leave together.

The story of the scene described in either version is accurate. During its short duration, two people, still highly respected by the world, begin to consider actions that are evil and that will irrevocably change their lives and who they are forever. A wife suddenly takes on the role and power of husband and a husband is suddenly dumb-founded and controlled by his wife. Both are about to begin a journey that, only moments before, they never would have admitted possible.

Though the scene on the printed page consists only of dialogue, the story summarized above is primarily told in terms of actions, or in other words, in terms of what the characters do. When read with a proper dramatic perspective, dialogue is always primarily about doing. Dialogue involves characters using words to express needs—needs that can be fulfilled either by characters who are present, or, as in the case of Lady Macbeth's soliloquy, by those who are not.

Notice that I have carefully selected action verbs to describe what goes on in the scene above, because well-selected action verbs suggest action rather than feelings, and the dramatic progression of a scene depends on its action. The verbs you will find above include "reads," "learns," "declares," "realizes," "beckons," "recovers," "praises," "dis-misses," "conjures," "enlists," "exchange," "flatters," "reveals," "betrays," "instructs," "silences," and "warns." Each verb suggests a playable action, and readers need to take their cues from these verbs and do what the verbs suggest.

Although several moments that I put into the story above have not been referenced in the dialogue, they are as important to the story as those explicitly mentioned. Take, for example, the moment Macbeth and his wife first see each other at the top of the scene. Given all that has happened to him, including a prediction of future greatness, and all that she has said in the previous moments, what might their first glances reveal or conceal? Then at the end of the scene, the future king and queen exit together. What has Lady Macbeth said to her husband, or better yet done to him, that allows this warrior hero to accept her leadership? Answering these questions clearly becomes an integral part of the scene.

I have also included several dramatic moments suggested but not emphasized in the dialogue. Lady Macbeth's references to her hus-band's facial expressions indicate his thoughts and actions, even though he never states them. "O never shall sun that morrow see," must pro-duce quite a reaction in the previously unsuspecting Thane of Cawdor. With practice, a careful reader will soon learn to recognize these kinds of dramatic moments.

As you and your students tackle a scene to find its cause-and-effect throughline of action, you will quickly discover that turning dialogue into specific actions can be messy work. Plots tend to be more slippery in reading than in performance. It is easy to miss significant actions and even easier to misinterpret a character's words. The most efficient way to overcome these analytical obstacles is to start at the end of the scene and work backwards. Cause and effect become quite clear when you turn it into effect and cause. If you start with "exeunt" and work your way back to "enter," your class will quickly become believers.

Analyzing the Language

Now it is time to examine the dialogue of the scene. Remember that I asked you to jot down any words and phrases you were not sure about. Were you my students I would also have asked you to look up the meanings of every word or phrase you had jotted down. (The most effective way to guarantee that your students do this is by using a carefully annotated version of the play, and for convenience, one with an easily accessible commentary, like the Folger or Signet editions which have the commentary on the same or adjoining page.)

It is essential that your students look up the meaning of every word they do not know. That may mean many words not annotated in their texts. You need to emphasize that, during the last four hundred years, the meanings and usages of many words may have changed. In some cases, words now denote or connote the opposite of their Renaissance meanings. Make sure your students examine archaic definitions for any unannotated words. (The best resource is, of course, the unabridged Oxford English Dictionary.) Their research can make for enlightening and fascinating discussions.

If you sell this process to your students as detective work, the task at hand will seem sexy rather than boring. You may want to put your students into teams where they can work together as in a scavenger hunt. Be sure to keep reminding them that in order to make the scene come alive, they will have to know exactly what the characters mean when they use specific words. Emphasize that they must not assume meaning. If anyone doubts the meaning of a word or phrase, he or she must look it up. (You might also want to create rewards for your best detectives.)

Here is a list I compiled while rereading the scene. Some of the words and phrases, when checked, proved deeper, more interesting, or more poetically complex than I first realized. In every case, the new and expanded meanings made the material more interesting and more dramatically useful than I first suspected. They also helped explain or amplify the reasons that Shakespeare chose a particular alliteration in a particular phrase.

•*day of success* - victory in battle

•*perfect'st report* - the accuracy of the report, suggesting the weird sisters'supernatural abilities

•*missives* - messengers (not messages as I first thought)

•*weird* - of or relating to fate, a more specific meaning than the "weird" we know today

•*nearest way* - easiest, or the way that is most available

•*illness should attend it* - evil quality (ruthlessness) that must go with great ambition

•*highly/holily* - (the use of an *h* sound emphasizes an ironic comparison)

•*wouldst wrongly win* - would be willing to win unfairly; again the alliteration emphasizes the importance of the phrase

•*hie thee hither* – the alliterative *h* sounds suggest speed

•*chastise/valor of my tongue* - scold with my tongue that is not afraid to say anything

•*golden round* – crown, but a phrase that associates the position with incredible wealth

•*metaphysical* - supernatural

•*seem ... withal* - that fate seems to have already given you

•*raven /hoarse* – the raven as a symbol of death combined with croaking and hoarse make an oddly funny but horrifying image

•*fatal* - meaning here directed by fate as well as deadly for the about-to-be- murdered king

•*unsex* - a frightening image implying losing all the natural characteristics that give her feminine qualities

•*make thick my blood* - thickened blood was believed to result in a ferocity of disposition

•*compunctious* - compassionate

•*fell purpose* - fierce and savage

•*take my milk for gall* - a gruesome antithetical image; see below

•*thick night* - besides the normal usage, thick also means morally corrupt

•*pall* - enshroud

•*dunnest* - darkest

•*keen knife* - besides sharp, keen also means bitter and eager

•*beguile* - deceive

•*solely sovereign sway* - alliteration for effect

•*alter favor ever is to fear* - to look other than normal will cause you to feel that people may be on to you

Skills for Reading Aloud

Now that we have examined the action of the scene and the meaning of the language, it is time to look at some of the skills necessary for reading Shakespeare aloud effectively. We will begin with what I consider the two most important: using the punctuation and identifying the operative words (i.e., those words that carry the most meaning in a phrase, line or sentence).

Punctuation and Other Traffic Signs

I tell my students that punctuation in a play by Shakespeare is like an organized system of traffic signs. If you obey the signs, you will reach your destination (or clarity of meaning) safely. If you fail to obey the signs, you will end up getting lost or having an accident. All those archaic words and figures of speech piled up on the page like cars at rush hour demand the use of traffic signs to prevent crashes and chaos.

The traffic rules are really quite simple. Your students learned them in grade school. But punctuation also offers actors a chance to work on their breathing. Periods, for example, indicate the end of whole ideas and require a stop. A stop is always a good place to take a breath. Commas indicate slighter pauses and usually suggest shifts in ideas or slight turns in direction, but they should not signal the complete ending of a particular idea. If a breath is necessary, the reader should take a short one. The ends of lines require the reader to follow the punctuation. If there is no traffic sign, then the idea continues and so does the reader's energy–at least until another traffic sign appears. This means that unless there is a sign, there must be no dip in energy at the end of a line. In fact, it is not unusual for the end of a line to contain an important, if not most important word in that line.

Too often American actors take pauses wherever they feel the acting urge to do so. They like to make moments. But this can be dramatic suicide when reading Shakespeare. Verse has a rhythm and music of its own that becomes apparent when read aloud with some degree of understanding. The playwright, who was also an actor, made sure each speech included all the necessary stops and pauses. He tells the reader if and when a pause is necessary. The best reading is invariably the one suggested by the provided punctuation. An unnecessary pause can kill the beauty and clarity of a line. So can ignoring pauses when they should be there.

There are a few more subtle traffic signals, and these involve the structure of the verse form that Shakespeare used. As you probably know, Shakespearean verse is written in iambic pentameter. When we get to scansion in a few moments, we'll talk about this in more detail. Iambic pentameter means that in a regular line (a line that does not break its established rhythm pattern) there will be five repetitions of an unstressed syllable followed by a stressed syllable. There is no magic here. Our language is made up of words in which some syllables are accented or stressed and some : Thy *let*/ters *have*/ trans*port*/ed *me*/ be*yond*/. In this regular line each of the five unstressed syllables is followed by a stressed one.

Sometimes, however, a spoken line is left uncompleted by one speaker and the next speaker finishes the pentameter on the next line.

> Macbeth: My dearest love,
>   Duncan comes here tonight.
> Lady Macbeth: And when goes hence?
> Macbeth: Tomorrow, as he purposes.
> Lady Macbeth: O never
>   Shall sun that morrow see.
>   Your face, my thane, is as a book where men
>   May read strange matters. To beguile the time. . . .

Notice that in lines three and five, Lady Macbeth completes the pentameter that Macbeth has begun. Since the rhythm has purposely been uncompleted in Macbeth's speech, the reader may assume that the author intended for Lady M to complete the missing beats. It also suggests that Lady M jumps right in with her lines. When properly executed, this gives the effect that Lady M is energized and taking control of the conversation. On the other hand, notice how the sixth line is left uncompleted just after Lady Macbeth lays down her bombshell. Since the line is intentionally left incomplete, it suggests that there is a long pause during which Macbeth produces some facial reaction to which Lady Macbeth refers in the next line. These are the kinds of traffic signs my high school teachers never told me about, but I certainly would have been fascinated had they approached the play in this fashion.

Finding and Using Operative Words

Now let's move on to operative words—the words that help to convey the meaning and dramatic purpose of each spoken line. As readers learn to identify the operative words in a piece of dialogue, they will have taken a major step toward reading Shakespeare with clarity and dramatic insight. When used in combination with a healthy regard for the traffic signs on the page, they may become serious threats to the Oliviers and Branaghs who are able to make a living from the skill.

So, how do readers of Shakespeare identify the words that most convey meaning and that move the action forward? A good way to start is by using scansion—the scanning of lines to determine where the naturally occurring accented syllables are.

> Come, thick night,
> And *pall/* thee *in/* the *dun/* nest *smoke/* of *hell,/*
> That *my/* keen *knife/* see *not/* the *wound/* it *makes,/*
> Nor *hea/ven peep/* through the *blan/ket off* the *dark/*
> To *cry/* "Hold, *hold!"/*

In this climactic moment from Lady Macbeth's conjuring of evil speech, you will notice that the second and third lines scan regularly. As I explained earlier, these lines are written in a normal iambic (i.e., unstressed syllable followed by stressed syllable) pattern. But lines 1, 4, and 5 do not scan perfectly. As a result of the natural stresses in a line in conjunction with their dramatic context, we get clear hints as to what syllables or words should be hit harder than others. In line two, we see that *pall*, *in*, *dun* (from dunnest,) *smoke*, and *hell* are all accented. In line three we see that *my*, *knife*, *not*, *wound*, and *makes* get the stresses. It then becomes important to rank the words according to their usefulness. There are no absolute rights or wrongs, but by going through this process, your students will begin a crucial evaluative journey.

Examine lines two and three further. In line two there is the verb *pall*. Verbs suggest action and we already know that in drama action is everything. In general, verbs are important dramatic meaning conveyers. Therefore *pall* is a useful word and definitely should be hit hard. Ends of lines also require an energy to carry the sense into the next line, so *hell* is also important. *Smoke* is accented, so next in order of importance. (After all, *dunnest* is archaic and therefore carries no meaning for a contemporary ear, while *smoke* of *hell* combine to make a phrase that creates a strong image. *In*, while only a preposition, which seldom carries a lot of power, will be hit slightly simply because of the natural rhythm of the line. Circle *pall*, *smoke*, and *hell* on your script. Now reread the line aloud stressing your circled words. The line probably sounded pretty good, didn't it?

Go through the same process with line three. We have a lot of room for discussion here. But my picks are *makes*, *wound*, *not*, and *knife* in that order. *Makes* because verbs carry action, *wound* because it is a visually provocative image, *not* because in combination with the unstressed "sees," it creates a dramatically effective cold heartedness in the speaker. If your order differs from mine, try it a few ways aloud and see which works best. Use the same process with your students. You will find that they love saying the lines aloud trying the words in different combinations of stress to make a dramatic impact. The ultimate result is that, through active participation, they will develop an appreciation for the words themselves, and for the art of the writer who provided them.

Because of its combination of one-syllable words, the first line comes out in a slow, sharp staccato. It is very difficult to say one-syllable words one after another too quickly, especially when there are no unaccented syllables between them. Dramatically, this means that all the words must be hit hard. Try saying the line aloud. Powerful, isn't it? Now say it as though you are really conjuring like Lady M.

Lines four and five are irregular, but the verb *peep* in line four with its accent and plosive sound clearly gets the dominant slot. The repetition of *hold hold* in line five speaks powerfully for itself. You will also notice that trying to scan lines four and five can be messy work because of their irregular rhythm. On the other hand, the irregularity gives a nice musical variety to the dialogue and keeps this section of dialogue from becoming unnaturally rhythmic or boring. Shakespeare uses iambic because its rhythm sounds very close to the way normal English is spoken. Therefore, when he chooses to break his established rhythm it still sounds right, yet he provides the variation necessary to avoid lulling the listener to sleep the way a childhood verse like "Twinkle, Twinkle" might.

Notice that at the top of the scene, Lady Macbeth is reading her husband's letter, a letter written in prose. Most of your students would not notice this, and those who do probably do so because of the way the prose looks on the page rather than the way the lines sound. Here again is proof that the difference between normal spoken English and patterned verse is a subtle one. Shakespeare often shifts from verse to prose and back again. Why?

When I studied Shakespeare in college as an English major, and later as a graduate student in acting, my teachers would hammer the importance of scansion. I think they overemphasized its place. No one wants to listen to lines that sound overly rhythmic, and the best professional actors would never even consider speaking them that way. Good actors make the language sound as natural as possible while at the same time using the language's dramatic and poetic imagery to make dramatic points. They use scansion, as we have, to find the heart and soul of the thought in the line.

Idea Units
Another effective way of determining how to read a line comes

from dividing up a passage into idea units or phrases, and determining which of those carry the most meaning.

> The raven himself is hoarse
> That croaks the fatal entrance of Duncan
> Under my battlements. Come, you spirits
> That tend on mortal thoughts, unsex me here,
> And fill me from the crown to the toe top-full
> Of direst cruelty. Make thick my blood,
> Stop up th'access and passage to remorse,
> That no compunctious visitings of nature
> Shake my fell purpose, nor keep peace between
> Th' effect and it. Come to my woman's breasts,
> And take my milk for gall, you murd'ring ministers,
> Wherever in your sightless substances
> You wait on nature's mischief.

By separating each line or sentence into the individual idea units they contain, your students will begin to see the power of each phrase. The result will be an opportunity to work with the colors and specific picture that each idea unit possesses. Breaking the dialogue into its stresses through scansion is effective for finding and delivering the clarity of the line, but picturing each idea unit conveys a far more nuanced meaning.

Dividing each line into phrases, as we have done above, does not mean that your students should take pauses (or find caesuras) in the line when they read a passage aloud. That is what the punctuation is for. However, if they take the time to separate the lines into their individual units, they will be able to explore not only the images themselves but the ways the images work in connection with each other. As they become familiar with what each phrase contains, they will become more proficient at painting the phrase images aloud without taking unnecessary pauses.

At this point have each student say some of the colorful phrases above aloud. Encourage them to repeat the phrases until they see and can convey a specific picture. Have them listen to one another and respond. Then have them put some of the phrases together. You will hear some very chilling readings. Notice, for instance, the power of the k and m sounds in connection with the blood images in *Make thick my blood*. Or the soft m-m sound of *my milk* when set against the hard contrasting g sound in the phrase that follows: *for gall*.

Alliteration

Alliteration, or a repetition of consonant sounds, offers another method for helping to find the words that should be stressed. The term has already been mentioned several times in our discussion. Shakespeare loved to use alliteration, clearly finding it an effective device for drawing attention to the images he painted in a basic and visceral way. His ability to use alliterative sounds in conjunction with the specific meaning of a line and the dramatic feel of a particular moment is truly remarkable. By acknowledging those repetitions vocally when they appear, your students have another effective way to make the drama in the lines pop out in their spoken work.

Have your students return to the scene above and underline the alliterations they find there. Ask them to explain why Shakespeare might have used alliteration when and where he did, as I did a few paragraphs ago in the discussion of phrasing. Then have your students repeat their chosen alliterative passages from the scene, emphasizing the alliterative sounds. They will be amazed at the cumulative power the repetitive sound can have dramatically. Remind them that English pronunciation has changed in the last four hundred years and a phrase like "my keen knife," which is no longer alliterative, would have been so in Renaissance England. Certainly the repetition of the hard k sound would effectively draw attention to Lady Macbeth's strength of intention.

Spending time going through this process will produce more skilled readers in the classroom which, in turn, will make the time spent reading vastly more effective. But perhaps more important is the fact that your students will discover for themselves experientially the language's power and beauty.

Apposition and Antithesis

I began my discussion of language with the topic of punctuation, the traffic signs for the eye when reading Shakespeare. But there are also some traffic signs for the ear that a reader must recognize and vocalize in order to comprehend the throughline of action and to get at the level of complexity in Shakespeare's characters. I will concentrate on two of those traffic signals: (I) antithesis and apposition, and (ii) transitions.

Apposition is a term that comes from the same root as opposite. It refers to ideas set against each other, ideas in opposition. Antithesis, a related term, refers to words and phrases of opposite meaning that are purposely placed in contrast to one another in a line or sentence and that balance each other when the two ideas are completed. The following example should make this point easier to grasp.

> Thy letters have transported me beyond
> This ignorant present, and I feel now
> The future in the instant.

In the example above, Shakespeare contrasts *present* against *future*. Later, Lady Macbeth's failure to separate present and future will take on a terrible irony. Consider another example:

> To *beguile* the time,
> Look like the time; bear welcome in your eye,
> Your hand, your tongue; look like the *innocent flower*,
> But be the *serpent under't*.

This passage contains two sets of images in apposition. Beguiling, or fooling the time, is very different from looking like or blending with the time. Contrasting the antithetical words when reading aloud produces a clarity and highly audible dramatic effect. The phrases *innocent flower* and *serpent under't* work in the same way. Recognizing and using such contrasts can turn a flat, black and white reading into a 3D comparison. Once students recognize appostion as a fundamental organizing device, they can look at its use in Lady M's speech as she categorizes her husband's strengths and weaknesses as a potential murderer. It is loaded with antithetical ideas.

Antithesis offers up another skill building opportunity for the detectives in your class, regardless of the Shakespearean play you are working on. Divide them up into teams of scavengers and offer a prize to the team that can find and then explain the largest number of antithetical phrases in a particular scene or passage. Then have them read the passages aloud. Your class can decide who does the best job contrasting the words, images, and phrases.

Transitions

Just one more term before we leave the subject of reading Shakespeare aloud. Transition is the term used by actors to describe the moment they shift from one idea to another. A transition to a new subject invariably causes a change of tone, a shift in color, a different use of energy, or a new purpose in what the speaker is saying. When a reader recognizes where these shifts occur, he or she can make an adjustment in the reading that will keep the listener's ear from being lulled to sleep and will keep the speaking character multi-leveled and interesting. Look back at that first speech by Lady Macbeth's after reading the letter from her husband and mark with a double slash the places you think transitions occur. Then check your choices against mine below. Don't read on until you have done your own work.

> The raven himself is hoarse
> That croaks the fatal entrance of Duncan
> Under my battlements./ / Come, you spirits

That tend on mortal thoughts, unsex me here,
And fill me from the crown to the toe top-full
Of direst cruelty. / /Make thick my blood,
Stop up th' access and passage to remorse,
That no compunctious visitings of nature
Shake my fell purpose, nor keep peace between
Th' effect and it./ / Come to my woman's breasts,
And take my milk for gall, you murdering ministers,
Wherever in your sightless substances
You wait on nature's mischief. / /Come, thick night,
And pall thee in the dunnest smoke of hell,
That my keen knife see not the wound it makes,
Nor heaven peep through the blanket of the dark
To cry "Hold, hold!"

(Enter Macbeth)

/ /Great Glamis, worthy Cawdor,
Greater than both by the all-hail hereafter,
Thy letters have transported me beyond
This ignorant present, and I feel now
The future in the instant.

Now compare your markings with mine. In the first section, Lady Macbeth makes a declaration about the future. In the second section, she begins to call on the spirits with an initial, but general call for their help in converting herself to evil. Next she lists specific things they can do to her to strengthen her resolve. Then she actually asks to be changed from her natural womanly nature. Next she asks for the protection of the darkness to shield her from failure. Finally, in the biggest transition of all, she changes tone and style completely to greet her husband properly. In your own analysis, you might have lumped Lady Macbeth's wish list together as one long playable action. That's fine, too. But either way, in a list like this one, there is a logical progression that must build vocally if the reading is to escalate dramatically.

Conclusion

Above all, it is essential for us to remember that all of these techniques are merely tools to help our students experience Shakespeare's plays more fully. Once we remember how much of his tradition was oral and how fully he lived his life in the world of the theater, we can appreciate more deeply the importance of the spoken word in his life and work. The better we understand the power and richness of spoken language, especially the ways Shakespeare's words play with and against each other, the more easily we can help our students blend them with a sensitivity to the dramatic situation in a scene to make his characters and stories come truly alive in our classrooms.

Act III

Playing with Productions

Suit the Action to the Word, the Word to the Action
Principles of a Good Director

Stephen Hollis

Stephen Hollis, an international director of Shakespeare and modern drama, defines the principles of a good director.

WHETHER I AM GIVING GUIDANCE to young men and women training to become professional directors or to school teachers who find themselves in the position of director of an annual school play, I always start with these basics. The first step, of course, is to have a full understanding of the script. In the case of a contemporary play, such as a thriller or a Wendy Wasserstein or A. R. Gurney script, the story is probably going to be straightforward. With a straightforward script there is no need for a concept, but a more complicated script (like a Shakespeare play) does require you, as the director, to ask yourself what the play means to you and what you want the audience to leave the theater thinking about. You may wish to reveal in, say, *Hamlet,* a young man attempting to reconcile with his mother or the problems of a prince who wishes to regain his "stolen" crown. I always study which dramatic conflicts in a particular play I wish to reveal because if I do not choose which of them I wish to emphasize, they will never come to life. So begin by knowing which dramatic conflicts you feel to be most important for this particular production.

The next stage is working with your fellow designers. First, the set designer. If you have a choice, you can have the luxury of choosing the person best suited to the particular play you are directing. Some designers are strong on naturalistic, realistic sets, while others are more imaginative. If you are visualizing a certain style to your production, you need to keep in mind whether you want a designer stronger in abstract sets or one more at home with representational sets. Remember, however, that most good designers will have their own opinions, so the better the designer, the more you will need to engage in a dialogue about the visual terms of the production. If, for instance, the play is set in a New York City apartment in 1975, you can choose to represent the apartment realistically with a complete box set or—if there is not a great deal of money, more likely the case for most productions, or you don't wish to clutter the stage with the set—you can suggest that apartment in simpler terms. For example, you can choose specific architectural features or crucial pieces of furniture that make a statement about 1975 or apartments or New York. Many plays take place in more than one location, as in *Hamlet*, where there are several locations both inside and outside the castle. In a strange way, the *less* set there is, the easier it is to suggest all the different locations in the play.

As the director, while you are in dialogue with the set designer you must also consult with the costume designer. Together, you need to discuss your opinions about the characters and their costumes. The costume designer should also have his/her ideas and show you thumbnail sketches of possible designs. Discussions between the director and the designers often will continue for some three or four weeks. After you make some initial decisions, the costume designer should present more careful renditions, often with fabric swatches to give a good idea of the colors and textures for the completed garments. Ideally, the set designer will be able to present a three-dimensional miniature model of the set. I should add that the design of any set can be drastically affected by the type of theater in which the production is to be mounted (e.g., proscenium, in the round, or thrust). A lighting designer can be consulted later in the process, as it is more important that set and costumes are ready by the start of rehearsals. The earlier an actor can have his/her costume, especially shoes, the better.

While you hold discussions with designers, you must also cast the play. Although many directors know a large number of actors they have worked with already in their professional lives, most directors will still consult with casting directors who know what actors are available and what their strengths and weaknesses are. Obviously, professional productions allow the director more choice than when directing amateur, or high school, or college productions. In any event, auditions can take place either by asking actors to prepare a monologue closely suited to the play in question (i.e., a classical or verse monologue for a classic play and a contemporary monologue for a contemporary play) or else you might ask the actors to simply read "sides" (certain selections from the play in question) if you have several people in mind for a part. If the actor is to read a scene, you can choose a "reader" to help the audition by reading the other character's lines in the scene. Initial auditions are usually followed up with callbacks when a few actors are selected for each role to come and work with you in more detail. This is especially important to make sure your cast members are capable of taking direction.

It is extremely important to have a reliable stage manager who will then mark out your rehearsal space according to the ground plan provided by the set designer. In a professional production, the actors should be called for their first read-through of the play in question. A read-through should be simply that; try not to give direction or comments to the actors as they hear the play read out loud for the first time. For amateur productions, the read-through may take a different form, as Stuart Omans (Chapter Two) points out in his essay. After this initial introduction of experiencing the text as a group, you should show everyone the models of the set and the costume renditions. Now you can talk a little bit about your feelings and ideas about the play, especially what the concept is and how you see the relationships. This provides an opportunity to excite and inspire the actors with your own enthusiasm about the forthcoming production.

The way that you structure the rehearsal process will depend on the length of time for the production, but, generally speaking, professional productions usually have three full weeks of rehearsal plus a week in the theater itself, onstage, for technical and dress rehearsals and previews. Amateur productions normally need several more weeks for rehearsal. In the first week of rehearsal it is common, but by no means obligatory, to block the play (i.e., give the actor some general moves as a basis upon which to proceed). When there are only two or three characters in a scene, blocking is not much of a problem because it does not matter much where actors are so long as their moves are justified by some particular action in the play or by some emotional need. However, in plays with lots of characters in a scene (e.g., in Chekhov or particularly in Shakespeare, when you might have 20 actors onstage at the same time), it is important to block the scene so that the major speakers are placed Upstage Center and the rest of the cast Down Left and Right. This Triangular Concept is a safe guideline, with the speaking actors always positioned at the apex of the triangle and other cast members down left and right of them. Blocking, of course, is always subject to change, but I find a rough blocking pattern very useful as a starting point. During the first week of rehearsals, when actors are still holding their scripts or books, a rough blocking pattern provides them some physical structure. It is also important to give actors a fixed date by which to be off-book (i.e., to know their lines), which for professionals is usually toward the end of the second or third week of rehearsal.

After initial blocking rehearsals, which can take three to four days, it is usual to go back to the beginning of the play and begin to work in great detail with the actors. By this I mean discussion of character, their background, their relationships to the other characters in the play, and their scene-by-scene intentions. Because an actor's through line in a play is always his intention (i.e., knowing what this character wants), it is one of the director's most important jobs to make sure all the actors know what their objectives are at any given point in the play. Most professionally trained actors already know this. There are, of course, several choices to make at any given moment, but the most effective choices are those which accentuate the conflicts in the play. Remember that it is the director's responsibility to resolve any differences of opinion about interpretation and to make the final decision about choices.

Actors expect from directors a combination of factors, including a knowledge of the text of the play, preparation, guidance, and support. Since actors come from a variety of training backgrounds, you must work with each actor individually while at the same time uniting the group into an ensemble of players. Although detailed scene work takes up most of the rehearsal time, it is crucial to have run-throughs as soon as possible to get some idea of how the production is coming together. The actors certainly need a complete run-through of the play by the third week of rehearsal.

Moving from the rehearsal room (if you are using one) to the stage is an important step in the directing process and it is imperative that enough time be put aside for technical rehearsals. During technical rehearsals a director should give over his concentration to all technical aspects of the production such as lighting, props, furnishings, costumes, sightlines, sound effects and the audibility of actors. Technical problems should be fully resolved during the technical rehearsals; there is usually no time to correct them later. You should also give the actors at least two dress rehearsals, which should be held totally without interruption—except for emergencies. Actors need to have the opportunity to go from the beginning to the end of the play, with all exits, entrances, and costume changes required of them. Under ideal circumstances a couple of previews should be scheduled so that the director and the actors can test the production in front of an audience. Throughout all of these run-throughs and technical rehearsals, the director should take copious notes and give them all to the actors at the end of the rehearsal, making certain that the actors, in turn, write these directions down in their scripts and incorporate them into the next rehearsal.

Beyond Playing Pirate
Alternative Methods of Staging Violence

Ian M. Borden

Ian Borden, a certified fight choreographer from Tallahassee, examines alternative approaches to staging violence safely.

ONE OF THE MOST DIFFICULT TASKS FOR EVEN the most seasoned of actors is to resist "playing pirate" the moment we grasp a sword. The desire to give in to the urges of an eight-year-old and begin waving our weapon around is almost overwhelming. Today, swords are barely recognized as dangerous. Compare picking up a sword to picking up a gun. We immediately recognize a gun's power as a weapon, even if we pick it up merely to examine it. In our society guns carry an inherent sense of danger about them, a sense no longer connected with swords.

This schism between what now feels real and dangerous and what was real and dangerous in Shakespeare's time is a very important one to overcome. If we cannot recognize that a sword fight had as much impact on his society as domestic violence, drive-by shootings, and terrorist attacks have on ours, we miss the impact of the violence on the story we are trying to tell. In fact, it is the impact of the violence that makes a stage fight both interesting and necessary to the story of a play. It is important for teachers as thespians to find ways to convey that emotional impact to our modern audiences. We must reach beyond attempts to recreate conflicts, particularly sword fights, as realistically as possible, and use all the possibilities of the theater. Carefully thinking through the way we stage fights will provide us with ways to make a tremendous impression upon an audience, while also taking into account the difficulties of staging fights in modern theaters, particularly in high school settings.

Violence generally comes into a story at the same time it comes into real life, at the moments that involve the highest level of emotional commitment, the moment when words have failed and violence seems the only alternative. Because of this, it is important that the violence onstage be connected to the emotional reality of the moment. The violence does not have to be realistic, but it does have to arise from the emotional truth demanded by the play. If you have ever seen a performance in which the violent moment lacked punch, it is because the moment failed to match the emotional heights of the scenes immediately before it. As spectators we are left feeling cheated, because our expectations have not been met, and the moment in the play that requires the actors' highest emotional commitment receives only a token effort.

Often the letdown is for reasons of safety. The director, choreographer, and even sometimes the actors themselves may realize that a full commitment to the violent moment may lead to an injured actor. Visions of sword-points sticking into scenery or young bodies make for a "safe" fight that isn't fully committed. In reality, however, such fights not only fail to capture the necessary quality of the moment, they are also far more unsafe for the actors. Research in athletics has recognized that the athlete who only commits 75% of his or her energy is the one who gets hurt. The same thing happens onstage. Actors assume they are safe because they are moving more slowly or committing less, and their concentration slips. Suddenly, someone has a sword-point in their belly or a cut on their hand. (Another factor for directors and teachers to watch for is the actor who has to "feel" the moment to act it. If one actor suddenly becomes slow and careful while a second decides to turn up the pressure, disaster looms.)

Unfortunately, even though these kinds of things occur at all levels, teenagers are especially prone to making mistakes with stage violence. Their concentration is often not as strong as that of adults; they do not yet fully control their bodies; and their lack of understanding the real consequences of violence can encourage dangerous behavior.

Teenage boys are especially prone to wanting to play pirate the moment they get swords in their hands. So how do we approach stage violence with untrained, young actors, especially when they have weapons that are inappropriate for stage combat? One answer is to avoid using the kind of weapons with teens that we might with trained adult actors.

The most important thing when approaching stage violence is not to worry about how to make the fight look real. It is the emotional truth, not the realism of the fight that has an impact on the audience. In other words, audiences focus not so much on the fight itself to tell the story, but the reaction of the characters to the fight. In fact, no one ever stages a truly realistic fight. If you want proof of this, watch Olympic fencing. Not only can spectators not follow what is happening, the participants must wear electric sensors to register a hit. The speed of the blades is such that no one can follow them without electronic scoring. Furthermore, traditional duels usually lasted about ten seconds, yet few stage fights have taken so little time. So even when "real" weapons are used and the fight has a semblance of reality, we are dealing with illusions.

The alternative to a real fight is to discover what makes a fight work onstage, what makes it exciting, and how it tells the story of the emotional moment. There are three components that all fights must have to make them exciting: intent, motion, and sound. If we explore each of these three in detail, we can begin to see how they might be used to create very exciting, yet very safe fights.

The first component is the intent of the characters. It is important to separate the intent of the character from the intent of the actor, while also remembering that, onstage, realism is not always important. After all, the stage has a tremendous number of conventions that we accept that have no basis in reality. It is very easy to create our own conventions with which an audience will go along. For this reason, actors do not need speed, real weapons, or even proximity to each other to show their intent.

The first and perhaps easiest approach is the slow motion fight. We have become so accustomed to television replays, with sports action footage slowed considerably, that slow motion offers a very accessible option to young actors. It also allows an audience to really follow the moves of a fight and to see the sense of fear or triumph or danger on the actors' faces. Remember it is the reaction to the fight that has an impact on audiences. And if we are looking for the reactions to a fight, then even the weapons themselves do not have to be real. What happens if you use imaginary weapons? Held convincingly and reacted to by committed actors, their reality will be provided by the audience's imaginations.

An alternative to slow motion in emphasizing intent is to place the actors on different parts of the stage. An actor on one part makes a violent action, while a second actor in a different part of the stage responds to the violence as the victim. There is also an assortment of less dangerous weapons that can be used. Sticks, poles, cardboard boxes, and cardboard tubes are examples of everyday objects that can be turned into weapons. One has to be especially careful with this, however, because even though it is hard to stab someone with a stick, those sticks can still break bones. In addition, some everyday objects have surfaces, corners, and edges that can cause a lot of damage.

Motion clearly helps in conveying intent. But it also helps in heightening the audience's sense of danger. Here again, though, the demands of the stage can draw us away from reality. If you have ever watched real wrestling, you can begin to understand why the fake professional wrestling is so popular. Like many real fights, collegiate and Olympic wrestling matches often seem very static as the wrestlers struggle to maintain or break a hold. Many matches strike the uninitiated as extended hugs. Onstage we cannot allow our characters to fall into the trap of a static fight. The two methods mentioned above both lend themselves to motion. A slow motion fight usually has tremendous movement. Separating the actors onstage opens them up, and does not allow the blur of a close-in fight. And imaginary weapons often heighten the sense of how an actor needs to move to make the weapon work.

Motion can involve not only the fighters but the objects and people surrounding them. I have had great success buying cheap sheets and tying them to poles to make flags. Actors then wave the flags from different parts of the stage to add to the excitement. The banners also help clarify for the audience which side is which in both large and small battles. A little imagination will allow spectators and other characters to add to the sense of movement of a fight, and thus the excitement of the moment.

This leaves the third, and perhaps most important element: sound. It is astonishing how much sound contributes to the energy of a fight. All you need to do to understand this is to watch an action movie with the sound turned off. The fights become almost silly without the sounds of the hits and the reactions of those who are fighting. There are two lessons from this. The first is that if we are using weapons, the sound of the hits is very important. The film version of *Rosencrantz and Guildenstern are Dead* has a wonderful example of this. During the film's sword fight neither of the actors actually holds a sword; they simply pretend to have the weapons. A third player holds two blades, and as the fight progresses, he adds the sound of the weapons contacting each other. The effect is stunning. As I watched the movie, I could have sworn that Hamlet's forlorn classmates were really fighting. This example reinforces the importance of illusion, convention, and expectation onstage.

However, it is not just the sound of the hits that is important. In fact, most of the examples discussed above have no need for such sounds. What is more important is the sound from the characters in the fight and the reaction of the characters around them. All of their voices must be engaged to make a fight exciting. If the actors stay mute, the fight will never reach its potential for excitement or sense of danger.

Sound can also be provided from other sources. Action movies prove how a sound track can add to the excitement. Percussion of various sorts can be tremendously effective, whether from drums, clapping, stomping, or pounding random objects that happen to be onstage. Part of the rehearsal process should be devoted to exploring how percussion can add to a fight.

Before examining how these factors can be applied to the fight in Romeo and Juliet, let me discuss a production that incorporated many of these ideas. Joe Price directed and choreographed a production of *Titus Andronicus* for the Professional Actor Training Program at the University of Missouri, Kansas City/ Missouri Repertory Theater. Anyone who knows this play understands that it is one of Shakespeare's bloodiest, with murders, battles, rapes, dismemberments, decapitations, and cannibalism. There is no more challenging play for a fight choreographer. Price captured all of these moments and made them emotionally powerful without bringing a "real" weapon onstage.

At the core of the production was a rectangular sheet of blood-red fabric, approximately forty feet by thirty feet. The actors' weapons were strips of cloths in lieu of swords, and as a character died, the central sheet was drawn over them, and then pulled back to reveal a hooded figure. The character who had just died became one of the faceless figures who manipulated the fabric. When the actors moved in slow motion during the rape and dismemberment of Lavinia, the sheet of fabric became part of each violent act. The sheet would cover her and then reveal blood-red fabric hanging from her sleeve, cover her again and then replace the other hand with a strip of fabric. Finally, the fabric engulfed her before pulling back to show her tongue replaced by cloth. The effect was so simple and yet so horrifying that it surpassed anything a realistic representation could provide. Price's fights had no realistic elements, yet they captured completely the emotional truth of the moment.

So how can these ideas work in our classrooms? Here is an exercise I have used in the Drey Summer Shakespeare Institute at Rollins College. Using very simple weapons and sound makers, the participating teachers working as a group constructed exciting, engaging fights that created emotional connections with their audience and told the story of the play extremely well.

Exercise: Act II - Romeo and Juliet (The Tybalt/Mercutio fight)

Equipment: two poles, percussive instruments, random objects
Players: Romeo, Tybalt, Mercutio, various members of the
        Montague and Capulet gangs

The first step is to have the actors playing Mercutio and Tybalt decide on what type of weapon they want to use. I suggest keeping it simple, either rapiers or daggers. The rapier, a sword with a three-foot-long blade used to poke or slash an opponent, can be held in one hand. Daggers are, of course, much shorter, and are primarily used to poke an opponent, although they can slash as well. Daggers might work better for the exercise, because the blade is less than one foot long and thus is in closer proximity to the hand. Once a weapon is chosen, have the actors stand facing each other. Remind them that they will *only* move in slow motion. (It is likely that they will need to be reminded of this several times.) It is also important that both actors find the same speed, the same pace, so that their motions match.

The next step is to put together three short fight sequences. These will match the three phases of the fight from *Romeo and Juliet*. The first phase is very playful. Even though Tybalt and Mercutio dislike each other, they are still only playing as they begin sparring. Mercutio needs to win this first sequence easily, perhaps with a tap on Tybalt's buttocks or some other humiliating move. This fight sequence should only have about five moves and end quickly.

The second sequence becomes a little more serious, particularly for Tybalt. However, Tybalt loses this exchange as well. Use no more than ten moves as a maximum, so that it is relatively brief but longer than the first. Finally, the third sequence becomes deadly as Tybalt's anger erupts and Mercutio responds. It is this sense of danger that brings Romeo into the fray and causes Mercutio to be slain under his arm. Once again ten to twelve moves are all that are needed. Remember that performing the fight in slow motion will make the sequences seem longer.

Now that we know what we are constructing, it is time to put the three sequences together. Have each actor state his actions aloud. For the first sequence, have Tybalt begin by saying aloud what his target will be. He should also state what type of attack he is making, for example, "I am slashing at Mercutio's shoulder." The actor playing Mercutio will then respond by slowly avoiding this attack and starting an attack of his own: "I stab at Tybalt's right side." Tybalt might respond by parrying the attack (blocking Mercutio's blade with his own): "I parry the attack with my blade." For the purposes of this exercise, we need Mercutio to win, so we will have him do the following: "I fake an attack to the other side, and as he responds, I pull my blade over his head and hit him on the backside."

With this approach the attacks become very clear, as do the responses.

As actors remember each new move, they can stop saying it aloud. In a way it is very much like learning lines, only this time they are physical lines of dialogue. Remember, though, that as they work in slow motion, they must always remain aware of their balance and of the fact that the emotion needs to register on their faces. It is very easy when doing an exercise like this to make the mistake of holding one's breath. Remind your students that it is necessary to go slowly and that it will take time to make the movements work, particularly for those new to the exercise. No one expects someone who has never done it before to leap up and tap dance. But students often feel that they should be able to do this kind of exercise instantly. Make sure they take the time to figure everything out.

Once these three sequences have been sketched out, you are ready to bring in the other actors. Separate them into two groups, the Montague faction supporting Mercutio and the Capulets supporting Tybalt. Give each side a pole with a sheet tied to it as a banner, and make sure that each side has its share of percussion makers. They are ready to begin.

The convention we will practice is that all the actors will be in real time talking and acting normally. Then as each fight sequence takes place, the actors playing Tybalt and Mercutio will move in slow motion while everyone else stays in real time. When each section is finished, Tybalt and Mercutio move back into real time and speak their lines normally with the other actors. Remember that while each fight sequence is taking place, the other actors are vocalizing, cheering their side on, waving the flag, and making percussive noise.

Let's start with a few of lines chosen from the scene:

    Mercutio: O calm, dishonorable, vile submission:
             Tybalt, you rat-catcher, will you walk? *[He draws.]*
    Tybalt:What would thou have with me?
    Mercutio: Good King of Cats, nothing but one of your nine
            lives.
    Tybalt: I am for you.

Notice that the tone is still playful. Let this be reflected in the response and vocalizing of the two gangs as they see the fight begin to take place. Now the actors playing Tybalt and Mercutio perform their first fight sequence in slow motion while the others cheer, wave flags, and make noise. When the sequence ends, the fighters return to normal time and interact with the other actors.

Romeo will attempt to stop the fight, but Mercutio will ignore him and call Tybalt to another exchange.

    Romeo: Gentle Mercutio, put thy rapier up.
    Mercutio: Come sir, your passado.

Once again, the actors playing Tybalt and Mercutio go into slow-motion time to perform the second fight sequence. The tone, a little more serious and dangerous, should be reflected in the reactions and sounds from the sidelines. When Tybalt is touched a second time, the fighters come back to real time. Perhaps Tybalt receives a slight injury. His pain, along with the humiliation of losing twice, draws him into a rage, and the scene's tone should turn more deadly.

For the last sequence, Romeo becomes more desperate. He will also enter the fray at the end, suddenly entering the slow motion world as he joins the other two: "Draw, Benvolio, beat down their weapons." As Mercutio and Tybalt enter their slow-motion world to start the third fight sequence, they begin to duel in deadly earnest. The actors on the outside of the fight this time work in concert. As one, every actor outside the fight should begin a very slow percussive rhythm. This rhythm will gradually accelerate during the fight, and if possible, increase in volume. Any vocalizing should support this rhythm.

When Romeo pleads, "Hold, Tybalt! Good Mercutio!," the young lover enters the fight, moving in slow motion. As he moves in, Tybalt stabs Mercutio underneath Romeo's arm. By this time, the accelerated rhythm of both motion and sound should be very fast and very loud. At the precise moment of the stabbing, every actor needs to freeze and the sound stop so that there is total silence. If we have been successful, this will be a very powerful theatrical moment that punctuates the story of the fight. It also allows the audience to understand what has happened within the fight. Have all the actors count slowly to three, and then have everyone continue in normal time.

Don't forget that the story of the fight isn't over yet. The reactions in the moment after the violence are very important. How do the different characters react? What do the Capulets do? How does that differ from the Montagues? Have everyone continue until the Capulet gang leaves, and then the exercise will be over.

At this point, you should find that you have accomplished the task of telling the story of the fight. Without weapons or trained actors, you will have created an intense theatrical moment. By using vocal support, movement and percussion, you will have made a stronger statement than if you had attempted to use real weapons and stage a real fight. Not only that, but everyone is safe and uninjured. Parents, the principal, the audience, and your actors will be delighted. And your fighters will have moved far beyond playing pirate and their fight scene will have come to life in the minds of their audience.

Where Shall This Music Be?

Daniel K. Flick

*Dan Flick, a composer and the former music director for the Ashland Theater
Festival, offers a series of exercises to help students discover the nature and
possibilities of sound and ways of integrating sound into productions.*

FREQUENTLY, WHEN I TELL PEOPLE that I perform music for a particular production, their response is "Oh, I didn't realize that the play was a musical." The use of sound and music is a valuable tool for conveying texts of all sorts, even when it's not necessarily called for by the playwright. Within the first few seconds of a musical introduction or prelude, an amazing amount of information can be established for the audience. Putting into the written text what can be said in a few measures of music would take paragraphs, but listening to a musical prelude automatically gives us a feel for the location and mood of the production.

For instance, a concert piano with string quartet can suggest socioeconomic bracket, educational level, geographic setting, and chronological setting. On the other hand, a fiddle, banjo and scrub-board sets its audience into a completely different space. By combining an evocative soundscape and set design, a director can captivate and transport his patrons with great specificity before a single line is delivered or a foot hits the stage.

Another way that music can enhance a production is to provide spatial transitions. It requires the same amount of time for each perceiver, actor, or viewer. If I, as director, need to change sets or move people onstage or offstage, the music will mask the sounds of the change while maintaining continuity.

One of the first questions for any producer or director is whether a production's music will be live or pre-recorded. Whichever is used, depending on resources, remember to err on the long side because things rarely take exactly the same amount of time in performance as they do in a technical rehearsal. I recall during a production at the Denver Center Theater Company, the stage turntable got stuck and I played a long solo. As usual, that night using live music covered our technical problems.

Because of its level of complexity, I will focus on live performance aspects of sound. These concepts, incidentally, can easily be applied to pre-recorded sound by using some basics of recording and editing. The following system is designed for teachers with little or no formal training in music. All you need is a willingness to stretch your students and yourself and an openness to new experiences.

As a prelude to discussing the uses of sound in theatrical productions, begin by imagining its opposite: silence. As you will quickly realize and as most scholars would agree, silence is very rare and difficult to experience. I will begin with a series of four practical–and fun–exercises to help students discover the nature and possibilities of sound, discuss ways of integrating what they learn, and finally explore some possibilities of connecting that knowledge with Shakespeare's plays.

I. Exercises

The Silence Game: To achieve silence, have your class pass a piece of notebook paper from person to person without making any sound. They will find this much trickier than they suspect. But the exercise will help them focus on sound awareness. When the paper has gone full circle, discuss what each person heard during the exercise.

Responses from the outside like cars and birds or from the inside like the ventilation system, the buzz from florescent lights, breathing, shoes shuffling on the floor are some fairly common answers. Students will realize that sound is present everywhere and that silence is elusive. With this in mind, point out to them that our only hope is to focus on the sounds we want to hear.

Sound Game I: This exercise and the next are designed to separate common sounds from their specific identities and combine them to create new textures. Begin by assembling the class or a group of students from the class in a circle, with the instructor or leader in the middle. Each person should then choose a noise that can be made with the body: a clap, a stomp, a click, a quick breath, two hands rubbed together–anything acceptable within the particular setting will work. Remind the students that there is no right or wrong sound; participation is all that counts. After each person has chosen a sound, he or she must produce it when the leader points to him or her. By pointing or circling from one person to the next at different speeds, the leader can show how sounds begin to produce a texture all their own. It is not necessary for the leader always to go in the same order or to include all of the sounds all of the time. In fact, variations work better here. The leader can "play" the sounds much as a conductor leads an orchestra. Try inserting rhythm and dynamics. Use your foot to stomp rhythm while raising and lowering a hand to indicate volume.

Sound Game II: The same exercise can be repeated using words. As each word is repeated and intermingled in a nonsensical pattern, the words tend to lose their individual meaning and become part of the overall soundscape. An analogy for both exercises is to see the specific words or sounds as threads in a tapestry.

Sound Game III: Using either objects you brought for this exercise or material already in the room, let the students bang, crumple, drop, smush, pound, and poke them. Here they are learning to explore the sound properties of their surroundings. And have them discuss what "this thing" sounds like when I do "this action" to it? After a few minutes of cacophony, break the group into sub-groups and tell them, "Using the stuff and the 'sound possibilities' you have discovered, create a short (2 to 3 minute) soundscape within your group." Give them five or ten minutes to collaborate and then present the creations to the entire group, bearing in mind that there is no right or wrong and no need to judge.

II. Integration

After exploring sounds for their own sake, the next step is to integrate them with a text in three steps:
•Choose a poem or a short passage from a larger work.
•Discuss the sounds that might be present within the setting.
•Decide how to represent or produce the sounds.

After pointing out that there are many books available on homemade instruments, ask them to discuss three questions:
•Where and when is the scene taking place?
•Would music be playing in this setting?
•Do you have musicians available?

As part of the background, either find a recording or have the students record appropriate sounds. They might want city sounds (e.g., traffic, horses, cars, feet, commerce, vendors, market sounds, and people's voices), country sounds (e.g., animals, cows, cowbells, distant church bells, birds, running water, splashes, wind, rain, or lightning), or seaside sounds (e.g., surf, waves, sea gulls, beach parties).

When the text and all of the sound devices are prepared, have them read the text with all of the desired pacing. Mark in the script where specific sounds might occur. Then try a read-through inserting the sounds/music. Remember that the story takes precedent over all of the extemporaneous elements. If an audience cannot hear an actor, something is wrong. These issues can be hashed out in the tech rehearsal. An important consideration, when choosing music for a production, is to make sure that the music never pulls the audience away from the show. Familiar tunes may conjure memories that take people out of the present and into their own pasts. In most cases you should try to elevate the emotion without breaking the continuity. One way to stay away from music that is too recognizable is to enlist a composer to write an original score for the production.

III. Explorations

In creating a score for a Shakespearean play, ask your students, "If music were a character in your production, what would it look like and how would you costume it?" This kind of approach can help to flesh out the character of the music. One of the most challenging and interesting requests I've heard from a director was "The music needs to be completely new. I'm trying to take the audience to a place where no one has ever been before." On the one hand, this request completely freed me from all limit; on the other, it implied new sounds, a new tonal system, and the ability to let go of all prior concepts of what constitutes music.

Assuming the students can give a clear description of when and where the production is to be set, choosing and composing the music should be fairly straightforward. Finding places for music in Shakespeare's *Twelfth Night*, based on such lines as "If music be the food of love, play on./Give me excess of it" can be obvious. In the stage directions from *Taming of the Shrew*, "the revelers enter," we can assume that the revelers don't sneak in but burst in with lots of music and merriment. In many instances Shakespeare includes songs and indicates that the passage should be sung, so the students simply need to supply a musical setting for the text. Scene changes, set changes, and other transitions are also excellent places for music.

Unlike more modern plays where the entire action might take place within a single room, Shakespeare's plays tend to make sudden and often dramatic changes. In minutes his location can shift from a battle scene to the local inn or pub. Music's fluid yet abstract nature can help give the play direction and avoid any sense of sections or cumbersome interruptions in the story line. Students will also find in their love and knowledge of music new and exciting ways to connect the plays and productions with themselves.

If Music Be the Food of Love, Play On

John Carpenter

John Carpenter, a professional musician and professor of English at the University of South Carolina, explores practical ways of integrating music into the plays.

AS TEACHERS WE KNOW THAT NO MATTER HOW IMPORTANT or relevant we may think our subject matter, if our students are not interested in it, all we can expect, at best, is the polite rote memorization of a few facts. One clear attraction of exploring the music in Shakespeare is that it is not only a legitimate, integral part of the plays, but most of our students have a personal investment in it.

An analysis of the music and musical allusions in Shakespearean (and other early modern) drama can take us deep into the complexities of its historical, political, and philosophical content. Any complete discussion of musical approaches to Shakespearean drama would take volumes. Instead, my purpose is to explore easily applied classroom techniques for using music and discussing music and to touch briefly on some of the ways in which music operated as a key part of Elizabethan culture in general and of Shakespearean drama in particular.

Music finds its way into the stage directions of every play but *The Comedy of Errors*. The most common type of musical stage directions calls for sennets or flourishes, specific short musical introductions announcing the entrance of a character. One way of taking advantage of these directions in stimulating our students' interest while deepening their understanding of the plays is to open a class discussion of what type of music might most fittingly introduce a character like Richard III or Romeo. We can approach this in a number of ways. One way is to ask students to associate the character with musical genres with which they are familiar. If a student suggests that a few notes of a grunge or rap tune might best introduce Richard, this can open up a conversation about which of his lines in the play might best support such an association. The class will find themselves searching for ways to discover a unified view of Richard that can be communicated through a genre of music that embodies for them and their contemporaries a specific emotional connotation.

Such a conversation could go in a number of directions. Should Richard's music represent his personality as well as his rank? If it suggests his rank, does the music change as he kills off his opponents and moves up the ladder? If so, how might we change it to reflect his new rank? Do some kinds of music sound more powerful than others, so that we hear something more powerful each time Richard enters after having had someone killed? If music can suggest his personality, how can we best describe that personality and which aspects of it can best be represented through music?

When the class begins discussing ways to stage the play, they will need to determine musical genres for each major character. They might then bring in recorded snippets of music to play upon for each character's entrance. Or they might discuss, instead of genre, what kinds of musical sounds best represent someone. Would they be major sounds or minor sounds (types of scales)? Would they be played quickly, slowly, or in between (tempo)? The questions are more important than the answers, because most answers can lead to provocative productions.

Once the nature of the music is determined, how will it be presented? On tape or whistled or sung or played on a musical instrument (e.g., a small keyboard, a kazoo, a wooden flute, an electric guitar)? Or do the students want to combine a number of these options? After trying out different possibilities, their discussion of what works and what does not—and why—can lead to an even greater understanding of what type of character Shakespeare has created and how we can interpret that character four hundred years after the fact.

Something to discuss with students before associating a specific type of music with a character is the idea of music as an agent of power. When considering such an association, the concept of relative power inevitably comes up, as it does with *Richard III*. One way of stimulating that conversation would be to suggest that the association of music with various kinds of power was a concept with which Shakespeare and his audience were familiar. The idea that different types of music could make people feel or act in different ways had been floating around for hundreds of years but had recently been clearly articulated in Baldesar Castiglione's *The Book of the Courtier* (1528), translated from Italian into English in 1561 by Sir Thomas Hobie. In this book Castiglione encapsulates and expands on elements of the sixth-century philosophy of Boethius, who discussed the influence that the music of the spheres—cosmic music, created by the vibrations of the planets, that orders the universe—can have on human beings:

The wisest of philosophers held the opinion

that the universe was made up of music, that the heavens make harmony as they move, and that as our own souls are formed on the same principle they are awakened and have their faculties, as it were, brought to life through music. And because of this it is recorded that Alexander [the Great] was sometimes so stirred by music that almost against his will under its influence he was constrained to rise from the banquet table and rush to arms; then the musician would play something different, and growing calmer he would return from arms to the banquet. (94-95)

The idea that Castiglione expresses here, that music can have power over the listener, comes up overtly in various Shakespeare plays. For example, Lorenzo explains to Jessica in *The Merchant of Venice* that music controls non-orderly impulses—that a "wild and wanton herd / Or race of youthful and unhandled colts," exposed to music, cease to view the world through "savage eyes" and take on a "modest gaze" (V.i.71-78).

How can we connect such ideas about music as an agent of power to class discussions of music and character? Let us return to Richard for a moment. Remember that he uses music to drown out what he does not wish to hear, espcially from Queen Elizabeth and the Duchess of York:

A flourish, trumpets! Strike alarum, drums!
Let not the heavens hear these tell-tale women
Rail on the Lord's anointed. Strike, I say!

Flourish. Alarums

Either be patient and entreat me fair
Or with the clamorous report of war
Thus will I drown your exclamations. (IV.iv.149-154)

But the situation becomes even more charged with the knowledge that certain kinds of music were associated in the day of the author with certain types of behavior, and the question of what this music should sound like acquires even more importance. We can, of course, expand this discussion into our own associations of music with power, from "Hail to the Chief" to college victory marches and national anthems.

Just as sennets and alarums allow an opportunity to discuss specific characters, other musical stage directions allow for differentiation not simply of one character from others, but of groups of characters from others. This is particularly true in *A Midsummer Night's Dream*, where we have four clear sets of characters: the Athenian lovers; Duke Theseus and his court; Peter Quince, Bottom, and the other rustics; and the fairies. This play is filled with music, and part of any real or hypothetical production of the play may easily entail discussion of what type of music is appropriate for each set of characters. We might ask our students, for instance, what the music of the fairies sounds like when they "rock the ground" or when they sing the "spotted snakes" lullaby to Titania. Again, to keep the discussion grounded in the text itself, they will need to look for clues in the language and behavior of each set of characters. This assignment works best as a group project, with each group focusing on a different part of the Athenian world. When the groups report, they can suggest music for their scenes.

One group might determine what the musical world of the rustics sounds like. This would of course entail a discussion of what type of people these characters are, and it would lead to, among other things, a look at Bottom's "Woosel Cock" song. Determining the general categories into which this music might fit—simple/complex, major/minor, on pitch/off pitch, loud/soft—could help them start. Once they begin, the possibilities are endless. They might sing the song in various styles, with various tunes and rhythms, and choose which one seems most appropriate. This could lead to various approaches to production. For instance, each rustic could carry instruments of their trades (e.g., tinker, joiner) and make "music" by banging on them in various ways.

Always remember that the central idea behind the fun is to characterize a specific group of characters through sound and to comb the text for clues as to how this should be done. One group of teachers in a Drey workshop performed *Romeo and Juliet* with this in mind and chose to focus on the kitchen scene, so often cut from productions. Setting the class of servants apart from other groups of characters through the sounds they made as they worked, they struck pots, pans, utensils, and glasses to specific rhythms. In the background, the upper classes worked against the more traditional music of a ball. All of this set a rhythmic interplay between characters and among groups of characters, underlining many of the conflicts that reverberate through the play.

The group interacting in the kitchen in this scene represents a certain socioeconomic class, and the students' inclination to separate classes through use of music makes sense in the light of history. For example, sennets and the like are generally reserved in the plays for members of upper classes. Just knowing this rule brings emphasis to its few exceptions, like the direction for hautboys, or oboes, that introduces the players in *Hamlet* (III.ii.123). A class discussion on this topic can lead students to interesting speculations about what this means. Was Shakespeare granting the players a social position that they would not have occupied outside of his theater? Would the original audience have found humor in this? More importantly, in a production, how would this music be similar to or different from the music announcing royalty? And in our productions should we try to recreate Renaissance music or find modern analogies?

Even more dramatic in its effect would be the flourish played for Peter Quince as the rustic actors take the court stage in *A Midsummer Night's Dream* (V.i.108). Would a flourish for a rustic produced by Theseus' musicians produce immediate laughter from the court characters onstage? (Think of Robin Williams entering to "Hail to the Chief.") What would it sound like? Would it be serious court-sounding music, or would it be the flatulent blast of a horn?

The association of music with class was as relevant an issue in Shakespeare's day as it is in ours—do business executives hang out at raves?—so focusing upon music reinforces the plays' original contexts. We might ask our students to bear in mind that Sir Thomas Elyot, in his famous tract on education, *The Boke Named the Governour* (1531), stresses the importance of a tutor playing music in harmonized parts for young children:

> He shall commende the perfecte understanding of musike, declaringe howe necessary it is for the better attaynynge the knowledge of a publike weale: whiche. . . is made of an ordre of astates and degrees, and, by reason therof, conteineth in it a perfect harmony. . . . In this fourme may a wise and circumspecte tutor adapte the pleasant science of musike to a necessary and laudable purpose. (42-43)

For Elyot, understanding music means also understanding that the "publike weale," or society of a commonwealth, is made up of "an ordre of astates and degrees," or levels of hierarchy, which makes it "harmonious," like the orderly music of the spheres.

This idea pops up in some of Shakespeare's plays, reinforcing the idea that different classes would be identified with specific music and the very idea of a class system resembled the way Shakespeare's audience understood music. For example, Ulysses, in *Troilus and Cressida*, ends his speech on hierarchical obedience with a musical metaphor: "Take but degree away, untune that string, / And hark what discord follows" (I.iii.109-10). For Ulysses, failure to adhere to a hierarchical class system is equivalent to musical discord. Similarly, Exeter, in *Henry V*, explains to Canterbury that "Government, though high and low and lower / Put into parts, doth keep in one consent,/ Congreeing in a full and natural close / Like music" (I.ii.180-83). He seems to be saying that a chain of command in social government is synonymous with musical harmony. Canterbury agrees, concluding that "therefore doth heaven divide / The state of man in divers functions, / Setting endeavour in continual motion; / To which is fixed, as an aim or butt, / Obedience" (184-188). In other words, obedience within a hierarchy is necessary if it is to be "harmonious."

This is more fertile ground for class discussion. If Shakespeare and his contemporaries equated music with obedience to a social hierarchy that included class structure, how does that affect its use on the stage? For starters, how does this idea impact the flourish for Peter Quince? If harmonious music represents obedience to class hierarchy, and Peter Quince represents a lower class, what type of music would musicians hired by the ruling class play for him? Would it be "harmonious," representing the concept of hierarchy, or would it be more noise than music, reserving more harmonious music for the class in power? Or would the flourish be supplied not by court musicians, but by the rustics themselves? If so, do they create their version of harmonious music in an attempt to please the court? Or is it cacophonous and subliminally subversive? And, returning to the idea of music as a representation for different sets of characters, especially in *Dream*, does such a representation take on even more significance if music is associated on some level for Shakespeare and his audience with class structure?

Even more class discussion can be generated by a spin-off from this idea of hierarchy-related music: the association of ballads with members of lower classes. For instance, Sir William Cornwallis, a friend of Ben Jonson's who served twice on parliament, warns in his *Essayes* (1600) against becoming familiar with ballad singers and the type of people who listen to them, and he claims to put broadside ballads to their best use in his privy (Achinstein 311-12, 316). Some literary historians claim that ballads were politically charged and therefore controversial; Bruce R. Smith argues that "from the standpoint of the authorities, ballads were dangerous not only for what they might say but for how they might say it. To ballet a subject was to commandeer the subject" (196). Smith's point seems to be that the very act of inserting subject matter into the musical ballad form made it threateningly political.

Class discussion of this idea can generate thoughts about singers of ballads in Shakespeare's plays and about their relationships with others. Take Ophelia in *Hamlet*, for instance. If ballads were controversial, politically charged, and generally representational of lower classes, is it meaningful that Ophelia, who is of noble birth, chooses ballads to express her madness to members of the court society who failed to protect her father? Or consider *Othello*'s Desdemona. Is there meaning in her choice to sing a ballad as she waits to be judged by her husband, who has already been physically violent with her? Or look at Autolycus in *The Winter's Tale*. Is it relevant that Autolycus, a thief and a liar who tries to manipulate others for his own gain, is also a purveyor of ballads?

Whether or not we choose to go as far as to discuss the politics of ballads with our students, we still might discuss the role of music in class and power relationships. Consider the song of Caliban:

> No more dams I'll make for fish,
> Nor fetch in firing
> At requiring,
> Nor scrape trenchering, nor wash dish.
> 'Ban, 'ban, Cacaliban
> Has a new master.–Got a new man!
> Freedom, highday! Highday, freedom! Freedom, high
> day, freedom!   (III.i.171-76)

Whatever his reasoning, Caliban, a slave, arguably *The Tempest*'s weakest character in terms of political power, chooses to express in song his intention to revolt against his master. Perhaps even Caliban senses the innate power of music. Our classes might consider this as they decide what Caliban's music should sound like. Once again, considering the type of music a character makes will lead our students to make a number of decisions about that character's identity. How human is Caliban? Does he sing on pitch? Does he sing loudly? Is his music pleasing to human ears, or is it jarring? Do words come easily to him as he sings, or does he struggle with them? What kind of rhythm does his song have? What does the language suggest?

Is this concentration on music a legitimate approach to Shakespeare? Given the vast number of stage directions for and references to music and sound, whether musically barking hounds or the music of the spheres, the answer must be yes. Using music in the classroom also recognizes our students' fascination with it. These techniques can encourage our students to enlist that fascination in a wide range of areas, from characterization and culture to politics and values. Ultimately, those discussions will return to the texts and help our classes recognize the remarkable level of integration and harmony Shakespeare achieved in all his work.

Resources

Achenstein, Sharon. "Audiences and Authors: Ballads and the Making of English Renaissance Literary Culture." *Journal of Medieval and Renaissance Studies* 22 (1992): 311-326.

Elyot, Sir Thomas. *The Boke Named the Governour.* 1531. Ed. Henry Herbert and Stephen Croft. 2Vols. New York: Burt Franklin, 1967.

Greenblatt, Stephen, ed. *The Norton Shakespeare Based on the Oxford Edition.* New York: Norton, 1997. 1823-1931.

Smith, Bruce. *The Acoustic World of Early Modern England.* Chicago: University of Chicago Press, 1999.

Romeo Rocks
New Tunes in Old Jugs

_C_

Susan Baron, Patricia Hagelin, and Mike Zella

Three teachers from St. Cloud High School discuss specific ways they have used music to interpret Romeo and Juliet.

_C_

"TODAY, CLASS, WE'RE GOING TO BEGIN WORKING on a performance of *Romeo and Juliet.*"

One student groans, "How come I have to read Shakespeare?" And then the chorus chimes in, "It's stupid! They talk stupid; they are stupid!"

The rhythm varies from class to class but the melody remains the same year after year.

As teachers, we know that when our students don't understand or identify with something they "think it's stupid." We also know that it's our responsibility to help our students understand and identify with the course material. Music, which in some form is loved by nearly everyone, is one way to help students understand and identify with Shakespeare's work.

Whether as flourished entrances, fairy dances, or rustic ballads, music plays a major role in nearly all of Shakespeare's plays. The two obvious ways of using dramatic musical opportunities in a class performance are (a) spending hours of historical research on Renaissance music and instruments for an authentic score, or (b) substituting music that speaks to our time. In the first case, unfortunately, there is no guarantee our students will appreciate all of our effort. This is why we suggest the second as a more effective way to connect students to Shakespeare's stage. Yet some might validly object, saying, "I can't put modern music into a traditional Renaissance drama; the music won't fit the characters, setting, action, anything!" Granted, such a combination would probably be odd. But if we can't put modern music into Renaissance drama, why not take the drama out of the Renaissance?

Put simply, why not move the play to another time and place? We believe that one of the best ways to engage students in a Shakespearean performance is to give them the freedom to move the drama in time and place and thereby create a dramatic world with which they can identify—complete, of course, with the appropriate musical accompaniments. How better to connect students with Shakespeare's timeless stories and themes? And don't worry; it's not as difficult or as time-consuming as you might think.

Here are eight simple steps in musically updating any traditional play:

1) *Decide the time period.* You have three ways to make a choice.

    a. Decide with your students. Ask them during what time in history would they like to fall in love, be rescued, fight a war, or defend their family's honor.

    b. Work in conjunction with what students are studying in other classes (e.g., history). This clearly offers a great opportunity for cross-discipline work and for interesting other faculty.

    c. Select it yourself based upon observations of what interests students.

2) *Decide the location:* The location will inevitably depend on the time period you and your class choose, but remember that students will be more enthusiastic if they are encouraged to have a voice in the decision-making process.

3) *Learn something about music and fashion during the period:* Discuss this with students. They can surf the Internet when researching the selected time period. This creates another excellent cross-curricular opportunity with history, home economics, music, and art.

4) *Decide what the characters are like in your new setting:* Read a portion of the play aloud to gain a basic understanding of characters' personalities and motivations. Try exchanging roles with shoulder tapping, hat-passing, or inner/outer circles.

5) *Transport the conflict to the new setting:* Keep the conflict consistent with the original play. For example, make sure both families, regardless of setting, are still "alike in dignity" if doing *Romeo and Juliet.*

6) Discuss how musical choices can reflect characters and conflicts.

7) Locate areas where music will enhance audience understanding of the way your students read the play.

8) Read. Discuss. Perform!

How We Applied the Process to *Romeo and Juliet*

1) The time period: Keeping in mind what might interest students, we decided to set *Romeo and Juliet* in the anti-establishment, free love period of the 1960s.

2) The location: We chose to move the play to America, specifically to a college campus as they were often the site of the civil protests that partially characterized the 1960s.

3) The music and fashion of the period: When researching music suitable for a 1960s version of *Romeo and Juliet,* we decided on music from the Beatles, the Supremes, the Beach Boys, the Righteous Brothers, Martha and the Vandellas, and Peter, Paul, and Mary. As to the fashion of the time, we chose straight hair, shoulder-length or longer for both guys and girls. Satin sleeveless dresses, accompanied by knee-high socks, was the style for the ladies. Pants, tunics, and long jackets were worn by the men.

4) The characters: As we developed our parts, we tried to work in or suggest movement and language reminiscent of the Civil Rights movement and the 60s dissatisfaction with Vietnam.

5) The conflict: As in the original play, our Capulets and Montagues of the 1960s were still "alike in dignity." They had similar wealth but very different lifestyles. Although Capulet is the one to throw the big party in Act 1, we chose to represent the Montagues—especially Romeo and his friends—as party animals. They embraced the then-popular belief in sex, drugs, and rock 'n' roll. Conversely, the Capulets were more conservative and less anti-establishment. Juliet, rebelling against her more conservative clan, was attracted to the "peace, love, and happiness" life and was, therefore, enamored with Romeo.

6) Areas for music: In addition to creating a mood, music also enhanced audience understanding of particular scenes or characters. We selected several areas of the play where music would add to the scene. Here is the song list from our performance, but remember these are only suggestions.

- Introduction: "Heroes and Villains" by the Beach Boys. (The play should open with music to set the mood.)
- I.iv. "Dancing in the Streets" by Martha and the Vandellas. (In this scene Romeo, Benvolio and Mercutio are making their way to the Capulet party.)
- I.v. "Stop! In the Name of Love" by the Supremes. (This is the party scene where Romeo and Juliet see each other for the first time and instantly fall in love.)

• II.ii. "For Lovin' Me" by Peter, Paul, and Mary. (Here any heart-wrenching love song would add to the passionate exchange of vows in this famous balcony scene.)

• III.i. "Nowhere to Run" by Martha and the Vandellas. (Here, we reach the climax of the play when Mercutio and Tybalt are both slain and Romeo is banished.)

• V.iii. "You've Lost That Lovin' Feeling" by Righteous Brothers. (Here, Romeo and Juliet kill themselves. We decided that the lovin' feeling was "gone, gone, gone.")

• Conclusion: "Let It Be" by the Beatles. The Capulets and Montagues "whisper words of wisdom" and resolve the conflict that results in the death of their children.

This is, of course, only one possible setting and musical adaptation of *Romeo and Juliet*. Be adventurous; maybe set *Romeo and Juliet* in 1920s Chicago where the Capulets and Montagues are rival crime families or in the old West with Tybalt and Romeo as gunslingers. Whatever you decide, the point is to find a connection for students.

The Soul of a Man Is His Clothes
Costume in Context

—☙

Sandria Reese

*Sandria Reese, a costumer, wigmaker, and choreographer who has worked
with the Royal Shakespeare Company and Blenheim Opera, examines costume
in the context of all aspects of a play's production.*

—☙

IF SHAKESPEARE IS RIGHT IN *All's Well That Ends Well* that our souls are
our clothes, we need to pay special attention to how we present those
souls onstage. Designing costumes is a group effort that involves a wide
range of talents. But it begins by assessing the task and making some
important decisions. I always start with a dozen essential questions.
Which play and why? How is the play to be done? Who will direct the
play? Who will design it? What kind of music and movement will the
production need? Where will the play be performed? Who are the performers? Who is the target audience? Will there be dressing rooms?
What space is available backstage? Is there a costume shop? And who
will help with the work?

As you address these questions, there are two more important
issues: time and money. Spending some time thinking through each of
these questions should give enormous direction and focus to your production.

Which Play?

Sometimes the reasons for choosing a play are very clear. You
might be discussing the relationship of men and women in society and
choose to present *The Taming of the Shrew* or *Measure for Measure* as an
exploration of the topic. Likewise, if your community is concerned with
racial issues, *The Merchant of Venice* or *Romeo and Juliet* or *Othello* could
make valuable contributions. Whatever your situation, it is vital to
know why you are doing this particular play and not another. What is
it about the play that inspires you to the Herculean effort involved, and
what is the effect you want it to have on (a) the cast and (b) the audi-

ence. Even if your aim is simply for a pleasant evening of fun and laughter, the stronger your vision, the more likely it is to succeed as a piece of theater. I have seen two children with glove puppets over the back of a sofa produce a marvelous show full of wit and insight, and conversely, a great international opera company send its audience away angry and mystified, so do not think success is all about resources and money. It isn't. The key to success is in how involved you can make the audience in the excitement of the tale unfolding before them. To do this you need both clarity and unity, and I shall try to show you some ways in which to go about choosing costumes to help clarify and unify your production. Of course, you will be concerned with acting skills, the memorizing of lines and delivery of the language, but a good design will completely support the cast in what they are trying to convey. I cannot stress too highly the importance of the things the audience *sees* onstage, as an aid to understanding what they *hear*.

How Is the Play To Be Done?

This may sound crazy, but you cannot just "do" a play. There is a raft of decisions you have to make about style if you are to communicate effectively with your audience.

Who Will Direct the Play?

The Director must choose the cast, and the designers for scenery, costume, and lighting along with composer, sound designer, choreographer, and stage-manager, getting them all working together on one vision. Of course, there may be only three, two or even one individual involved, but all these *functions* must be covered. This is how it is generally supposed to go in a fully operational theater and recognizing that your situation will have its inherent limits, you should strive to get as close to the ideal as possible.

1. **The Concept Meeting:** Usually, it is the director who chooses the play and the style. Everyone involved discusses the idea, considers available resources, and talks through all the consequences. Planning well at this stage and controlling your ambition will make for a happy and smooth production. I found when doing Shakespeare Festivals I had to keep saying, "This is not the Royal Shakespeare Company." That meant, of course, that we didn't have their budget and facilities, though our passion for excellence was equal or greater. You may choose to set the play in historical period, or have a strong sense of a particular location or country, but why? Well, look at your play. Do you *need* to do *A Midsummer*

Night's Dream in Grecian costume? Shakespeare might have been using the concept of "Athenian" to mean "cultured," but you will find that a domestic comedy like *The Merry Wives of Windsor* cries out for Elizabethan costuming in a way that *Macbeth* does not. Because it is a timeless story about military men, for *Macbeth* you could use modern army uniforms. *Othello* and *Julius Caesar* offer excellent opportunities for uniforms also. The concept meeting also allows you to explore the implications of choices. In *Julius Caesar*, for example, you will have to decide if you want to put blood at the heart of the play. That decision would be hopelessly impractical if costumes were rented, or if you had no way of washing them after each performance. Because real stage blood made with food dye, glycerin, and sugar will wash out of fabric if soaked immediately in cold water, white bed-sheet togas would be spectacular, but only if you can do laundry. If you can't wash things, best avoid blood altogether and use a theatrical device like streams of red ribbons or a flood of red light to represent blood. Do you see what I mean about decisions and choices? It is not necessary to be realistic; just find some way to indicate to your audience that they are to imagine blood. You are sure to come up with some exciting solution. Sometimes you need do nothing at all except act! For instance, in *Romeo and Juliet* the gore on Tybalt is so eagerly described that you don't need to show it as well. So do not be disheartened by lack of modern theater facilities and resources, and remember to let Shakespeare do the work with words: he did not have much in the way of laundries either.

2. **Budgets:** Make clear how much money you have and what can be spent in each category. That way everyone knows what money (if any) is available. Once everyone has agreed on the finances, the set and costume designers make sketches, cut out designs from magazines, and/or make models to prepare a presentation of what the play should look like on the stage.

3. **Production Meeting:** This is the critical meeting when all department heads discuss ways to achieve the design within the budget and in a realistic time frame.

4. **The Readthrough:** (See Omans' essay). Your actors will expect you to thrill them with your ideas for the play, so this is the opportunity to fire their enthusiasm; it is also a time for their ideas and input, no matter what their age or experience. Remember that it is the actors who will have to make the play come alive, so they should feel that they are a vital part of the design process.

5. **Rehearsals:** As rehearsals begin, the costumer must fit each actor, choose or begin to make the clothes, and find accessories. Your cast will bless you for giving them their shoes to rehearse in as soon as possible. Shoes—even more than cloaks and hats—help build character and make actors feel secure onstage. Remember that movement is more governed by footwear than by any other factor. Choreographers take note!

The Paper Tech:

A useful device that can save you hours of time on the set, the "Paper Tech" offers an overview of the production if you are experienced enough as a director to know what you want—or do not want—without needing to see everything through first. All the technical team go through each cue to establish the order of events. The heads of departments then write their own plots giving their cues numbers which will all be written into the stage manager's prompt script against the relevant bit of text, so he or she can "call" the show. It will help the costume crew if your stage manager is able to make a plot of who is involved in each scene (characters might be there even if they have no lines to say) and how many minutes they have between an exit and their next entrance.

Generally it is considered to be the actor's responsibility to know where and when to enter and how to achieve a costume change. However, it must be the job of the costume crew to have everything ready to put on, in the right place, at the right time. Shakespeare needed to craft his plays so that major scene and costume changes could be easily achieved, but there are some classic quickies. These occasionally happen because our modern theater conventions indicate costume and set changes that Shakespeare would not have bothered with. If you are doubling roles, you need to plot each shift carefully and be especially wary when making text cuts: some apparently rambling speeches may have been included by Shakespeare for technical reasons. Have a look at *As You Like It* V.iv in which Touchstone has an odd long solo about "the quarrel on the seventh cause." Woe betide a director tempted to cut it. If you have ever tried to get the entire cast changed into fantastical costumes for the Masque of Hymen that follows, you will know how essential Touchstone's speech is and you can picture a wonderful old comic actor keeping the punters rolling in the aisles whilst watching for a signal that all is ready backstage.

The Technical Rehearsal:

Sometimes called the first dress rehearsal, the technical rehearsal can be handled in a range of ways on a continuum between two extremes.

One end of this continuum is the "crash through." In this method the director gets actors into costumes with complete makeup and hair style, together with the musicians, lighting, scenery and props. Begin with the opening sequence and try not to stop whatever happens until the interval. Do the second half the same way. After the entire production, the director spends a long notes session with the actors. Meanwhile the technical team tries to resolve its problems with the help of the stage manager. (The techs can sometimes benefit from having a "dry tech" after the run, a process which involves going through the show cue by cue, without the actors.)

A crash through is very valuable for the stage crew and technical team, but it is of no help at all to the costume crew who can seldom snatch even a morsel of time to really *practice* a difficult change with the actor, in the right place in "real time." In fact, from the costumers' point of view, it is a system designed to wreck costumes with panicky actors and dressers confined in tight spaces in the dark. Because the needs of the costume department differ so much from those of the other techs (e.g., costumes are so vulnerable to damage and actors apt to get injured), a sympathetic director will give wardrobe, props and especially weapons an absolute priority on the first costume run, checking that the actors are ready to continue, and going back over a change if necessary. Because actors have had weeks of rehearsal; it is only fair to allow the crew a practice too.

If you are the costumer and your director is determined to be a "crasher," you would be wise to take precautions. It is essential that you have a costume parade in good time to check that everything is ready, to adjust fastenings, to try out hem lengths, and to let the actors generally strut about and get the feel of things. You might even try to schedule a costumed run-through all of your own in the rehearsal space, where you can stop as much as you like and sort out any problems that arise.

At the other extreme we have the "endless tech," which begins at the beginning and works slowly through the opening sequence, going over it several times until all departments know exactly what to do and have written it down. You plot the cues through the first scene sorting out problems as you go and making sure everyone is secure before moving on. Actors hate an "endless tech" because it is boring. They must hang around for hours while the costumer steps in at every pause to make necessary adjustments. The dressers can set up the next costume changes in an organized and thoughtful way and occasionally whole costumes are remade between one entrance and another. While all this is happening, the lighting technicians decide with the director on the best effects to use. Of course, it can quickly become very indulgent, especially with perfectionists on the loose.

A good director will know how to find a mean between the extremes of "crash" and "endless" and move the rehearsal on, deciding which problems can be sorted out later. One important caution: Please, please do not worry about people's sense of "a run." A run of the play should be held *before* the technical rehearsal. This is not the time to worry about anything but technical matters. (Have your crew watch this pre-tech run if you can. Many people believe that it is often the best and most moving performance the actors will give until after opening night). If your show is complicated and has moving scenery, it is necessary for staff to ensure everyone is coordinating properly and that the stage manager calling the show understands the sequence before running it. Of course, the technical rehearsal will not give you a sense of how the play as a whole is shaping up. But technical matters should go very smoothly during the next run through, with only minor adjustments needed. I have known shows at Stratford to open successfully to an audience after a long and thorough tech, without every having had time for a dress rehearsal at all!

6. **The Final Dress Rehearsal:** The final dress sometimes takes place before an invited audience, which can be helpful to the actors and director and give a sense of reality to the event. Try hard to keep the same people working on your show crew till after opening night at least, even if not through the run. One very important rule: *Never* change anything technical in your costume plot between the dress rehearsal and opening night. If something does not seem to work, alter it on the second night when nerves are less frayed.

7. **Opening Night:** This should be an exhilarating experience for a cast and crew who are well prepared. Don't neglect to organize a schedule of maintenance for your costumes because there will be

mending to do and regular laundry of shirts and stockings. However small your number of costumes, appoint a wardrobe head and make her or him responsible. It is good practice to have a list or plot of all the costumes and accessories and check this off before the actors arrive for each show. It is amazing how often things get lost. I once had a leading actor's entire costume disappear only to be found next day in the dumpster. It had accidentally slipped from the hanger into a bin beneath and been thrown out with the old tissues and Coke bottles.

Please do not forget to put on a good cast party afterwards and never let the "Friends of the Theater" get to the food before any actors and crew have time to arrive. Remember, with nerves and overwork they will not have eaten all day and will be *hungry* (the actors, not the Friends).

8. **The Run of the Show:** It is critical to consider every audience as important as the first. Commit yourself to maintaining and even improving the quality of the costuming during the run. And make sure every scrap of costuming is either put away or thrown away after the last night. There is nothing more depressing than going into a theater space where bits of past productions still lurk in the corners.

Who Will Design the Play?

It is the designer's job to look after everything the audience will see onstage and even around it. As the production's arbiter of taste, the designer must work intimately with the director to preserve the unity of the entire experience. It is not theater design to draw some pretty pictures and then run away to another project, leaving the cutter guessing at what the costumes look like from the back. Because no one can plan every detail and because the rehearsal process invariably produces new ideas and new problems, the designer must be with the crew and cast to make on-the-spot decisions right up to opening night and beyond.

If you decide to rent costumes, go to the stores and pick them yourself, character by character. If you begin thinking about using a set of costumes from a past production, change your mind immediately. Your show will be a tired old has-been. Throw them away and think afresh. Take your cast to a thrift shop. You can have fun trying on one thing after another until everyone has found clothes to make the character come alive. A designer I know bought old suits for an entire opera chorus and then painted them with a bucket of violet scene paint, transporting everyone into an entirely new, imaginative realm. The only exception to this rule is in adapting costumes from an entirely different play, a process which should provoke you to rethink some of your ideas. Nothing will be quite perfect but that is OK. Compromise is a very interesting discipline.

What About Clarity?

Costume will inevitably help your audience to understand what is going on in the story. In *A Midsummer Night's Dream*, for instance, where there are two sets of lovers, you should make Hermia look like Lysander in some way (color?) and Helena like Demetrius so the mix-up of partners is more apparent. A famous designer at the R.S.C. one year dressed all of the characters in white. As a result, hardly anyone in the audience could tell one from the other, creating a respectful but puzzled silence during some of the funniest scenes ever written.

Emblems are very important in making an immediate statement, so be liberal with the icons of the era in which you set the play. Dress beggars as beggars and kings as kings and try to place each character exactly in the hierarchy of his society. In period dress the Fashion Victim, the Cool Dude and the Godfather should be as easily recognized as in modern dress. Think your characters through as if they lived today. If you can translate that effect into your period costume, you will help your actor to bring a character to life.

Costume should never be an add-on. Sometimes it is your performance. In one production of *The Winter's Tale*, the coat worn by Autolicus was as full of pockets as a conjurer's: the objects that came out of it and the places they got to will live on in my memory far longer than some of the human performances. Always assume that the spectators of your play know nothing about the story, and remember to have every aspect of the production . . . Tell the Tale.

What About Unity?

To achieve unity, you must acknowledge that everyone and everything belongs to the same show. As difficult as it may be, find a way of narrowing your choices to present a unified design. A very obvious way to do this is with period costume, a reason why period productions are so popular. Setting a date for costume reference will create either a stylistic straitjacket in which to tie up your play or a strong sense of unity. Above all, be careful that everything has been made to the same standard. No matter how beautiful it may be, one fantastic costume will stand out and may become an eyesore if it appears on a home-made set among poorly made costumes. I know of no professional designers in

England who are the least bit interested in historic costume as such, even though many glory in the sumptuousness of bygone ages. They invariably look for other ways to "tell the tale." You can be clever too and do it with modern costumes, but you can't just have the actors turn up in their own clothes. It is not that simple. You need to think of something to unify your design and make a theatrical statement.

Here are a few ideas that have worked well for me:
• Find or make all your costumes in denim / calico / patchwork / leather.
• Make your garments mainly out of plastic sacks / foil / newspaper.
• Use only costumes that are some shade of blue / brown / red.
• Use blocks of color, no patterned fabric.
• Make your stage a riot of glorious color.
• Keep the color palette very cool and earthy.
• Go "ethnic."
• Paint all the costume details and designs onto a basic unit costume (e.g., T-shirts / overalls / pajamas / leotards).
• Have everyone in winter-wear / beach-wear.
• Use masks.
• Have everything very glossy and new-looking.
• Distress garments or use layers of garments, one over another.
• Have something sparkling, stripy, or flowered for every character.
• Use strong imagery such as circus or space-age.
• Take a vacation in Thailand and purchase bales of silk at extraordinarily low prices!

Now read over what I said earlier about clarity and you will see how careful, clever, and inventive you have to be when designing a show. The movie *Get Over It* did a good job displaying unity in its high school play, but I would say the clarity was wanting because all the characters were dressed alike. (Remember, though, that we, the movie audience, unlike the play's audience, were already familiar with the cast members and also that we were seeing it all in close-up.) In that context, the film's production worked well for the film's audience but you might want to make other choices for your play.

What Kind of Music and Movement Will the Play Use?

Pay careful heed to the design concept, because suiting music and movement to it will really help to set the scene. Writing a pastiche of period music is rather difficult to do and you are almost always better off taking original tunes as your foundation. At this stage everyone needs to communicate their ideas and discuss developments. You cannot dance a two-couples English country dance if your ladies are wearing Scarlet O'Hara crinolines; nor can anyone waltz successfully in panniers or rock 'n ' roll in a Charleston dress. This might seem obvious but you would be surprised at how often the choreographer forgets to check or the costume designer fails to attend rehearsals. It is a fabulous feeling to walk onstage with your robes trailing behind you, but you cannot then be expected to dance a farandole hand in hand in a line, because someone will certainly tread on your train. Tell the actors they must learn how to walk backwards in costume, wear the right foundation garments, and most importantly, practice the curtain call.

The dance sequences in Shakespeare plays often do not exist; they are described as happening offstage as in *Romeo and Juliet* or are cancelled as in *Love's Labours Lost*. The only real opportunity is found in *All's Well* where the characters have to meet on cue in a masque. Curiously, the only two dances ever demanded by Shakespeare in the plays are the measures and the burgermasque, and these occur in the closing moments of *As You Like It* and *A Midsummer Night's Dream*. The measures, a formal procession dance for couples with walking steps in sequences of singles and doubles, resembles the earlier pavane and almain and is normally used for big displays and formal occasions. The burgermasque, a rough rustic dance that we do not know much about, is usually depicted by dancers in clogs or with staves as in a Morris dance. There are many dance courses and classes in university dance departments. If you are producing a period Shakespeare production, you might call the nearest large campus and ask, or get on the Internet. You will find that there are some wonderful teachers of period manners and movement too.

Even if a play may not call for dancing, you can certainly put some in, for example, to accompany songs. There is much revelry to be made in the household during *Twelfth Night* and in the Forest of Arden during *As You Like It*. And even though the big dance scene in Romeo and Juliet occurs offstage, many directors feel compelled to put it into their production.

Where Will You Perform?

You may be lucky and have a theater in which to perform your play, but it can often be much more exciting to use some other space. (See Ben Gunter's essay.) Shakespeare's characters spend a lot of time speaking directly to the audience and a thrust stage is very workable for the actors. Think seriously about using the floor of your theater or hall, seating the audience all round. If your stage is not too high, flowing on and off it gives marvelous scope for spectacle. Be imaginative, have your actors move amongst the watchers, make the audience into your crowd and even have them follow your scenes from place to place. The peripatetic production and the "site specific" are rather fashionable just now, so why not transform the whole of your local high school into Elsinore or your arts center into the Forest of Arden? And why not set *A Midsummer Night's Dream* in a real wood? You might commandeer a floating rig or lay out your stage cloth in a large chldren's sand box surrounded by swings and slides. Because in intimate settings you need to consider a greater degree of detail in costumes and props, you might want to use a natuaralistic or modern design unless your costume shop is of the highest standard. Remember that heavily stylized or fantastical costumes need distance and theatrical lighting to make them live. Certainly, your location may inspire the design concept and set you on a new train of thought.

Whatever you do, when thinking about costumes you must match the scale of the design to the size of the space. I found it helpful in large spaces to pay attention to clarity. And consider how helpful it is when following a complicated plot to have a subliminal link between characters. It would be rather obvious to dress all the Capulets as Bikers for instance. But how about portraying the Montagues as Aliens! (Yes, I saw this on a tour of England recently. Although it didn't quite come off, it was a brave try. I still remember it fondly and with mirth.)

Who Are Your Performers?

When you plan costumes for the play, you need to accurately assess your actors' level of competence. Are they professional actors or school children, high schoolers or university students? Experienced actors really love having things to play with, so give them a cloak, crown, boa, or cane and it will inspire all sorts of activities. Be careful, though, or you will find yourself directing a scene about a hat! An actor is an actor. Directors sometimes abandon costumes that are too magnificent because they can distract the audience's attention from the dialogue. This is very distressing as most of your time and half the budget can disappear at a stroke. Better to be discreet then, when creating costumes, and sensitive to the effect you are trying to achieve.

Dealing with your clothing onstage is not easy. When designing for inexperienced actors, make everything as simple and "actor-proof" as possible. If an actor is struggling with the lines and the furniture, she won't remember to control her shawl, beads, and bag as well. Take special care with armor. Fighters are very focused on their weapons and will not thank you for loose, floppy bits of costume. Put a belt over the tabard, tie sword scabbards to the thigh and fix chains of office onto both shoulders. Cloaks and heavy coats should always have "hug tapes" so the weight is supported on the shoulders, rather than on the fastening. Nearly everybody likes hug tapes: they are made with webbing tape or a bagged strip of fabric, stitched on under the center of the shoulder seams where they hang straight down the front and are tied firmly by the dresser.

Consider these ideas for securing clothing and accessories:

• If you have beads that flop about, fill in the neck of your dress with a layer of flesh colored net and stitch them to it.

• Put tie tapes on your petticoat or underskirt, never a hook which could come undone. If you must use a hook and bar, back it up with a snap.

• Almost never use velcro for a dress fastening. Use a good quality zipper and it will only get stuck if the placket or lining becomes caught in it. Check any zippers before each show and make sure any loose fabric is stitched down. If a zipper is a bit stiff, run the point of a pencil down it. The best thing for a quick change is big hooks and bars (not eyes) for tight garments, big snaps for loose ones, or any combination of the two.

• To secure your shoe laces, make a double knot, but do not tie the two bows together or you will fumble to undo them again. The better way is this: tie your knot and make your first loop as usual but after you have formed the second loop, keep your finger in the hole and you will be able to push the new loop through the knot a second time. Pull it as tight as you can; it will not scuff loose, yet a good tug on the ends will release it.

• If a hat or wig won't stay on, make some flat pincurls in your hair secured with two crossed bobby pins, spray hairspray into them and allow it to dry. Secure the hat by pushing big hairpins or a hatpin in under the curls. Sew a thin strip of lace around your hat brim as an anchoring point. Hair too short? The tiny elastic bands you get from dental suppliers will make an anchorage for pins. Wigs need pincurls and then a crepe bandage wrapped once tightly around the head; you can pin securely into that.

Who Is Your Audience?

Playing to people who are coming along to give support is not the same as dealing with a commercial paying audience (although it is part of the pretence of theater to make believe that it is). Is the audience there for your benefit or are you there for theirs? No, really! It is an important question, and not easy to answer. Many professional companies are not very clear on this and would be hard pushed to justify their choices if asked. You might make people pay for their tickets, but unless you intend to make a profit or pay your cast they might still be in a supporting role. So, allowing that the audience is there for *your* benefit can give you a great deal of freedom to experiment. No one is going to ask for their money back if you do the show in your old jeans or wrapped in tin foil. You can be wild and show as much creativity as possible.

In educational theater and amateur productions, you have a license and freedom to experiment that is only shared by the big subsidized companies. As you are planning costumes and settings, think of what will really give you pleasure and added value. You might have a fantastic art department that can't wait to get the brushes out. So why not bring white T-shirts and paint everything on? If your group is mainly interested in the acting, set the whole play in a rehearsal room and have someone represent the stage crew who can bring on the props and furniture, as the play demands. This way you can use your everyday clothes and the classroom furniture, adding fun bits of theatrical tat and old gems from past productions. The important thing is to be very clear in your concept with no half measures, and you will be astonished how the audience will respond.

Will There Be Dressing Rooms?

A large open space is preferable to dressing rooms that are cramped, ill lit, or too far from the stage. Even if you can manage enough costume rails, it is worth giving everyone two chairs. Lay the costumes out on the first one, in reverse order, and discard on to the second chair as you change. If you have a costume crew, they can sort out the discards and re-set for the next change. Almost always with Shakespeare you have a larger than normal cast and dressing tables have to be shared. This can be hard for the makeup crew, so make a special station and have the actors go to them.

A word about makeup: consider leaving the men without makeup, unless you have a really old character to portray. Once you apply foundation, the natural contours of the face are obscured and have to be put back with shadow and highlight. Try leaving it off. Just bringing out the under-eye a little with dark pencil and re-shaping the eyebrows is usually enough to make the face visible under light.

What Space Is Available Backstage?

I find it is usually better for the actor to run another few yards to an area where there is light and space than to fumble about in the wings. If you really can't get to a dressing room, persuade the stage crew to make you a booth out of three flats where you can have a table, mirror, lights and a chair. The secret of a successful quick change is not the speed at which you do it but the rhythm. Have the actor's costume laid out on a chair in reverse order (i.e., coat, jacket, tie, pants, shirt). Choreograph all movements. Be balanced and graceful because it is as much a part of a performance as the next scene. Change in exactly the same way every time and, if you have a dresser, practice the change with him/her till it is slick. Make sure both actor and dresser know their tasks, then relax and trust each other.

Hints for Quick Changes:

• Tie your tie in advance, but 2" looser than your neck, cut it through at the back and fasten with a big snap. Or pre-tie it and slip it over your head.

• Cuff buttons or links can be stitched onto elastic so you can slip in your hand without undoing them.

• Shoe laces can be replaced by round-cord elastic.

• Overdress one costume with another or underdress. I know professional actors who, when wearing robes, underdress all their street clothes for the curtain call so as to be first in the bar—the quickest change of the show!

• Wedding rings cover easily with a band aid or paper tape, a little makeup foundation completes the camouflage. Do the same with stud earrings.

• Put a little talcum powder in your shoes and use a shoe-horn for speed.

• Fasten necklaces and bracelets with velcro.

Is There a Costume Shop?

Even if you have a real shop with proper facilities, you will need a "show-running station" close to the stage for emergency repairs, laundry and storage. You can use a box for your equipment in the wings, or the dressers can carry a kit with them. Someone needs to be in charge, because it is unlikely you will get through any show without a costume incident of some sort and actors need to know who to go to. Carry safety pins, needle and thread, scissors, sticky tape such as band-aid, ribbon tape or shoe laces, shirt buttons, hooks, tissues and other items specific to the show. Be prepared and the worst may never happen!

And now a brief word about wigs. They are best avoided unless you have someone on the staff who really knows what to do. A handmade theatrical wig with European hair currently costs £800 and upwards in London. It will need constant, careful maintenance which requires the right blocks, stands, and equipment. The theatrical wigs available in catalogs have far too much hair. If you buy from a catalog, never be afraid to take out some hair. First, look at how the wig is made. Usually the hair is sewn in as a weft and you can unpick the bits where it is too thick without cutting the hair. Commercial wigs are better than ever these days. Do not be afraid to cut and style them. But do not use hot tongs on synthetics. The original curl has been made with hot steam so to strengthen or increase the curl, you must use steam. Set the hair wet in rollers and dry in a hot place or steam them with a pressure steamer. Incidentally, almost any man's natural appearance is better than a synthetic wig. If he is young and bald, go with it—or give him a hat. Remember that the best advice is to avoid wigs altogether.

Who Will Help?

Volunteers are always a challenge. If you get good helpers you will save yourself time and achieve much better results. But be prepared for them not to show up. Remember that this is true of all volunteers, even parents. We used to have a notice on our wall, "Lack of planning on your part does not constitute an emergency on mine." People in their daily lives are pulled in many directions and you cannot expect them to make your show their absolute priority, in the way you can. Try to match jobs to people's talents and try not to expect too much, or even more importantly, too little. There are some fantastically talented people around and you can harness their enthusiasm to make a wonderfully fulfilling project for them and for you.

Keeping control of style and quality is never easy. There is always someone who will make more work than they save. In the interest of standards you may have to be ruthless and turn them out. On the other hand, ask yourself the question, "Who is the show for?" and listen carefully to your answer. It may actually be the performers and team members and those volunteers. If so, that understanding could color the relationship you have with your helping hands, the standards of work you will accept, and the approach you take to getting a working party together.

And Two Truths

The Truth about Budgets: There is never enough money. Are you building your costumes? Whatever your fabrics cost, you should budget at least as much again for general haberdashery and whatever you expect to pay out for labor, double it!

The Truth about Time: There is never enough time. I do not know any way to accurately predict the amount of time a task will take. Apply Parkinson's Law that "work expands to fill the time available." I have colleagues who vow always to do the less important (and prettier) jobs first because the vital ones will certainly get done somehow. Try to give people the next job before they finish the current one. But recognize that overloading some people can bury them in stress. Try to make sure that everyone understands what they are doing and how long it should take. If a helper spends three days stitching one hem beautifully when there are 20 to do, remind them that hems can be machined.

Some Time- and Budget-saving Tips

• Measure twice and cut once.

• Use the same basic shape for everyone and it will be much quicker to cut the show.

• Never machine with a short stitch unless you have good reason. Use big stitches and if you have to re-do it the thread will come out easily.

• Avoid stitching on fasteners. Buy hook and eye tape.

• Close all petticoats with tie-tapes that can be machined on.

• Petticoat frills? Don't gather them with a running thread but shove a strip of fabric directly under the machine foot and push the gathers in as you sew. Use a long stitch and you can gather some more afterwards if you want by drawing up the back thread.

• Pin pattern pieces together with the pins at a right angle to the edge so you can stitch straight over them and remove afterwards. This process is good for frills too.

• Skirt too long? Take it up with a machined tuck, far quicker than a hem.

• Dress bodice too big? Take a tuck in the back at each side to save moving all the fastenings.

• Too small? Let out the under side seams and stitch a triangular gusset into the sleeve seam. Or you could unpick the sleeve underarm, finish off the raw edges and leave it as a gap. This gives much more freedom for arm movements.

• Garments to be lined? Flat-tack the lining to the goods and sew the garment up as one piece. (Tack exactly on the sewing line and you will have an accurate mark when matching the pattern pieces. You will not need to tack the pieces together, just pin and sew. This is how the professional workrooms do it). Use 1" stitches for flat-tacking and leave it in until the garment is finished. Don't sew around corners; fasten on a new thread for each side of your pattern piece.

Conclusions

It is your show and you must do it your own way. The important thing, I think, is to be joyful and creative. Even if the design doesn't quite work, an exciting imperfection can often be far more watchable than a boring masterpiece!

Be not too tame neither, but let your own discretion be your tutor,
suit the action to the word, the word to the action, with this special observance,
that you o'erstep not the modesty of nature. (Hamlet III.ii.16-19)

Why Do You Dress Me in Borrowed Robes?
Creating Renaissance Costume

—⟶

J. Ann Singleton

*J. Ann Singleton, a costumer and costume consultant, provides a comprehensive
guide to creating Renaissance costumes within limited budgets.*

—⟶

"WHY DO YOU DRESS ME IN BORROWED ROBES?" Macbeth asks Ross
after being told that he has been named Thane of Cawdor though he
thinks that Cawdor still lives and so still wears his own title and the
clothes that mark it (*Macbeth* I.iii.109). As the play advances, we, the
audience, realize that Macbeth means robes in both a literal and a more
far-reaching metaphoric sense as well. Literally, he has been handed the
chain of office for Thane of Cawdor, part of the title's ritual "robes," and
we probably see him put the chain on. But we also understand that he
has been fighting against his recurring ambition to be king, a king and
mentor who still lives and wears his own. Both attracted to and repulsed
by these fantasies, Macbeth here wonders why if one change of a garment and status can occur so dramatically and without warning,
whether the other might not also be possible.

Shakespeare fills his plays with references to appropriate and inappropriate dress. In *Richard III*, the plotting, misshapen Richard jokes
about successfully wooing the recently widowed Queen Anne, whose
husband and father-in-law he has murdered, and decides either seriously or facetiously to change his clothing so that his outer attire can match
his new status as a handsome lover: "I'll be at charges for a looking
glass/And entertain a score or two of tailors/To study fashions to adorn
my body" (I.ii.256). And the drunkard Sir Toby Belch in *Twelfth Night*
boasts that the clothes he is currently wearing are "good enough to
drink in" (I.iii.11). He needs nothing fancier or even cleaner.

What clothes a character wears and how he wears them often provide clues to the way the character thinks and feels. Clothing is important as a clue to the character's sense of his status in the world he inhab-
its either onstage or in his mind, and it can also allow the audience to

enter that world, to suspend disbelief to a time and place distant from the present.

Student actors are no different from professionals in this regard. They must come to believe that what they wear are not borrowed robes, but clothes their characters have chosen. The Roman toga from *Julius Caesar* must become as natural as a pair of jeans or sweatshirt. But each character must also see himself or herself as an individual. Thus, Brutus would choose a more conservative toga than Cassius, while Calpurnia's gown must be far more elaborate and royal than Portia's. It is my experience that even as early as the readthrough, a simple piece of clothing can move the student from classroom and self into character. A length of fabric can become the beginning of the right cloak or cape, while a carefully selected hat or necklace can help the student make the leap into character.

Most Renaissance actors, including Shakespeare's, wore garments from their own time, and most contemporary audiences expect to see Shakespeare's characters dressed in the fashion of the late sixteenth or early seventeenth centuries. This article is generic in that it describes the typical clothing of the nobility and the ordinary citizens of Shakespeare's time. It also describes in some detail how an adequate seamstress can construct effective facsimiles of these garments for the stage. It is then up to you and your actors to individualize the garments so that they become not borrowed robes, but the distinctly individualized clothes of each character onstage.

I want to make it clear that this article presents the ideal situation. In many cases it might be preferable to simply rent what you need from a local costumer and gain permission to temporarily alter it with ribbons or buttons and jewelry, or borrow what you need from a large theater company, if there is a generous one in the area. But if you are ambitious and have the time, skills, budget, and talented parents, it is a great advantage to design and construct as many costumes that meet your specific production needs as time allows.

Male Costume

Most of the lead characters in Shakespeare's plays are of the upper class. Often they are members of the court, and no one was more style conscious then the male courtier. He was a trendsetter and proclaimed his station in life by the style and richness of his attire. In fact, dressing below or above one's station in life was quite literally considered fraud.

Let's start with the order of a gentleman's dressing as he arose in the morning.

The Supportase

Over drawstring-type boxer shorts a gentleman would put on a shirt of fine linen, silk, or cotton (a luxury fabric) nearly always with a stand-up collar edged with a little ruffle. This was called a supportase and its function was to support the ruff that was put on later. For very large wide ruffs, an extra supportase was worn with a wire frame built into it. The shirt had full, gathered sleeves with either a closely fitting cuff usually with another little ruffle on the edge, or a drawstring at the wrist. Black embroidery was very fashionable for collar and cuffs. These cuffs closed with a tie or two, as did the collar, to guard against their coming untied, which happened often. Clearly, a servant was necessary just to keep a person from coming undone. These shirts reached to the knees and many men used them as nightshirts as well.

Upper class men and women wore outer ruffs made of fine linen. Often they were edged with a fine lace, a luxury fabric affordable during the Renaissance only by the wealthy. A gentleman also wore hose of knitted fabric or fabric cut on the bias and fitted to the leg. The hose came very high on the thigh and tied to a belt. (Remember that men were the first to wear hose and garter belts.) Alternately, they would wear tights where each leg was separate, which is why we now speak of a pair of pants. The hose crossed in the back for coverage and were not sewn together through the crotch for sanitation. In the front of the hose a triangular flap called a codpiece covered the open space. The codpiece, which looked very much like a thong bikini or "G" string, later in the Renaissance became decorated and grew larger and larger. Much of the apparently incomprehensible joking between Romeo and Mercutio in *Romeo and Juliet* when they meet the Nurse in the street becomes clear if we realize that it is connected to jokes about virility and the codpiece that both of the young men are wearing. Here an awareness of style makes text clear.

Knee Breeches and Slops

Over the hose, a gentleman would wear knee breeches and sometimes slops or pants that look as though one is wearing a pumpkin on each hip. Slops were often stuffed with sawdust, bran, old clothing or an extra shirt. Students can achieve this look by using tulle or nylon netting for stuffing because it is lightweight and will wash.

Trousers

A gentleman might also wear trousers, cut in panes (strips) with shirt-like material slopping out between the strips of fancy fabric. These trousers would be sewn in the crotch, but open in the front. Normally, they would have buttons or hooks and eyes to close them.

Jerkin

Over his shirt a man would wear a jerkin or jacket cut a couple of fingers above the natural waist in the back and a hand below the natural waist in the front. Tabs on the jerkin hid all the things tied together underneath and many times had eyelets so that the trousers and hose could be tied to the jerkin to keep everything in place. Tabs were also placed around the lower edge of the jerkin, which hid all the ties at the waist and created a smoother transition.

Sleeves were usually not sewn to the jerkin; instead, they laced into the armhole and a roll, tabs, or wing on the shoulder hid the ties. Sleeves were also mix and match. Richer and more costly fabric was often used for the sleeves and often trimmed with jewels or fancy braid. (For theatrical purposes, velcro may be used for closure and attaching sleeves so long as there is no need to remove the sleeves onstage unless, of course, you want the sound of tearing fabric during a rough-and-tumble fight scene. For a following scene where a greater degree of informality is indicated, the use of velcro attachment allows the sleeves to be removed quickly offstage, the shirt loosened at the neck, and the jerkin opened or removed.) Capes were often worn over the jerkin.

Caps

All men wore caps of some sort. The lower classes wore a baby cap–type "biggins" tied under the chin. A courtier would wear either a Tudor flat cap or a short crown, narrow brim Spanish hat. Most men of middle or upper class wore the flat cap until about 1570.

The Ropa

Over the jerkin in cold weather, a man might wear a short or ankle-length A-line overcoat called a "ropa." A man's ropa often had a flat falling collar and could have sleeves or not, similar to the jerkin. If sleeves were not attached, the ropa usually had wings or a padded roll to decorate the armhole. It could be worn open or closed. A man might wear this without the jerkin at home in informal situations. Older men usually wore ropas most of the time.

Cloaks

Cloaks were also worn. The higher the wearer's class, the more decorated the cloak. A courtier in any public situation usually wore a thigh-length, half-circle or three-quarters-circle cloak with a collar. Many times it was worn sideways over one shoulder and tied under the other arm. This would allow him to draw a rapier without tangling it in the cloak or to take a lady's arm when they were together in a formal situation like a procession. While traveling or in bad weather a full-length cloak might be worn.

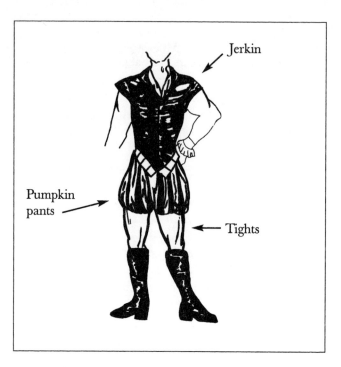

Gloves

Gloves were also a mark of the upper classes. Usually gentlemen wore gauntlet cuffs decorated according to class. If a person wore rings, the gloves' fingers might be split over the ring so that it would be visible to all. Again, the higher the class, the more elaborate the decoration.

Footwear

Footwear might be anything from a simple, low slipper cloth shoe to thigh-high leather boots. The later into the 1500s, the higher the heel. Riding boots had heels to hold the stirrup, while boots worn on shipboard had low almost flat heels to more easily grip the rolling deck. So King Alonso at the beginning of *The Tempest* will probably look awfully foolish stumbling around on the deck of the foundering ship in his high heels while the mariners will be more sure-footed. In this case fashion not only reveals who you are, but whether you are in the wrong place and situation.

Jewelry

Courtiers in this period wore plenty of jewelry. Officials wore a chain of state that draped around the shoulders but was attached in such a way as to not hang down like a necklace. The chain of state should dip only slightly across the chest and back. Jeweled pins were very popular and worn on the chest, shoulder, and sleeve. Men also wore a drop-type earring in the left ear.

Colors and Status

Black was a favorite color. It hid the dirt, showed off the jewelry, and was costly. A true black was difficult for the dyer to achieve. Other favorites were straw, tan, peach, russet, gray, red, green, and medium and light blues. Dark blue was usually worn by the lower classes because wood and indigo dyes were inexpensive. Lower classes used vegetable dyes and natural undyed cloth. They were usually seen in dull yellows, ochers, dull greens, and dull grays.

Female Costume
The Chemise

The first garment a high-born woman put on in the morning was the chemise. She may have slept in it as well. There were two major styles. It could be as simple as a long "peasant" blouse with drawstrings at the neck and wrist. Or it could resemble a square-yoked high-necked "granny nightgown" with full sleeves and drawstrings at the wrist. Both styles were made of fine linen, silk, or cotton. Neither style had ruffles on the bottom. The high-necked style had a little ruffle at the neck that was used to support the ruff, a fashion favored by women as well as men. Next, the gentlewoman put on knitted

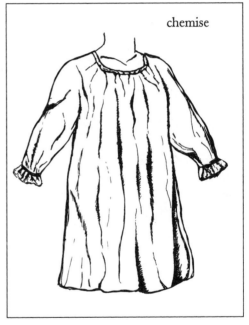

chemise

stockings that went to just below the knee. Alternately, she could wear thigh-high stockings, worn with garters that tied around the leg. Drawers or panties were worn for horseback riding to the hunt before side saddles were in general use and when needed for medical reasons, but were considered a hindrance for natural functions.

The Corset

Over the chemise she would put on her corset. The ideal female Elizabethan silhouette was one of a small cone balancing upon a larger one. In order to achieve this look, all women except the lower classes wore corsets. Little girls were put into the corset at about four or five years of age. This early corseting did not allow the lower rib cage to fully develop. As a result of corsets and different nutrition, most women's bodies were much shorter and slimmer than people of our times. (A note of warning: If your ladies are going to wear corsets, make sure that measurements are made for the outer clothing after the corset is fitted. The lines of the torso will be quite different from those we are used to in ready-to-wear. The actress's bust line will be in a completely different place and of a different shape.)

The Busk

A lady wore a busk down the front of her corset. This was a piece of wood, whalebone, or metal, shaped much like a wooden paint stirrer and rounded on the bottom. It fitted in a pocket down the front of the corset and kept the wearer in a very upright posture. Two holes were drilled in it that aligned with two eyelets in the corset. A lace or ribbon threaded through it to keep it in place. The little bow in the center of many bras is a remnant of this. A busk might also be used alone in the lower classes to stiffen the front of their bodices.

The Farthingale

The lady also wore a farthingale or hoop skirt to support her outer skirts. After 1580, the wheel or French farthingale came more and more into use instead of the hoops. The wheel farthingale was high enough on the sides to serve as arm rests and dipped lower in the front. In order to achieve this look, a series of bum rolls were worn around the hips starting with a smaller one and increasing in size as they went up. Topping them off were concentric hoops—usually about three to make the top of the farthingale look like a centerpiece on a round tabletop. A bum roll was a sausage type stuffed bag with its widest circumference in the back tapering to nothing at the front where it tied to allow the elongated bodice to plunge past.

The Underskirt and Overskirt

Over all of this she wore an underskirt consisting of a highly decorated or rich panel of fabric for show in the front with the rest of the fabric of lesser quality. It might have a slit or pocket opening at the back or the side.

Next came the overskirt, usually of the same fabric as the bodice. It could be as simple as a long straight piece of fabric gathered at the waist with a drawstring or in the extreme upper classes several blunt pie-shaped pieces pleated to a waistband. In any event, if you are trying to effect this style, it should measure at least four yards around the hem. The overskirt opened down the front to show the fancy panel of the underskirt.

The Bodice

The bodice, an outer vestlike garment that covers the body from neck to waist, could be high-necked or lower with a square neck opening. It was largely similar to the men's in cut and styling. It might open down the front or down the left side under the arm. Sleeves were laced to it at the shoulder and, like the men's, were interchangeable. A wing, tabs, or a roll on the shoulder hid the laces. Tabs were also placed around the lower edge of the bodice. These hid all the ties at the waist and created a smoother transition.

The Lady's Ropa

Over all of this, in cold weather, women often wore a ropa similar to the men's. A lady's ropa usually had a standing collar and, if she was pregnant, nursing slits that started at the mid-shoulder and went halfway to the waist. All the openings were heavily trimmed and had buttons and loops for closure.

Hats

Men and women wore the same styles of hat after Queen Elizabeth gained the throne. Before that they wore a Tudor gable-style headdress or a French hood. Under all the hats, a muffin cap like a baby cap or a circle of fabric gathered to a band kept the hair in place. This was usually white or off-white. Later in Elizabeth's reign, hats became smaller and eventually disappeared. Short curly wigs replaced them.

The Woman's Ruff

Ruffs were worn at the neck and wrists and were so precious and

Ruff

Lady's bodice

hard to maintain they were kept in specially built containers called "band" boxes.

Women's Gloves and Accessories

As in men's style, gloves were a mark of class and were often carried when they were not being worn. And like their men, Elizabethan women loved jewelry. Long pearl necklaces were popular. Brooches of all kinds were pinned to the bodice, sleeves, and near the top of the skirt. A lady also wore a fan, mirror, and/or keys suspended from her waist on cords and possibly a prayer book or a pomander to perfume the air. Popular colors were the same for men and women.

Female Theatrical Costume and Available Patterns

If you have personnel with solid sewing skills, you can obtain good costume patterns at a fabric shop. The Simplicity brand looks good and the cut is close to period. I recommend Simplicity for good home sewers.

The Alter Years catalog also stocks many brands of historical patterns, but you need to be cautious with these. They may not be standard sizing, have seam allowances, or have complete directions included. When dealing with an unknown company, get some advice from a professional. Please remember that pattern sizing has very little to do with off-the-rack ready-to-wear sizing. As an example, I wear an off-the-rack 6, but the patterns I use may be 10 in regular sewing patterns or even 12 in historical patterns. Measure your actors while they are wearing the undergarments they will be wearing in the production. I am going to repeat a warning I gave earlier because it is crucial. If your ladies are going to wear corsets, make sure measurements are made for the outer clothing after the corset is fitted. The lines of the torso will be quite different than what we are used to in ready-to-wear. The actress' bust line will be in a completely different place and of a different shape. If you choose to corset actors, I suggest buying corsets because corset construction is a very exacting art and not for the average sewer.

A serviceable, adjustable corset can be ordered from Frederick's of Hollywood, which has retail stores in most large malls. It is only an approximation and not truly period, but will serve. Make sure that it is a corset (no bra cups) not a body briefer, which is a type of girdle. The correct corset laces up the back and has hooks and eyes down the front to make it easier to put on, but a dresser should be provided for the actress because getting into the garment is not easy. If your actress is slim and small busted, then it may be possible to dispense with the corset and bone the bodice. In any case, all bodices should be interlined with at least 60 and above weight material like Pellon® sewn-in nonwoven interfacing or the equivalent. (I like nonwoven rather than woven because it does not wilt under perspiration. This is especially important if the play has a long run.)

A good test is to place the bodice on the floor and see if it stands up by itself. I bone all my bodices even when worn with a corset. They last longer, can be laundered, do not wrinkle as much, and give a smoother line.

Simple Suggestions to Create the Period Look

The most basic chemise is that of a peasant blouse mid-calf or ankle-length with a drawstring at the neckline and wrists. You can also use an old-fashioned clown costume pattern. Put a standing band collar on the neckline instead of the drawstring called for and remove the leg section and drop the waist to thigh level. Try not to use a polyester blend as it will not drape well and will be very hot for the actress under stage lights.

A high-necked style chemise can be made from a high-necked blouse pattern. Slit the sleeve lengthwise and add at least eight inches to the width of the sleeve.

Hoop skirts may be found in resale shops or bridal shops or a historical costume company such as Amazon Drygoods. Make sure the ones you use have drawstring waists for use with a variety of sizes and at least four adjustable hoops in the skirt. They should expand out to a circumference close to ten or twelve feet. No skirt should be less than four yards around the hem. Even in earlier periods this four-yard rule is a good one to follow. It allows free movement so that the actress will not tangle in brisk movement scenes, and it will allow the actress to step up steps without showing her underthings. (See Sandria Reese's essay which discusses clothes and movement.) Skirts may have drawstring waists, as the bodice will cover the waist.

A plain, dark, low-heel flat shoe will serve for ladies of all classes. Jewelry adds much to the costume and helps define class. Earrings are usually drop or French wire–style. Long necklaces of pearls and many brooches are important for your upper class ladies.

Male Theatrical Costume

Lower class men in the cast could wear drawstring-waist pants in dull colors over plain boots or low cloth or leather shoes without laces.

Upper class males will probably want to wear cotton tights in gray or white. (Vermont Country Store stocks this type of tights.) If you cannot find cotton tights, you may have to have your actors wear two pairs of nylon or polyester opaque male dancers' tights. They will need two pairs, because leg hair protrudes through a single layer and looks very strange onstage. They could also shave their legs, but that is usually not an option with student actors.

If your upper class gentlemen are going to wear "pumpkin pants," you may get by with cotton stockings sewn to drawstring short shorts. If they are going to wear knee pants, you may get by with cotton stockings sewn to drawstring shorts ending just above the knee. "Pumpkin pants" may be made out of the lower part of the clown costume mentioned earlier. Cut the pattern just above the waistline and cut the legs off just below the knee. Gather the lower edge to a pair of drawstring short shorts. Do not put any gathers on the portion on the inside of the leg or your actors will not be able to walk normally. Fill the space between the two layers with handfuls of netting (i.e., tulle). Luckily, this is inexpensive, as you will need plenty. Although some costumers use pillow stuffing as stuffing, I strongly advise against it. It is lumpy, hot, and hard to move in.

Jerkin patterns and hat patterns may be located at your local fabric shop as mentioned earlier in the discussion of female costume. In the same way, the clown pattern shirt mentioned earlier will also work for all men's shirts.

Chains of state can be made from large link chain from the hardware store or even from a woman's metal belt with the buckle and extra links removed. Large pins that look a little military can decorate the chest or the top of the sleeve.

Historical Background for Italian Renaissance Costume
Female Costume
Because Renaissance Italy was a collection of warring city states rather than a unified country, each city had its own styles and favorite colors. They differed in some subtle but important ways from Elizabethan costume.

On the whole, the bodice for Italian styles had a much higher waistline and a lower neckline. The waistline was only a little longer in the front than in the back where it was still two or three finger widths above the natural waistline. An underdress was worn under the outer gown. The outer bodice and skirt were often of the same fabric and the bodice did not have tabs. The bodice and skirt could be constructed as one unit and many times opened down the front to allow for pregnancy. Colors were similar to those mentioned earlier. Courtesans wore red, so avoid this color for your ladies' gowns.

Because Italy was much warmer than England, the wearing of hats and high necklines was not in as much favor. Hoop skirts were rarely used. After about 1580, Spanish styles were popular in Italy and the highest classes dressed much like the Elizabethans. The "peasant" blouse style of chemise is a good choice for these low square necklines. An ankle-length "A-line" sleeveless collarless vest like a very simple ropa over an ankle-length chemise makes a nice costume for a bedroom scene such as in *Othello*.

Male Costume

Italian men started the fashion for men in tights. They wore short, fitted jackets that buttoned down the front, and styles got shorter as the 1500s wore on. By 1580 they were wearing the Elizabethan-style jerkin over just a pair of tights and codpiece. The very fashionable also took to "pumpkin pants." Older men wore a ropa over their inner clothes. The Italian male ropa is the same style as our graduation gowns, ankle length in dark colors. A flat cap was often worn with it. Other men wore brimless felt hats with a rounded top. Households many times wore similar colors and badges of their house on the upper sleeve. Favorite colors remain the same.

Summary

Because few people in your audience will be knowledgeable in period costume, don't let yourself get upset if the costumes are not perfect in every detail. Even professional companies rarely have costume departments with the funds or skill to recreate a period style with perfect fidelity. The key should be to give the flavor of a period. If you must conserve money, think about spending the most time, effort, and money on the main characters.

Clothe the rest of the cast in duller, complementary colors. It may be possible to borrow costumes from another school or local college and gain permission to temporarily alter these with appropriate accessories to fit your conception of character if you commit to returning the costume to its original state. Even a civic theater may have costumes that you might use. If worst comes to worst, you may find funds to rent some of the costumes.

Costumes are exhilarating and crucial to the actor's realizing character and to the production's taking on its unique life, so never let costuming become a chore. Hopefully, the suggestions in this article about how to build the look you want will make the task of costuming a traditional production of Shakespeare easier and more exciting for you.

Bibliography

Arnold, Janet. *Patterns of Fashion 1560–1620*. New York: Drama Book Publishers, 1985.

———. *Queen Elizabeth's Wardrobe Unlocked: The Inventories of the Wardrobe of Robes Prepared in July 1600*. Leeds, England: Maney, 1988.

Betzina, Sandra, et al. *Fabric Savvy: The Essential Guide for Every Sewer*. Newtown, CT: Taunton, 2002, 1999.

Boucher, Francois. *20,000 Years of Fashion*. New York: Harry N. Abrams, 1987.

Bradfield, Nancy. *900 Years of English Costume 1066–1960*. New York: Crescent Books, 1970.

Cunningham, Rebecca. *The Magic Garment: Principles of Garment Design*. Prospect Heights, IL: Waveland, 1994, 1989.

Davenport, Millia. *The Book of Costume*. NewYork: Crown, 1976.

Dearing, Shirley. *Elegantly Frugal Costumes: The Poor Man's Do-It-Yourself Costume Maker's Guide*. Colorado Springs, CO: Meriwether, 1992.

Holkeboer, Katherine Strand. *Patterns for Theatrical Costume: Garments, Trim, and Accessories from Ancient Egypt to 1915*. New York: Prentice Hall, 1987.

Hunnisett, Jean. *Period Costume for Stage & Screen: Medieval to 1500*. Studio City, CA: Players Press, 1996.

Ingham, Rosemary. *The Costume Designer's Handbook: A Complete Guide for Amateur and Professional Costume Designers*. Portsmouth, NH: Heinemann, 1992, 1983.

Jackson, Sheila. *Costumes for the Stage: A Complete Handbook for Every Kind of Play*. New York: New Amsterdam, 2001, 1968.

Kidd, Mary T. *Stage Costume Step-by-Step: The Complete Guide to Designing and Making Stage Costumes for All Major Drama Periods and Genres*. Cincinnati, OH: Betterway, 2002, 1996.

Norris, Herbert. *Tudor Costume and Fashion*. Mineola, NY: Dover, 1997, 1938.

Rogers, Barb. *Costuming Made Easy: How to Make Theatrical Costumes from Cast-Off Clothing*. Colorado Springs, CO: Meriwether, 1999.

———. *Instant Period Costume: How to Make Classic Costumes from Cast-off Clothing*. Colorado Springs, CO: Meriwether, 2001.

Winters, Janet and Carolyn Schultz Savoy. *Elizabethan Costuming for the Years 1550–1580*. Oakland, CA: Other Times Publications, 1987.

Resources

1. *Simplicity*. 901 Wayne St., Niles, MI 49121. Phone: 888.588.2700.

www.symplicity.com
2. *Alter Years*. 3749 E. Colorado Blvd., Pasadena ,CA 91107. Phone: 626.585.2994. www.alteryears.com
3. Amazon Drygoods. 2218 E. 11th St. Davenport, IA. Phone: 319.322.6800. www.amazondrygoods.com
4. The Elizabethan Costuming Page. www.costume.dm.net

We Will Every One Be Masked

_—ᘓ_

Theo Lotz

Theo Lotz, an artist and curator of the Cornell Museum in Winter Park, offers ideas about using masks in Shakespearean productions and practical advice on making the masks.

_—ᘓ_

IT GOES WITHOUT SAYING THAT THEATER IS LARGELY VISUAL. Hamlet's advice to the players to suit the action to the word offers a microcosm of each effective theatrical moment. But Hamlet might have gone on. "Be certain," he might have continued—if he had been less a poet and more a teacher—"to see all the possibilities for costume, for makeup, for masks as ways of revealing personality and take care not to lose the masquerade."

Is it sacrilegious to suggest these few extra words for the prince? Perhaps. But maybe not. After all, Hamlet himself chooses to put on an "antic disposition," to disguise his deeper motives, to wander the corridors of Elsinore in the dramatically effective costume of depression with his "doublet all unbraced," with "no hat upon his head," and with "his stockings fouled, ungartered, and down-gyved to his ankles" (II.i.78-80). As he plays his multiple roles, this student unwillingly kept home from the University of Wittenberg ironically reveals his deep fascination for all things theatrical.

As teachers, directors, and students of Shakespeare, we stand to lose many opportunities to explore character, theme, and environment if we fail to join Hamlet in recognizing the extraordinarily rich world of visual possibilities in the plays. Like costumes, masks and masquerade offer an endlessly fascinating way of engaging Shakespeare's plays. However we construct them and whether we choose realism or abstraction, masks offer ways to establish or reinforce themes, comment on characters, or suggest entirely new meanings.

We need not look far for provocative examples. In a recent Drey seminar, "fair is foul and foul is fair" suggested a complete production idea that began with the witches in grotesque masks that progressively grew more beautiful. Hecate appeared before and during the banquet scene dressed in a beautiful white, translucent costume wearing an angelic mask. The "fair/foul" distortion of *Macbeth*'s world quickly took on new meanings.

In another Drey exploration, Bottom in *A Midsummer Night's Dream* appeared as quite an ugly man, with overly large ears, protruding teeth, and an unruly, scraggly beard. Later, his ass head exaggerated those features: his human ears became much longer, his teeth much larger, and his beard a full mane. But as a donkey, all of these features worked wonderfully and, of course, delighted the enchanted Titania, played by an actor who would earlier and later appear also as Hippolyta. At the play's conclusion, after Bottom, restored and now playing Pyramus, has delivered his melodramatic death scene, Theseus' response–"with the help of a surgeon he might yet recover, and yet prove an ass"–received a nostalgic look not only from Bottom but from Hippolyta/Titania as well. Exaggerating Bottom's features in his donkey mask and having those features admired in one context but not the other emphasized the production idea that all things are transformable and beautiful in some dimension. When Bottom is most Bottom–as a donkey–he is also a substitute king of fairyland, and he is more passionately loved than the genuine king.

One other example from a Drey workshop should suffice to illustrate the power and possibility of masks and masquerade. A production of *The Merchant of Venice* conceived the world of the play as a Christian society gone terribly wrong, with Shylock its outsider, its challenger, and, eventually, its victim. During the trial scene, the duke led a procession of black-robed inquisitors from the back of the theater, each holding an oversized, brutally distorted white mask in front of his or her face. When the court/inquisitors arrived at the stage, they placed their masks in a row of mute, demonic, heraldic witnesses to the trial. Before a word was uttered, it was clear that Shylock, the only character without the protection and disguise of a mask, was doomed.

To explore the use of masks in Shakespeare is to simultaneously explore character, circumstance, and environment. It is one more way to understand that all the world truly is a stage and all of us merely–both consciously and unconsciously–players. Masks have a universal appeal to adults as well as children. As we grow older, we recognize that, like games, masks allow us to extend and explore our personalities. Who among us has not revealed some hidden personality trait by donning a mask? And who has not witnessed the surprise of another person's appearance drastically altered–and enhanced–through masquerade?

The following simple technique offers an opening strategy for helping students to build masks. Your colleagues who teach art and the students themselves will immediately find ways of elaborating on these ideas. Blending the masks into your production is, of course, up to you and your actors.

Tools Needed:
>   Wire cutter
>   Pliers
>   Utility knife or X-acto knife
>   Straight edge

Materials Needed:
>   One sheet of 32" x 40" 4-ply mat-board
>   Masking tape
>   2 wire shirt hangers
>   Newspaper
>   (And miscellaneous materials to paint and decorate the mask)

1. Cut a 3-inch strip from the long side of the mat-board. To make the outside perimeter of the mask, bend the 3-inch strip into an oval, slightly larger than your head. Using the masking tape, tape the ends where they overlap the oval. Be sure to tape both ends well; from the inside as well as from the outside. This is the foundation of the mask, so it is important that it is fastened together well.

2. Cut a length of the wire hanger about 14 inches long. This will be the brow of the mask. Bend the wire into a shallow u-shape. Tape each end to the outside of the oval, about 1/3 from the top. Again, it is important to secure the structure together well. Burnish the tape with your fingers right up to the wire, so that it doesn't slip or move.

3. Next, a support for the front of the forehead and nose is added. Cut another piece of wire, about 18 inches long. Three inches from one end, bend a gentle curve—considering the structure of your character's head. Carefully wrap the long end of the wire around the "brow" wire. Try to make this wrap as tightly as possible. Tape the end of the wire to the inside of the cardboard oval. Carefully form the profile of the nose using the rest of the wire beneath the wrap. Remember to think about the physical characteristics of your mask. Will it have a large nose? Protruding forehead? Or, will

it have more delicate features? Look at the profile of what you have constructed, and imagine the mask "fleshed out." Cut off any extra wire.

4. Take another piece of 12" wire and bend it to form the cross-section of the nose and cheekbones. Lay the nose piece across the middle of the "nose profile" wire you made in step 3. Tape the ends to the outside of the oval.

5. Cut another strip of mat-board, this time about 1" inches wide, and about 12 inches long. Hold the mask facing you. Loop the strip of board and place it in the back of the mask. While looking at the front, position this piece so that it forms a structure to support the mouth. Be sure to leave an opening large enough that lines spoken will be heard. Tape the ends of this piece to the inside oval and to the wire you placed in step 4. Cut off any extra board.

6. Take 2 or 3 sheets of newspaper and fold them in half. On the edge of the fold, tape the newspaper to the front of the "brow" wire. Be sure to place the newspaper right along the wire, and wrap only the tape around the wire. This will keep the paper from slipping and making it difficult to work with. Now, working with the mask facing you, carefully fold the paper to conform to the shape of the head. This may require you to fold the paper in on itself, or to cut sections out of it to lay the way you want. This can be tricky, so work slowly. Think about the structure of a human skull: it has a large frontal plane in the front and smaller faceted planes on either sides which together make the head appear round. Keep this in mind as you fold the newspaper. Once you have folded the paper, cut any extra off the back. Tape this down along the back of the oval and inside across the wire. What you have now should somewhat resemble a human skull.

7. Cut another strip of mat-board, about 2" inches wide and 14 inches long. In the center, about eyes-distance apart, cut two large holes. Place this inside the mask and position it so it looks right. Make sure you can see out comfortably.

8. Cut a small triangular piece of mat board to form the nose. Bend it in half and place it over the wire nose structure. Tape it to the "cheekbone" wire and from inside.

9. Using small pieces of wadded-up newspaper and the masking tape, you can now flesh out your character. Build up areas by twisting bits of newspaper, placing them where you want and taping them down.

Resources

Grater, Michael. *Paper Mask Making.* New York: Dover, 1984

James, Thurston. *The Prop Builder's Mask-Making Handbook.* White Hall, VA: Betterway, 1990

———. *Maskmaking Introduction* (Video). Aspen, CO: Crystal Video, 1991.

———. *Maskmaking Workshop* (Video). Aspen, CO: Crystal Video, 1991.

Sivin, Carole. *Maskmaking.* Worcester, MA: Davis, 1986.

Act IV

Playing with Texts

The Most Unkindest Cut of All
Editing *A Midsummer Night's Dream* for the Classroom

Joyce Rose and Andrew Smyth

⎯ↅ

Two teachers, Joyce Rose of West Orange High and Andrew Smyth of Lake Highland Preparatory School, discuss a set of guidelines for editing the plays for classroom use and model their principles by applying them to A Midsummer Night's Dream.

⎯ↅ

GIVEN THE NEAR-SACRED STATUS OF SHAKESPEARE among English teachers and the literati in general, it is not surprising that many high school English classes in the U. S. continue to incorporate at least one Shakespearean drama into their curricula each year. Shakespeare's reputation as the prince of playwrights has so ensconced his works in our canon of worthy literature that many would think a year without Shakespeare unacceptable. Such approbation is appropriate; Shakespeare should remain high on the list of "must-reads" because of his enormous impact on English and American culture (literary and otherwise), the beauty of his dramatic poetry, the genius of his interwoven plots, and the power of his drama to reach people throughout the world and make them view their lives anew. Nevertheless, Bardolotry has its downfalls, especially the intimidation it imposes on Shakespeare's texts.

Most modern editions of the complete works of Shakespeare weigh more than five pounds. They contain lengthy introductions, all the poems and plays accepted as belonging in the Shakespeare canon, copious explanatory notes, and textual notes and variants either at the bottom of each page or in the back of the book. These last items are most often ignored by high school teachers, since they usually consist of cryptic references to *Q1, F1, Malone, This Edition,* and most frustrating, *See Note.* Of course, all of these standard abbreviations and references are spelled out clearly in the section of the introduction often referred to as "Textual Note" or "Textual Introduction," but without some training in Shakespearean textual bibliography, even many college teachers tend to ignore the textual notes, accepting them as nothing more than further proof of the authority of the edition they have so skillfully chosen.

Authority is the key term here, for as most of our students can probably attest, Shakespeare's plays are frequently presented as divinely inspired texts that should not be questioned under any circumstances. Thus, few students and even fewer teachers will feel comfortable about reshaping the plays of the Bard to fit the needs of the classroom. This essay will attempt to alleviate some of that anxiety and demonstrate how active involvement of teachers and their students in editing Shakespeare can produce not only slimmer, more presentable plays for classroom usage but also a much greater understanding of Shakespearean theater and its relevance to high school students today. After all, in editing Shakespeare's texts, our students are actually joining a tradition which began in Shakespeare's own theaters and has continued for over four centuries.

Teachers of Shakespeare should take a few cues from their students. Whenever the unit begins, countless students run to a local bookstore to procure copies of *Cliff's Notes* or, if they wish to retain an air of respectability, *Shakespeare Made Easy*, a series that provides facing page "translations" of Shakespeare's verse and prose in Modern English. If these students were asked why they would choose such "shortcuts," some frank responses might include, "I can't understand a word of Shakespeare without these!" or "It tells me all I need to know for the test." A large part of students' inability to approach Shakespeare "head-on" without such aids might derive from the very authority with which we have endowed Shakespeare's texts in the first place. The problem is that we give them Shakespeare to read, but we forget that the text of Shakespeare gets rewritten every time it is "read" in theater performance. Most of us know that each performance of a play reinterprets—that is, rewrites—the play in numerous ways, ranging from the interests of the director to the space available for production to the actors and actresses playing the parts to the audience for which the play is intended. For students to move beyond their fear of Shakespeare—a fear that drives them to rely on "Cliff" to "explain" the play for them—they have to be engaged in that same process of revision that has characterized Shakespeare studies for four hundred years. They need to edit the play for performance.

Acting as a pedagogical method works extremely well with modern teens who need visual and motor stimulation to maintain their interest in a subject for even short periods of time. So, it is quite convenient that Shakespeare's plays were made for just such an audience—people who wanted to see a good show, have a few cries or laughs, think about what they saw, and move on to the next play. The actors and directors (including Shakespeare himself) who produced these plays knew that if *King Lear*, for example, was too long and showed signs of losing the audience, then it would have to be altered to continue to bring in ticket money. If we can convince our students to approach Shakespeare's plays with that same philosophy—one that values performance over textual analysis—then their experience with Shakespeare will be active, enlightening, and enjoyable. Performing a Shakespearean play, however, requires a large amount of time, energy, space, and good fortune for students to participate fully in it and learn from the performance. With planning books already crammed with myriad duties that must be covered during a quarter or semester, English teachers have to question whether they can budget the time and resources to allow each class a chance to perform all or even part of a given play. One way that teachers can ease the rigors of performing a play in class is to edit the play, reducing its size so that a class can make their way through it in the time it takes for a normal literature unit. While many will look on this task with dread, as pointed out above, if the instructors will allow their students to get involved in the process, the process of editing Shakespeare will itself be a significant part of the learning experience.

One way to break the ice for editing Shakespeare is to show the students the numerous variations between different modern editions of their text. With a little time spent comparing a page or two from five or six different editions, the pupils should recognize clearly that professional editors disagree over their control texts, their textual emendations, their interpretations of key passages, and even their conceptions of the major themes of the play. Especially if a class is using a play found in their classroom anthologies, they need to see how many options are available for their own working "edition." For example, the version of *Macbeth* found in Harcourt Brace's *Adventures in English Literature* makes no reference to the textual history of the play, nor to the principles behind the editing of the text, and even neglects to mention who edited the play. If one searches assiduously through the copyright information, one will eventually find this entry: "Notes for *Macbeth* by G. B. Harrison from *Adventures in English Literature*, Classic Edition, edited by Paul McCormick et al."

G. B. Harrison, a noted Shakespeare scholar, apparently only contributes explanatory notes to this book, leaving the textual editing a mystery, for Paul McCormick appears to be one of the editors of the textbook, not of the play itself. If we wish to learn more about how this text was edited, the textbook refers us to an earlier edition of itself for a clue! When students compare this irresponsible editing with that of the recent Oxford and Arden editions of a play, they will quickly discover how carefully professional editors must work to establish an authoritative text. Simply scanning the table of contents of the New Oxford edition of *A Midsummer Night's Dream*, edited by Peter Holland, will illustrate to teachers and students the importance of textual editing. Holland takes two pages to establish the date of the play, seven pages to discuss the merits and problems of the first two quartos and the first folio editions of the play, and three more pages to explain why he is using Q1 (the first quarto, published in 1600) as his control text, with a significant emendation from the first folio in Act V (to which Holland devotes a twelve-page appendix).

Perhaps the greatest surprise for students will come when they read Holland's statement, "*A Midsummer Night's Dream* presents probably fewer textual problems than any other Shakespeare play published both as a quarto and as part of the Folio of 1623. . . . The text of *A Midsummer Night's Dream* does not leave the editor tearing out his/her hair in anguish." With all of those pages devoted to explaining his textual policies, Holland's declaration of the text's relative simplicity must come as dramatic understatement to thoughtful students. This preliminary exercise should give teachers and students much more confidence when they approach their own task of editing Shakespeare's plays for classroom usage. Students will see that the decisions they make with their version of the play should be rational, consistent, and carefully thought through.

As noted above, time seems to be the most significant factor in the decision of whether or not to use performance-pedagogy, and time will usually become the goal of teacher–and student–editors. Faced with the difficult task of cutting a play down to a realistic ninety minutes of performance time, teachers will appreciate having a set of principles to guide them through the editing process. In addition to the guidelines, we suggest that teachers involve the class immediately in the project, asking them to generate criteria for cutting the text. The primary decision will be whether to cut whole scenes and/or subplots or to trim lines from individual speeches and scenes while retaining every scene. In editing *A Midsummer Night's Dream*, we chose the latter, but teachers and classes will have to reconsider this question for each play they edit. In making our editing decisions, we followed four primary principles:

1. **Keep the story intact.** If you cut a whole scene, you will obscure a crucial connection between the main plot and subplot or between characters. The students need to see how Shakespeare weaves so

many different strands into a five-act play. In *MSN*, for example, Shakespeare includes four groups of characters whose words and actions are interconnected by the theme of love and marriage: (1) Theseus and Hippolyta; (2) the four young lovers; (3) the fairies: and (4) the rustics or "rude mechanicals." When such thematic parallelism exists, editors should take care not to disrupt it by cutting out a crucial component.

2. **Maintain and emphasize the visual elements of the play.** Often, props, scenery, or a small dance in the background can convey plenty of atmosphere and information regarding the plot, without taking up actual speaking time. Samuel Pepys observed in 1662 that *MSN* was "the most insipid ridiculous play that ever I saw in my whole life," but he appreciated its inclusion of "some good dancing and some handsome women." The visual aspects of a play often leave the most lasting impressions.

3. **Eliminate redundancies.** While the transitory, oral nature of narrative delivery in a play necessitates some repetition, in a shortened version of a play we can rely on the fact that our students have read, studied, *and* performed the play. They should have enough experience with it to ensure that they know what is going on. In *MSN*, Helena's protests provide ample opportunities for cutting away some text, since she demonstrates a remarkable talent for whining about the same injustice in a variety of ways. On the other hand, some redundancies may prove necessary; the comical play-within-a-play, for example, relies on repetition for much of its comic effect. Decide which repetitions are necessary.

4. **Eliminate arcane language and lost-context passages.** Especially in the comedies, some serious jokes that would have appealed to an Elizabethan audience require extensive footnoting just to make sense to modern readers (see, for example, the famous "widow Dido" sequence in *The Tempest*). Great care should be taken, however, to distinguish between understandable Shakespearean dialogue and irretrievable context.

In our own recent editing of *A Midsummer Night's Dream*, these four principles proved helpful, simply because we had some guidelines with which to work. It would certainly facilitate a more efficient group-editing project if the class decided on some similar set of principles before the read-through stage of encountering the play. Then, they can stop and suggest cuts and revisions as the play unfolds, suggesting movements, songs, and dances to supplement or even supplant certain portions of dialogue. The key is for the students to keep in mind, even in the early read-through stage, that the performance must guide their reading and editing of the play.

Our edition of *A Midsummer Night's Dream* focuses on keeping the story intact while reducing certain speeches that might prove troublesome for students, who are often daunted by memorizing long passages, and that do not contribute significantly to key developments in plot and theme. Often, we noticed that the fairy scenes allowed for a reduction in lines, precisely because their visual potential is so strong. Such potential enables an audience to see (rather than listen to) the magic and mystery and, of course, the mischief, that is developing. When the enchanted Titania falls in love with the ass-headed Bottom, for example, Titania's instructions to her accompanying fairies (while certainly ludicrously poetic and therefore tempting to retain) can be eliminated, as well as their responses. When Titania tells Bottom, "I'll give thee fairies to tend on thee" (III.i.158), a simple wave of her hand or wand can send Peaseblossom, Cobweb, Moth, and Mustardseed to work, scratching and feeding Bottom. Thus, lines 163-201 can be deleted, with a brief dumbshow providing an equivalent amount of fairy humor in the scene.

Even among the human characters, teacher and student-editors will probably discover numerous areas where they can reduce the number of a scene's lines while maintaining its passion. Most teenagers can readily identify and empathize with Helena in her utter frustration as she finds herself suddenly transformed from an object of derision to the hottest item on the planet (or at least in the forest). Thanks to the misapplied magic love potion, both Demetrius and Lysander are now madly in love with her, and their flagrantly overdone Petrarchan rhetoric of praise nearly pushes her over the edge. The students will understand how Helena's interjection, "O spite! O hell! I see you all are bent/To set against me for your merriment" (III.ii.145-46), works well in response to Demetrius's sudden deification of the woman he had scorned in contempt an hour earlier. Any teenage girl should know how much meaning an appropriate facial expression and gesture of outrage can carry in this situation. Thus, an editor might very well reduce Helena's boiling rage by ten lines (III.ii.151-61), where her vehement protests become redundant. Indeed, Helena is given to fits of outrage throughout the play. While much of her whining and protesting is essential to her character, most student-editors will find many such outbursts that can be shortened.

Teachers and students will notice, of course, that whenever they make cuts in the text they will have to adjust surrounding areas and compensate for the lost dialogue. In other words, the community of readers, performers, editors, auditors, and learners that has developed through this process of editing the text for production will need to judge what has been lost and how newly formed fissures can be filled–either with a few words of dialogue, a well-placed look or gesture, a prop that connects the remaining action with a continuing theme, or any other device that they can imagine and implement. Ideally, all of those involved in the play will become what Stanley Fish describes as an "interpretive community," one that feels comfortable making affective readings and thus bringing to realization the symbolic potential of the play as an interpretive experience. With performance as the driving force behind each class's "reading" of the play, that reading experience empowers the community of learners to produce their own "text" of Shakespeare. Edward L. Rockin sees this performance-oriented production of text as a necessary bridge between writing and literature classes:

> The transformation in the study and teaching of literature is in some ways a mirror image of the transformation of composition, for it also starts with reconceptualizing the text and continues with a reconception of the role of the reader and the community of readers who respond to that text.

Most students only equate Shakespeare and writing when they are forced to write an essay on a play they have been fed, and they usually end up guessing in their essays what the teacher intended them to learn from the play. Rockin's thesis, on the other hand, is that students can learn more from Shakespeare when they view the play as a work in progress, a first draft of a paper that they must complete:

> Thus literary criticism has shifted from product to process by beginning to look at the writer as a composer of a text that is also a draft, even as it has also begun to look at the reader as a recomposer who enters into a transaction with the text.

Textual editing becomes much more than a matter of painfully cutting away some of the Bard's words to make the play fit one's class constraints (e.g., time and size); it draws the students into the process of *creating* drama, conflating reading and writing into one act of learning. When done properly, with the whole class involved, the process of editing Shakespeare recreates the social power of Shakespeare's presentations and enables the students to discover how drama is a shaping factor in their own lives and communities. An example of the transformative power of even one major editorial change is the middle school production of *A Midsummer Night's Dream* by the American School in Japan in 1997. For whatever reason—practical or theoretical—that this community saw fit, they changed the gender of the character Egeus. Suddenly, the sexual politics of the play are radically transformed, for when Theseus admonishes Hermia, "What say you, Hermia? be advised fair maid:/To you your mother should be as a goddess; Demetrius is a worthy gentleman" (I.i.46-48), the patriarchal power against which Hermia, Hippolyta, and Helena struggle throughout the play is instantly complicated. This textual emendation compromises the dramatic subversion of Athenian/Elizabethan patriarchy developed so carefully in Shakespeare's original text, but for this particular group of learners and performers, the change may teach them more about sexual and textual politics than any lecture could ever do. Given the large number of single-parent families in contemporary U. S. societies, a situation that impacts the classroom dynamic in middle school and high school, the transfer of parental power to a female Egeus (Egea?) creates a dramatic situation with which many of our students can identify. In a play that self-consciously scrutinizes the place of gender on the stage and the politics of marriage both on the stage and in the audience, such a sexchange seems quite "natural."

Why teach Shakespeare in high school? Many students would come up with some interesting, if painful, responses to this question, but few would probably say that Shakespeare comes "naturally" to them. Given the power of editing for performance, however, students will more than likely grasp the amazing currency of Shakespeare, not as an impossible author that every English teacher insists on teaching, but as a text that is malleable and fully capable of having an impact on their own lives.

Example: *A Midsummer Night's Dream* Edited for the Classroom

As a model, the following lines have been cut from the Peter Holland edition of *Midsummer Night's Dream*. These deletions should result in a running time of approximately ninety minutes. Teachers who want to adapt this particular "edition" should feel free to preserve any cut lines that they feel are particularly worthy of study, and they will most likely wish to make further changes based upon their classes' perceptions of the play.

Act & Scene	Lines deleted
I.i.	32-36; 141-155; 230-41
II.i.	51-57; 77-80; 88-114; 124-35; 161-64; 255-56,

	265-67
II.ii	11-26 (shift to background music); 90-99; 137-42
III.i	51-55; 115-20; 163-201
III.ii	19-23; 25-30; 151-61; 203-19; 307-16; 339-44; 356-59; 378-95
IV.i.	5-28; 50-53, 56-59; 115-28; 176-79
V.i	7-22; 93-105; 231-37; 239-256; 261-63; 289-91; 308-25; 359-62; 377-80; 413-22

Resources

American School in Japan Middle School Players. *A Midsummer Night's Dream*. Internet. http://iris.asij.ac.jp/msdrania/msnd.html

Brooks, Harold F., ed. *A Midsummer Night's Dream. The Arden Edition of the Works of William Shakespeare*. London: Routledge, 1994. (The Arden editions contain full introductions discussing the critical and historical background to the play, with thorough textual editing notes and appendices.)

Clemen, Wolfgang, ed. *A Midsummer Night's Dream. The Signet Classic Shakespeare*. New York: Penguin, 1998. (The Signet edition includes an overview of the play and seven critical commentaries. The edition also has an excellent bibliography and suggestions for further reading.)

Doran, Madeleine, ed. *A Midsummer Night's Dream. The Pelican Shakespeare*. NewYork: Penguin, 1987. (This slim edition, not overburdened with critical commentary, laces textual variants from Q1 [i.e., the first quarto] in an appendix.)

Durband, Alan, ed. *A Midsummer Night's Dream. Barron's Shakespeare Made Easy*. New York: Barrons, 1985. (The complete original text is laid out side-by-side with a full, modern "translation." This edition can be useful for conversations about "modernizing" Shakespeare's language and rhythms.

Fish, Stanley. *Is There a Text in This Class?* Cambridge: Harvard, 1980. (Fish's classic critical text offers a thorough investigation of reader-response criticism.)

Holland, Peter, ed. *A Midsummer Night's Dream. The Oxford Shakespeare*. Oxford: Oxford, 1994. (Holland's thorough introductory essay provides relevant background information together with an appraisal of critical views and of the play's effects in performance. A section on editorial procedures is particularly helpful.)

Rockin, Edward L."An Incarnational Art: Teaching Shakespeare." *Shakespeare Quarterly* 41 (1990): 147-59. (In the leading Shakespearean journal, Rockin spells out the benefits of performance-centered teaching of Shakespeare.)

What's in a Name?
Behind-the-Scenes Language in Romeo and Juliet

‿ᝍ

Alan Nordstrom

Alan Nordstrom, an actor, poet, and Shakespeare professor at Rollins College, uses his poet's eye and ear to show how the language and meter of Romeo and Juliet *help create and convey character and idea.*

‿ᝍ

> Servant: But I pray, can you read anything you see?
> Romeo: Ay, if I know the letters and the language.
> (I.ii.60-61)

SHAKESPEARE'S EVIDENT AIM WAS TO WRITE IMMORTALLY, to write so beautifully that the works of his verbal art would live indelibly in human consciousness—"So long as men can breathe or eyes can see, So long lives this, and this gives life to thee." To write for an audience is one thing; to write for posterity is another. Shakespeare obviously meant to do both, as if he were writing not only for men but for the gods, aiming over the heads of his Globe Theater spectators to still higher ranks in the celestial amphitheater. It must have been so with his plays, cast in a language too rich and rarefied ever to be apprehended fully by human hearing in a theater. What four centuries of subtle teasing out by scholars and poets have found packed into his dialogues could never be grasped in the Globe or the Blackfriars or the Court. Shakespeare knew he had another audience, whether in the sky or in the future. Either way, he courted immortality and won its hand.

When we see Shakespeare on stage and screen, we hear speech, we hear dialogue, but most likely we do not immediately or easily hear prose or poetry or varieties of poetry. Making that latter recognition requires a copy of the script, the text, to read at leisure and aloud. In the theater, we may somewhat feel the effects of the different styles and manners Shakespeare uses, responding to them subliminally, as we do to music of different rhythms, keys, and modes; nonetheless, modern actors often homogenize those differences that we can see and hear when reading to ourselves because they hope to bring the sounds of

Shakespeare as close as possible to our familiar idioms of speech. This was Baz Lurhmann's obvious aim in his Verona Beach *Romeo*, the effect of which was to steamroll the language, squeeze out the undulations, and flatten the patterns of verse. What's lost in translation, Robert Frost said, is poetry. What's lost in most contemporary acting of Shakespeare is, to say it briefly, poetry.

I would like us to take some time to look at and listen to the "poetry" in the first act of *Romeo and Juliet,* by which I mean the various modes and dimensions of language that our students are likely not to recognize or distinguish among, either when they attend performances or when they read the playscript. I want to point out how Shakespeare employs a full gamut or wide palette of styles (to use two common metaphors) or (to use a more modern one) shifts his stylistic gears frequently throughout the first act, as he does throughout the whole play. When we move *Romeo* from the page to the stage, it's too often like Wordsworth's reluctant passage from prenatal immortality to imprisoning mortality. Though the embodied performance still trails clouds of transcendent glory, it sheds perforce much of its immortal splendor, for actors have not the voice to say nor we the ears to hear the full linguistic spectrum Shakespeare exercises.

> Such harmony is in immortal souls,
> But whilst this muddy vesture of decay
> Doth grossly close it in, we cannot hear it.
> <div align="right">(<i>The Merchant of Venice</i>, 5.1.63)</div>

Therefore, before we move too hastily in the direction of performance, I want us to linger a little on the less evident and more poetic glories of Shakespeare's achievement to make more manifest the full, if unrealizable, richness of the script. Listen, first, to the opening prologue.

> Two households, both alike in dignity,
>   In fair Verona, where we lay our scene,
> From ancient grudge break to new mutiny,
>   Where civil blood makes civil hands unclean.
> From forth the fatal loins of these two foes
>   A pair of star-crossed lovers take their life:
> Whose misadventured piteous overthrows
>   Doth with their death bury their parents' strife.
> The fearful passage of their death-marked love,
>   And the continuance of their parents' rage,
> Which, but their children's end, naught could remove,
>   Is now the two hours' traffic of our stage;

The which if you with patient ears attend,
What here shall miss, our toil shall strive to mend.

What could be more formal, dignified, orderly and resonant than this opening monologue? To recognize it as not only verse but as a measured, balanced, rounded sonnet is to sense a controlling artistry shaping what we see. This play is framed by the authorial presence of a sentinel-like narrator presaging in miniature all that will ensue: how rage enflamed will ultimately be quenched by love sacrificed. Thus this play of impetuous motion and emotion begins at a still point of high and sober order, just where it will also end, though in a wounded way, with Prince Escalus' envoy:

A glooming peace this morning with it brings.
The sun for sorrow will not show his head.
Go hence, to have more talk of these sad things:
Some shall be pardoned, and some punished;
For never was a story of more woe
Than this of Juliet and her Romeo.

(V.iii.307-12)

Fittingly, the play ends with this truncated sonnet signifying both order restored and happiness lost.

The second act also begins with a choral sonnet, where once again we sense a sentinel-like guard coolly supervising the events he narrates and predicts; yet by the time Act III begins, events have heated up so hectically that Friar Lawrence warns Romeo how "violent delights have violent ends," at which point the sentinel sonnet vanishes and all hell breaks loose as the mercurial Mercutio enflames the fiery Tybalt, and amorous Romeo falls into the furnace of their fury.

One other sonnet that appears early on, within Act I, also serves to signify order, poise, and harmony in high degree.

Romeo: If I profane with my unworthiest hand
This holy shrine, the gentle sin is this;
My lips, two blushing pilgrims, ready stand
To smooth that rough touch with a tender kiss.
Juliet: Good pilgrim, you do wrong your hand too much,
Which mannerly devotion shows in this;
For saints have hands that pilgrim's hands do touch,
And palm to palm is holy palmer's kiss.
Romeo: Have not saints lips, and holy palmers too?
Juliet: Ay, pilgrim, lips that they must use in prayer.
Romeo: O, then, dear saint, let lips do what hands do!

They pray; grant thou, lest faith turn to despair.
Juliet: Saints do not move, though grant for prayer's sake.
Romeo: Then move not while my prayer's effect I take.
(I.v.93-106)

Woven within the duet of dialogue celebrating Romeo and Juliet's first encounter, this sonnet links and binds the lovers instantly. Romeo's quatrain pairs with Juliet's quatrain, then quicker repartee concludes in a shared couplet and a kiss. Thereafter begins another stichomythic quatrain, perhaps headed toward another sonnet, except for the spell-breaking interruption of the Nurse: "Madam, your mother craves a word with you." Romeo continues the sonnet:

Thus from my lips, by thine my sin is purged.
[Kisses her.]
Juliet: Then have my lips the sin that they have took.
Romeo: Sin from my lips? O trespass sweetly urged!
Give me my sin again.
[Kisses her.]
Juliet: You kiss by th' book.
(I.v.107-110)

As we feel the fusion of these youngsters' souls implicit in their interfolded words within the sonnet's form, we also sense the tension of contrary motives. Their sonnet is not only a dialogue but a dialectical dance of yin and yang, of the sacred and the secular, of Apollo and Dionysus, of Diana and Cupid, of the ascetic and the erotic—all emblemized in the image of two smooching saints. Such passionate extremities, tempered and contained within a sonnet's timeless monument, represent a momentary stay against confusion (to steal a phrase from Frost), yet confusion is the main theme of the play, the chaos that raging hate introduces into the garden paradise of transcendental love. This exquisite sonnet shared by Romeo and Juliet at their meeting is a crystal image of pure human love, too fine to last in so rough a world.

So now let's return to the opening scene that follows the dignified prologue sonnet. The shock of linguistic counterpoint here is palpable. Sampson and Gregory, two of the Capulets' servants, banter and jostle in crude, choleric prose.

Sampson: Gregory, on my word, we'll not carry coals.
Gregory: No, for then we should be colliers.
Sampson: I mean, an we be in choler, we'll draw.
Gregory: Ay, while you live, draw your neck out of collar.
Sampson: I strike quickly, being moved.

Gregory: But thou art not quickly moved to strike.
Sampson: A dog of the house of Montague moves me.
Gregory: To move is to stir, and to be valiant is to
                                                    stand.
        Therefore, if thou art moved, thou runn'st
                                                    away.
Sampson: A dog of that house shall move me to stand.
        I will take the wall of any man or maid of
                                                Montague's.
Gregory: 'Tis true; and therefore women, being the
        weaker vessels, are ever thrust to the wall.
        Therefore I will push Montague's men from
        the wall and thrust his maids to the wall.
                                            (I.i.1-17)

Sex and violence—a sure-fire attention getter at the start of the dramatic action. And so the scene continues, prosaically, until Benvolio enters with a line of blank verse:

        Put up your swords. You know not what you do.

Tybalt retorts in the same style:

        What, art thou drawn among these heartless hinds?
        Turn thee, Benvolio! look upon thy death.

Thus does the dialogue continue in unrhymed iambic pentameters as Lord and Lady Capulet then Lord and Lady Montague join the fray.

        Officer: Clubs, bills, and partisans! Strike! Beat them
                                                        down!
        Citizen: Down with the Capulets! Down with the
                                                    Montagues!
            Enter old Capulet in his gown, and his Wife.
        Capulet: What noise is this? Give me my long sword, ho!
        Wife: A crutch, a crutch! Why call you for a sword?
        Capulet: My sword, I say! Old Montague is come
            And flourishes his blade in spite of me.
            Enter old Montague and his Wife.
        Montague: Thou villain Capulet!—Hold me not, let me go.
        Montague's Wife: Thou shalt not stir one foot to seek a
                                                            foe.
            Enter Prince Escalus, with his Train.
                                                (I.i.70-78)

Note how those last two lines gear up to a couplet, a greater formality that ushers in the outraged Prince.

At this point I'd like to focus for a while on the varieties of blank verse in Act I. All blank verse is not equal. Though each line typically contains ten syllables and each line usually pulses five times with the *te-DUM* of the iambic beat, what Shakespeare makes of this basic scheme is like what a master carpenter can make of a 2x4. Listen first to the imperious tones of angry Prince Escalus.

> Rebellious subjects, enemies to peace,
> Profaners of this neighbor-stained steel—
> Will they not hear? What, ho! You men, you beasts,
> That quench the fire of your pernicious rage
> With purple fountains issuing from your veins!
> On pain of torture, from those bloody hands
> Throw your mistemp'red weapons to the ground
> And hear the sentence of your movèd prince.
> Three civil brawls, bred of an airy word
> By thee, old Capulet, and Montague,
> Have thrice disturbed the quiet of our streets
> And made Verona's ancient citizens
> Cast by their grave beseeming ornaments
> To wield old partisans, in hands as old,
> Cank'red with peace, to part your cank'red hate.
> If ever you disturb our streets again,
> Your lives shall pay the forfeit of the peace.
> For this time all the rest depart away.
> You, Capulet, shall go along with me;
> And, Montague, come you this afternoon,
> To know our farther pleasure in this case,
> To old Freetown, our common judgment place.
> Once more, on pain of death, all men depart.

> > (I.i.79-101)

Blank verse this is, but straining to be more, almost bursting into rhyme. Note the first three lines that end not quite in rhyme but in assonance with the resounding vowels of *peace*, *steel*, and *beasts*, followed by *rage* and *veins*, then *hands* and *ground*. In fact, the Prince does round off his oration with a resolute couplet:

> To know our further pleasure in this case,
> To old Freetown, our common judgment place.

After this brouhaha, the scene changes key as Lady Montague inquires from Benvolio of Romeo's whereabouts. Here is what Benvolio might have said had Shakespeare given him mere prose to speak:

Madam, an hour before sunrise, my troubled mind drove me out to walk where I spotted your son in a grove of sycamore west of the city. I headed toward him, but when he noticed me, he slipped into the woods for cover. Thinking that he felt as unsociable as I did, I gladly joined him.

Now, hear why the word "prosaic" implies dull, unspirited writing. Hear this same thought colorized:

> Benvolio: Madam, an hour before the worshipped sun
> Peered forth the golden window of the East,
> A troubled mind drave me to walk abroad;
> Where, underneath the grove of sycamore
> That westward rooteth from this city side,
> So early walking did I see your son.
> Towards him I made, but he was ware of me
> And stole into the covert of the wood.
> I, measuring his affections by my own,
> Which then most sought where most might not be
> found,
> Being one too many by my weary self,
> Pursued my humor, not pursuing his,
> And gladly shunned who gladly fled from me.
> (I.i.116-128)

Unlike the Prince's peremptory, oratorical blank verse, this verse is lush and lilting, ornamented with rhetorical configurations, balances and antitheses:

> Pursued my humor, not pursuing his,
> And gladly shunned who gladly fled from me.

In the passion of youth and friendship, Benvolio falls into a florid style.

More florid still and more contrived is Romeo's first long speech, which proves a veritable catalog of oxymorons, as far from common speech as one can go.

> Here's much to do with hate, but more with love.
> Why then, O brawling love, O loving hate,
> O anything, of nothing first create!
> O heavy lightness, serious vanity,
> Misshapen chaos of well-seeming forms,
> Feather of lead, bright smoke, cold fire, sick health,
> Still-walking sleep, that is not what it is!
> (I.i.171-179)

In utter contrast to Romeo's poetry is the rambling, lumbering blank verse of Juliet's Nurse. Shakespeare's game here is to deflate her verse so that it sounds as close as possible to prose and yet still sings, as only the Nurse can sing.

> Even or odd, of all days in the year,
> Came Lammas Eve at night shall she be fourteen.
> Susan and she (God rest all Christian souls!)
> Were of an age. Well, Susan is with God;
> She was too good for me. But, as I said,
> On Lammas Eve at night shall she be fourteen;
> That shall she, marry; I remember it well.
> 'Tis since the earthquake now eleven years;
> And she was weaned (I never shall forget it,)
> Of all the days of the year, upon this day;
> For I had then laid wormwood to my dug,
> Sitting in the sun under the dovehouse wall.
> My lord and you were then at Mantua.
> Nay, I do bear a brain.

> (I.iii.16-29)

It's hard to interrupt her unstinting monologue, as Lady Capulet discovers. It lurches along tipsily, sometimes squeezing extra syllables into lines, sometimes falling short, and always playing fast and loose with meter. Even at this relatively early point in Shakespeare's artistry, he's learned to imprint the speech and the verse of his inimitable characters with unique verbal signatures as distinct as modern voiceprints. The Nurse is the Nurse is the Nurse.

And Mercutio is Mercutio. A very different cadence and sensibility. Listen.

> O, then I see Queen Mab has been with you.
> She is the fairies' midwife, and she comes
> In shape no bigger than an agate stone
> On the forefinger of an alderman,
> Drawn with a team of little atomies
> Over men's noses as they lie asleep;
> Her wagon spokes made of long spinners' legs,
> The cover, of the wings of grasshoppers;
> Her traces, of the smallest spider web;
> Her collars, of the moonshine's wat'ry beams;
> Her whip, of crickets's bone; the lash, of film;
> Her wagoner, a small grey-coated gnat,

Not half so big as a round little worm
Pricked from the lazy finger of a maid;
Her chariot is an empty hazelnut,
Made by the joiner squirrel or old grub,
Time out o'mind the fairies' coachmakers.
And in this state she gallops night by night
Through lovers' brains, and then they dream of love;
O'er courtiers' knees, that dream on curtsies straight;
O'er lawyers' fingers, who straight dream on fees;
O'er ladies' lips, who straight on kisses dream,
Which oft the angry Mab with blisters plagues,
Because their breaths with sweetmeats tainted are.
Sometimes she gallops o'er a courtier's nose,
And then dreams he of smelling out a suit;
And sometime comes she with a tithe-pig's tail
Tickling a parson's nose as 'a lies asleep,
Then dreams he of another benefice.
Sometimes she driveth o'er a soldier's neck,
And then dreams he of cutting foreign throats,
Of breaches, ambuscadoes, Spanish blades,
Of healths five fathom deep; and then anon
Drums in his ear, at which he starts and wakes,
And being thus frighted, swears a prayer or two
And sleeps again. This is that very Mab
That pats the manes of horses in the night
And bakes the elflocks in foul sluttish hairs,
Which once untangled much misfortune bodes.
This is the hag, when maids lie on their backs,
That presses them and learns them first to bear,
Making them women of good carriage.
This is she—

(I.iv.53-95)

A dynamo of imagination, a rhapsodic, ecstatic, vatic Bard, Mercutio, with his quick-silver mind and mercurial humor, makes blank verse sound enchanted, conjurational, as he transports us into Faeryland in phantasmagorical detail. This is blank verse that flies like Icarus.

Finally, there's old Capulet as the frenetic, distracted host, decked out in yet another fashion of blank verse.

Welcome, gentlemen! Ladies that have their toes
Unplagued with corns will walk about with you.

Ah ha, my mistresses! Which of you all
Will now deny to dance? She that makes dainty,
She I'll swear hath corns. Am I come near ye now?
Welcome, gentlemen! I have seen the day
That I have worn a visor and could tell
A whispering tale in a fair lady's ear,
Such as would please. 'Tis gone, 'tis gone, 'tis gone!
You are welcome, gentlemen! Come, musicians, play.
          Music plays, and they dance.
A hall, a hall! Give room! and foot it, girls.
More light, you knaves! and turn the tables up,
And quench the fire, the room is grown too hot.
Ay, sirrah, this unlooked-for sport comes well.
Nay, sit, nay, sit, good cousin Capulet,
For you and I are past our dancing days.
How long is't now since last yourself and I
Were in a mask?

                                        (I.v.16-33)

My point is clear if you have heard something of the variety of uses to which Shakespeare puts blank verse, fashioning it to suit many kinds of occasions and to represent the idiosyncrasies of many characters. And my larger point has been to illustrate the gamut or palette or gears of Shakespeare's dramatic language, some of which we may catch on the fly in the theater as the dialogue zips by our ears, but most of which we can appreciate only in the repose of the study and the classroom.

A primary goal of teaching Shakespeare must be to win students to a love of the words, words of his plays, and to a love of how these words compile into phrases, clauses, sentences, lines of metrical verse, and into wonderful concatenations of sounds, sounds that ring in our ears and linger in our memories. Shakespeare is not Shakespeare without his words and the artful orders of language he constructed of them. Though we can insightfully discuss his plots and themes and characters and stagecraft, language is his primal element and his most eminent accomplishment. To lead students into recognizing, comprehending, and loving Shakespeare's ways of singing English is our first job.

His Letters Bear His Mind
Re-Writing Shakespeare

Maurice O'Sullivan

Maurice O'Sullivan, Kenneth Curry Professor of English at Rollins College and a cofounder of the Drey Shakespeare Institutes, offers an exercise in finding Shakespeare's characters' voices by creating their unknown letters, diaries, and journals.

> "What says Romeo? Or, if his mind be
> writ, give me his letter."
> (*Romeo and Juliet* V.ii.4)

Attempting to write a character's mind can be frustrating, challenging, and engaging. When Mary Cowden Clark wrote the three volumes of *The Girlhood of Shakespeare's Heroines* (London, 1851), a series of fanciful Victorian recreations of the early lives of such figures as Juliet, "the white dove of Verona," and Hermione, "the Russian princess," she merely followed a long history of speculating about the lives of Shakespeare's characters outside their plays. In doing so, she joined a rich tradition that includes such diverse works as Franklin Harvey Head's marvelous *Shakespeare's Insomnia and the Causes Thereof* (1886), with its letters from the moneylender Mordecai Shylock dunning Shakespeare for his loans and Nicholas Bottom complaining about his fellow Stratfordian's plagiarizing of Bottom's version of Pyramus and Thisbe in *A Midsummer Night's Dream*, and Tom Stoppard's mildly absurdist *Rosencrantz and Guildenstern Are Dead* (New York, 1967), in which those two simple-minded courtiers try to work out their place in both *Hamlet* and the universe. While these fictions about fictions offer amusing and occasionally provocative insights, they invariably reveal far more about their authors than either the characters or Shakespeare himself.

As a pedagogical traditionalist, I believe our attention should always focus primarily on the text. But one way I have found of exploring how well my students actually understand those texts is to give them creative writing exercises that allow them to play with the texts. As they play with the texts, I gain invaluable insights into their understanding of both the plays themselves and of the ways individual characters see each other and themselves. Aside from the irritation that some students express about any assignment, most students find these opportunities fun. They serve both as a welcome respite from traditional essays and as a way for students to explore their creative sides. Recently, a number in one class on Shakespeare's early plays even praised me for encouraging them to "think outside the box." (Of course, as I regularly remind them, if any Shakespearean play is a box, it is the intricately decorated, beautifully lacquered box from which a magician pulls a kaleidoscopic variety of treats. Unfortunately, some prefer to see it as Forrest Gump's box of chocolates.)

In most cases I set the first couple of topics. A few have always seemed fairly obvious. Surely Romeo sent love letters to Rosaline, the girl who kept him walking the streets of Verona all night and to whom he lay siege with loving terms, assailing eyes, and saint-seducing gold. After all, the characters in *Romeo and Juliet* mention letters about twenty times. And would not Juliet have kept a diary detailing her thoughts about Paris and her coming-out ball? But teachers' imaginations always pale in comparison with our students'. They will invariably find the most curious, most obscure, and most outrageous possibilities. I encourage them to think about nuance, to put themselves into the minds of the character whose persona they adopt. And I often advise them to write from the perspective of someone for whom they have little or no sympathy. Trying to recreate Iago's or Lady Macbeth's mind can offer surprising insights.

Taking the last piece of advice, one student decided to try to reimagine Lady Montague as her own mother negotiating a conspiracy of peace with Lady Capulet:

> Lady Capulet,
> Although we are two of the many involved in the wars between our families, I write to you with the hopes that you may relieve the pain in my heart. Please, consider this a plea from a fellow mother not an enemy, for I feel you are the only other soul in fair Verona who can truly understand my grief. We are two women, caught in the center of the storm raging between our houses, watching our families destroy one another.
> Here in this letter, I ask that you throw aside your

hatred of my name and help me to bring our families to a resolution of this constant fighting. I know your heart longs for peace. During yesterday's disturbance in the street, I heard your pleas to your husband to calm his temper and restrain his sword. I, too, cried words of peace into my husband's ear. Although our families live in conflict, I believe our hearts are in agreement; let us stop this nonsensical hatred before one of us must walk the streets of Verona as a member of a funeral procession. We can no longer be satisfied with our positions as silent observers and whispering beggars!

With the Prince's last judgment lying heavily on the heads of our husbands, we must act soon. I am sure you are wondering how I plan to bring about this feat of peace and tolerance. Well, my dear Lady, I share your curiosity, for I do not have a plan yet. But, I have a proposition. What would happen if we were to join our houses together through a bond of matrimony? Unfortunately, my only son, Romeo, has been struck by Cupid's scathing bow and constantly aches from unrequited love. He is useless to my plan. But, my nephew, Benvolio, is of the perfect age to take on the role of husband, and I know your daughter, Juliet, is of the age to marry. Their matrimonial vows would serve as a bridge between our families, one we could use to cross over all the hatred and bitterness of the past. I know my plans make me look like a raving lunatic, but I beg you, in the name of those you love, to consider my proposal.

Lady Capulet, please say you'll join with me in my attempt to bring peace back to our households and the streets. I am waiting anxiously for your reply.

In hopes of future friendships,
Lady Montague

In much the same conciliatory spirit, a similar-minded student created a letter from Benvolio to Romeo's father, asking for advice:

Old Montague,
I am writing this letter to you in the hope that you may be able to reach out to young Romeo, for his

somber humor is more serious than I originally thought. We are glad that he did not witness the last fight for fear that he would have become enraged, but I feel that his mind has become occupied with deeper thoughts, deeper troubles.

When I saw him wandering in the sycamore grove, I knew something must be troubling him. But I felt it best to leave him alone to work it out. After my most recent conversation with him, however, I feel he is in dire need of advice. A woman has engulfed his soul and is tearing him apart, and I feel something rash on the horizon.

He desperately feels that Cupid's arrow has struck him deep. But the one he loves has the wit of Diane and vows to live chaste. I advised him to forget her, but his love is too strong. I am concerned, Old Montague, and unsure how to proceed. I want what is best for Romeo, but I cannot get through to him. Please counsel me or address young Romeo yourself, for he is in dire need.

Benvolio

In a lighter vein, another student created a note from the surprised friar upon hearing of Romeo's infatuation with Juliet:

Dear Romeo,

Holy Saint Francis! Romeo, is it really true that you have fallen for the daughter of a Capulet? What of dear Rosaline, so pretty and fair? She is the perfect match for you, a perfect pair. Why Romeo, do you consort with thy enemy? There are so many beautiful maidens that your eyes may feast upon.

Romeo, remember that a young man's love may come and go like the wind. Good God, Romeo, love is so blind. I, however, will stand by you in your hour of need. After all, it is better to love thy enemy than never to love at all. I'll assist you in your quest for passion, and marry both of you at once. Perhaps your true love for each other will unite your enemy households and restore peace. Through the power of love, hate is destroyed. My only advice to you, Romeo, is to proceed with patience. Those who leap before they look find themselves in a deep hole. Go with God.

Fair well my son,
The Friar

Because students invariably find Shakespeare's language and metrics daunting, I encourage them to begin in any style they feel comfortable with. At first, most choose simple prose letters or diary entries. But as they become more comfortable reading the plays and the Bard's image undergoes its inevitable demystification, I begin suggesting experiments with poetry, both rhyme and blank verse. One very talented young man found rhyme an effective tool for capturing Tybalt's frustrated attempts to balance and control his volatile emotions in a diary entry immediately after recognizing Romeo at the masked ball:

I seek only to spare our family's name
From any trouble, bloodshed, or great shame
That well may rise from uninvited guests
As Romeo and his team of masked pests.
He enters in, intrudes upon our feast
And good intentions shows his family least.
But dear old Capulet says I should hush
While rather my command would be to rush
Those rascals out so far from off our grounds
And chase them back to where they should be found.
But Capulet, his word I must obey,
And though I may argue, do what he say.
He is the wise old head and I the boy
But surely Montague will bring no joy.

Occasionally this creativity turns comic, as when a male student decided to recreate a personal ad placed by the Nurse in the Verona *Sentinel.*

To the beefcake of my dreams:
I am in need of a strong man, I am.
Many be the long night I spend alone
Since the departing of my dear 'usband.
Though my bones may ache and my back may 'urt,
Used up I am not. I do crave but just
A bit of naughty fun by the moonlight!
A trim twenty and two stone do I weigh.
The healthiest in Verona some say!
Italian Stallions need not apply.

Ah! and I prithee, a non-smoker please.

Nursie

Students' creativity appeared in some ways I had not anticipated. A surprising number of letters arrived in envelopes, some sealed with wax and one with a home-made seal featuring a heart enclosing an intertwined R and J. Students often used font options on their computers to recreate handwriting or gothic script. Addresses on the envelopes often revealed a sense of humor, as in the one I found attached to the door of my office (Room 209), addressed to the deposed Richard II ("King Richard, Prison Tower, Room 209, London, England 90210"). Obviously a television fan. One letter by the distraught Ophelia in *Hamlet* came ripped into jigsaw pieces and another stained with tears. At least, I hope they were meant to be tears. And for her last project on *The Tempest*, one of my most consistently creative students gave me a bottle containing the letter Miranda had set adrift in hope of someone finding it and rescuing her and her daddy, Prospero.

In *1 Henry IV* the fiery nobleman Henry Hotspur, furious with King Henry IV's demand for the rebel Lord Mortimer, whom Hotspur had captured after what he recalls as an epic fight, decides he will refuse to turn over his prisoner. In his ranting, the young warrior promises to train a nightingale to haunt the king by screeching Mortimer's name over and over. Hotspur's temper tantrum inspired a student to imagine a speech for the nightingale:

EERRAAHH!! Mortimer, Mortimer, MORTIMER!
My master has instilled in me, a task
That is born of hostility and wrath.
Be it known'st unto you and your minion,
That I am given to you by Hotspur,
So that you shall never forget "Mortimer!"
A sly and cunning plan it is indeed,
I surely hope that you shan't need earplugs
To sleep while I screech my boisterous cry,
And violate your repose whils't you lie.
But be sure to keep your calm while I fly
Through the vestibules of your disturbed home,
For if my feathers are attacked only once,
I most certainly shall be forced to cry
All the louder, "Mortimer, MORTIMER!"

Contemporary concerns inevitably work their way into the students' projects, as when one student decided to have the ultra-macho Hotspur reflect in his diary on one of the nineties' more curious athletic heroes:

> Dear Diary,
>> Today I find this wretched NBA
>> To be in quite a sad state of affairs.
>> 'Tis great folly to see upon the court
>> Players adorned with multi-colored hair.
>> This Dennis Rodman is the worst of them
>> By far. I hath heard he doth prance about
>> In the most un-manly dresses and wigs.
>> Is this the example we wish to set
>> For young boys who are to become soldiers?
>> This Rodman is no better than Prince Hal!
>> Is armour to be replaced by knight gowns?
>> And our swords to be replaced by purses?
>> Were I to meet this vile Dennis Rodman,
>> I would surely have him drawn and quartered
>> Just to see if he was indeed a man!

Combining a contemporary fascination with the psychology of death and the possibilities presented by computer fonts, one of the most talented of the writers in the class used an assignment on *Hamlet* to recreate Ophelia's suicide note. Finding a visual metaphor in the computer's fonts for the conflicting thoughts and emotions competing in her mind, he blended details from the play, contemporary imagery, and a suggestion of an additional motive in a possible pregnancy to create a clever and poignant image of a young woman who can see no options in her life:

Ophelia's Journal
Why should **everyone** *think I am* **insane**,
When all **I DEAL with** *is terrible* **pain!**
MY Father **is dead**, and my **Hamlet gone**,
THEY THINK I BEHAVE as if I were **blonde**.
YET, pity is harsh. **Hamlet** has **no love**
For me. AS black **is no col'r** f or **a dove**
'Tis rotten **shame that** I should bear his child,
With no **love** from him as if I **were** *wild*.
Life has no end, *but cease to* exist **I will**,
Perhaps I **will** drown, or jump <u>OFF A HILL</u>

For life without *Hamlet* or Dad is none,
I certainly wish THAT I HAD *a gun.*
Oh well. Life'S dull and so is apple *pie.*,
I *surely see now's* the best **time to** die!

While these exercises very clearly have their limits, they have offered me some wonderful insights into how my students read the plays. In addition, a surprising number of class discussions have sprung from ideas embedded in student letters and diary entries. For some students, as always, these projects will appear merely one more obstacle to hurdle or scramble over, one more exercise by teachers intent on frustrating their evening or weekend plans. Even those students, however, occasionally find themselves fascinated with creating a letter or diary entry by one of the characters in a play. Most students find irresistible the opportunity to engage the play on a more personal level and work it into their own frames of understanding. Far more than traditional assignments, such creative explorations into the minds and souls of Shakespeare's characters offer students the kinds of insights into Shakespeare's mind and art that once motivated Mary Cowden Clark to re-imagine the childhoods of his heroines and Tom Stoppard to recreate the hopes and fears of even his most minor figures.

Act V

Playing with Challenges

Words, Words, Words:
Shakespeare for Students with Limited English Proficiency

Silvia Hurtado de Mendoza

Silvia Hurtado de Mendoza, an Orange County school psychologist who works as a diagnostician at the county's Early Intervention Center, discusses strategies for working with students of limited English proficiency.

ONE OF THE MOST DISTINCTIVE FEATURES of contemporary teaching is the number of students from varied cultural backgrounds in our classes. With one of the most diverse populations in the nation, Florida's schools have become an exciting and often challenging patchwork of backgrounds, values, and languages. Teachers no longer face the homogeneous, monolingual classrooms that characterized the state only a few decades ago. Instead, our students can have first languages that range from Spanish and Arabic to Yoruba and Tagalog, from Vietnamese and French to Mon-Khmer and Haitian Creole. Congress has pointed out that American students speak virtually all world languages, in addition to those indigenous to the United States (H.R. Act 6, Sec. 7102 [1994]). In Florida alone, students speak 219 languages, including the state's native Muskogee and Miccosukee dialects.

All of us face a number of challenges in introducing Shakespeare to this new world of the American classroom. Although 83.7% of Florida's students enter school with some proficiency in English, their levels of ability can vary significantly. Many of these students, as well as those acquiring English as a second language, are also learning new cultural norms. If we want to provide the optimal educational experience for all our students, we need to recognize the cultures and languages represented within the classroom and to develop lessons that challenge students sensitively and creatively.

Before teaching language arts to students of limited English proficiency (LEP), we first need to recognize how any second language is acquired. Like all new residents whose first language is not English, our students progress through three clearly defined processes in learning a second language: (1) automatic habit formation; (2) conscious rule learning; and (3) the natural acquisition of meaningful language (Hamayan & Damico 39). Habit formation is a fairly simple and natural process which involves making the phrases frequently used in everyday language part of our verbal repertoire through repeated use. We learn the grammar, phonology, and semantics of a second language, on the other hand, through a conscious study of rules. While engaged in habit formation and conscious rule learning, we acquire meaningful language in a process very similar to the way we learned our first language. Language development typically begins with a silent stage, technically referred to as the pre-production phase. Once production emerges, it does so systematically. Single words are followed by short phrases, which eventually merge into longer and more complete sentences. Remember that errors are an essential part of this acquisition process, and, as teachers, we need to develop strategies for correcting our students without discouraging them.

The speed at which a person acquires a second language depends, of course, on a variety of factors, including but not limited to proficiency in the first language and the age at which the second language is learned. Students having difficulties with a second language, for example, may lack a solid foundation in their native tongue. And, as many of us have come to realize, younger children are more adept at picking up second languages. Because English proficiency may vary greatly from student to student within the same class, it is important to be aware of all of our students' backgrounds and levels of exposure to English by inspecting cumulative records and engaging in dialogues with them.

Although language proficiency, a multi-faceted, multi-leveled phenomenon, has a variety of theoretical and practical definitions, practically speaking, it refers to the degree of control one has over a language. That control focuses on four major skills: listening, speaking, reading, and writing. Because these skills have some level of independence from each other, they may develop separately (Hamayan & Damico, 40-42). In acquiring a second language, as in the primary language, social language develops before academic language. People visiting other countries for extended periods of time, for example, generally develop the social aspects of a country's language (i.e., listening and speaking skills) first. Generations of immigrants to the United States from non-English speaking countries, including many of our own parents and grandparents, used these skills to conduct their daily lives.

Teaching Shakespeare to any secondary student is challenging;

doing so with LEP and/or bilingual students presents unique challenges. Shakespeare's language, for example, seems foreign to all high school students, even those whose native language is English. Filled with unfamiliar words and figurative language rooted in Elizabethan England, many of his words have multiple meanings and special connotations. To our bilingual students, it seems as unlike English as their native tongue. For them, the difficulties are compounded. Moreover, there may well be many varying levels of skills within any one classroom. Recognizing all of this, it is clear that the most effective way to teach Shakespeare's plays is to use multiple methods. An effective way to begin is to focus on the themes of the plays. Although our students may not have base knowledge of Shakespeare or Elizabethan England, Shakespeare's themes are universal.

Before presenting the texts themselves, introducing such universal themes as love, family, and betrayal can provoke lively discussions among teenagers from any culture. Because of the nature of social language development, LEP students might especially benefit from these classroom conversations as a primary method of instruction. They allow students to bring their own experiences and cultures into class discussions, greatly enriching the conversation. Teachers, of course, should take care to include all students and check for comprehension among those of lower proficiency levels.

Shakespeare's more popular plays can be especially useful with lessons and homework assignments revolving around cultural differences among students within the same classroom and differences between the present and the Renaissance. Since *Romeo and Juliet* is known worldwide, most students are already familiar with some parts of the story. An effective early homework assignment is to have students discuss with their families the differences between their ideas of an ideal mate and their parents' ideas. Begin with classroom discussions that have students describe the qualities of their ideal mate and rate those qualities in order of importance. At home the students can ask their parents and even grandparents to share their ideas of the ideal mate. Exercises that allow students to relate Shakespeare's plays to their lives and families are an ideal way to stimulate interest and provide fascinating conversations both within and beyond the classroom.

Knowledge of Shakespeare's historical period can be invaluable for LEP and second-language students studying his plays. One or two lessons covering the Renaissance will provide students with an understanding of the culture in which Romeo and Juliet lived. Be sure to use the many informative videos and booklets on Shakespeare's life, Elizabethan customs, and costumes. Visuals such as posters and examples of costumes are particularly useful. Additional assignments may include casting the play with today's actors or students' cultural icons and creating marquees with alternate titles to the drama.

When beginning discussions of the play itself, always present the story first. Because of the difficulties the language poses, all students will benefit from familiarity with the plot before being exposed to the text. The story can first be presented through a variety of methods, including summary and simplified editions. For the text itself, many editions of Shakespeare give plenty of information about both vocabulary and meaning. Some teachers also use supplementary works like *Cliff's Notes Complete Study Editions* in combination with excerpts from the original text.

Language arts teachers often wish to present the original text in its entirety. For LEP and/or bilingual students, teachers need not choose between modified versions and the original text. The golden rule is never to have students read the text on their own. They should be introduced to the text only after they are familiar with the story line. One technique that always works well is to allow students to listen to an audio recording while reading the text, a practice which allows them to hear Shakespeare's poetic language without constantly struggling to read *and* understand it. If students are already familiar with the plot, an audio version can help them follow the story, while the actors' inflections and tone will add to their understanding of the play. It is important to provide students with the opportunity to hear and see the traditional text without requiring them to read it without assistance. Reading and discussing *Romeo and Juliet* should be done as a class, and students should be encouraged to talk about scenes and predict subsequent actions of the characters involved in those scenes. Such interactions promote understanding and interest in the drama.

Because *Romeo and Juliet* was written as a play, it can best be experienced by students as a production. Like all learners, LEP students benefit from participating in dramatizing scenes as both performers and audiences. By this point in the Shakespeare unit, learners have interacted with each other in discussion of themselves as well as of Shakespeare's characters. Since the class is now a culture in and of themselves, dramatizations should be done within the classroom. At this time, the teacher can use many of the techniques discussed in other essays in *Shakespeare Plays the Classroom*. If you divide a class with a variety of different cultures into small groups, those groups should be heterogeneous to provide for differing viewpoints within each group. These mini productions within the classroom stimulate imagination and interest in other cultures. Once each group is assigned a scene and develops props and costumes, consider allowing–or even encouraging– students to take some artistic license. Strict adherence to the text may not be the purpose of this exercise; it may, for example, offer them a chance to further explore the universal themes presented in Shakespeare's plays. Cultural differences will often emerge as themes within scenes, especially when students draw parallels between their own lives and those of Romeo and Juliet. Many students may also choose to use a mixture of their native tongue in combination with English when producing their scenes. If they do, make sure they provide translations into English within the dramatization. After discussing Elizabethan history and theater practices, the teacher may want to experiment with males playing female characters and vice versa in the classroom as an alternate way to dramatize scenes.

As a final lesson within the unit, teachers should try to take the class to a production of the play or present a VHS or DVD version of the play. Because the students are now familiar with the play and have discussed it in several contexts, they will usually find a traditional interpretation fascinating. Of the many versions available, those which are most faithful to the standard text are usually best. While popular among students, many modern versions take a good deal of license with the story, adding or deleting from speeches, scenes and the story line. If you cannot find a traditional interpretation and need to rely on a version that alters the text in significant ways, make sure you preview it and note where the movie varies from the original text. Discuss these changes with the class before viewing the movie. While native English speakers may not find these differences distracting, LEP and bilingual students may, depending on the level of their English proficiency.

Depending on time constraints, instructors may also opt to present modern adaptations of the plays, both movies and musicals. *West Side Story* has proven an especially popular adaptation for Hispanic students because it allows them to identify with many of the play's cultural conflicts. During classroom discussions of these films, students often raise intriguing comparisons and connections among the play, the movie, and their lives. Not surprisingly, the early homework assignment involving their parents' ideas versus their own frequently resurfaces during these discussions.

Finally, when evaluating LEP students, alternate types of assessment should supplement traditional tests, with grades combining tests and assignments. In determining how to test an LEP student's knowledge of any unit, keep in mind the fact that the social aspects of language are the first to develop during second language acquisition.

Therefore, traditional paper/pencil tests may prove the least effective method of evaluation. Oral tests, class projects, and homework assignments can offer a more accurate measure of an LEP student's knowledge and should supplement any written examinations. Because the academic language of LEP students remains at the concrete stage longest during the process of second language acquisition, written tests should concentrate on factual information regarding the unit.

Although challenging, teaching Shakespeare in a multi-cultural, multi-linguistic setting can be a fascinating and rewarding process. Both teachers and students are likely to learn unexpected things from each other. Anyone willing to approach Shakespeare's work in its full richness and universality will find that, rather than detracting from the learning process, diversity within the classroom enriches and deepens the experience for all of us.

References

Fradd, Sandra H., ed. *Creating Florida's Multilingual Global Work Force.* Tallahassee: Florida Department of Education, 1999.

Hamayan, E.V. and J.S. Damico, eds. *Limited Bias in the Assessment of Bilingual Students.* Austin, Texas: Pro-Ed, 1991.

Improving America's Schools Act of 1994, H.R. 6, 103d Cong., 2nd Session. Sec. 7102 (1994).

Setting the Stage for the Reluctant Reader

___☙

Noelle Morris and Andrea Moussaoui

Noelle Morris of Corner Lake Middle School and Andrea Moussaoui of Boone High outline a detailed lesson plan to help reluctant readers engage with A Midsummer Night's Dream *and* The Tempest.

___☙

I. Focus

Our focus in preparing these units was to create something for the reluctant reader in grades 7-12. It was our intent to create activities which invite the at-risk student into finding enjoyment with two of Shakespeare's plays. The direct experience that we had with at-risk students coupled with the limited amount of challenging teaching materials gave us the inspiration to create these plans. We know that as teachers of reluctant readers, our mission is to expand our students' backgrounds and increase the number of personal experiences that they have with the cultural and literary world.

II. Rationale

To read Shakespeare or not to read Shakespeare? Our students would say, "Is there really a question?" However, given a valuable opportunity to take ownership of Shakespeare's plays, they too could address him on a one-name basis.

The majority of our students today are not college bound, but our greatest intention is for them to become life-long readers. We know that students who read on a regular basis have better communication skills, increased creativity and critical thinking skills. They also gain the ability to escape their perceived limitations and create visions from the author's imagination. An experience with theater heightens all of these abilities. Therefore, we should use the same preparation and perspiration to help students become life-long admirers of theater. After all, a coupling of reading and theater education will allow the student to experience and participate in the interpretation of literature, consequently furthering students communication skills, creativity, and critical thinking skills.

The Task Force on Reading from the 1986 National Council of Teachers of English Conference stated that English teachers need "an extensive body of literature and literary types in English and in translation by people of many racial and ethnic groups, and by authors from many countries and cultures" and that teachers need to desire to "use the English language arts curriculum for helping students become familiar with diverse peoples and cultures" *(Guidelines* 9-11). Clearly, these guidelines hold that a teacher who has the job of increasing the background knowledge and reading ability of reluctant readers should not shy away from Shakespeare (even though some of our contemporaries insist that his writing is too difficult for students to understand). The teacher may find that with some help and interesting lessons the students are able to construe meaning and even admit having enjoyed the experience.

A Midsummer Night's Dream and *The Tempest* are two of Shakespeare's plays that offer much opportunity to the teacher or the reluctant reader. Most important, both are great fun and incredibly imaginative. Our lesson plans are constructed in a four-week unit for a traditional block of time. The plans give the students ample time to have hands-on experience with the plays and for the teacher to help and participate with them as they have fun, gain excitement, and increase their understanding.

III. Objectives

A. To provide students with background knowledge which will invite the reluctant reader into enjoying the reading of a Shakespearean play.

B. To provide students ample opportunities to express themselves both orally through discussion and creatively in written form while exploring character, themes, and story.

C. To provide students the opportunity to enhance their speaking and listening skills through the use of role-playing and music to bring about meaning and understanding.

IV. Units on *Dream* and *Tempest*

(Since teachers generally have the opportunity to use one or the other of these plays in the classroom, the first five days in both lesson plans are the same. The units are left open to such individual teaching styles as journaling and reflecting where necessary and desired.)

Week I: Introduction

Days 1 and 2: Introduction

Introduce Shakespeare and his plays through visuals and tangible objects such as pictures or models (e.g., the Globe Theater, the groundlings). Following are the suggested activities for the introduction:

1. Share a created portfolio of pictures, articles, artifacts, and playbills.

2. Discuss societal structure and have students draw from a hat to find their place in the established hierarchy of the period. Create a diagram which would display this hierarchy clearly. Show pictures of royalty, the land barons, the guilds, the working class, etc.

3. Visit Stratford-upon-Avon and the Globe Theater via the World Wide Web.

Day 3: Introduction to the Play and Parade of Characters

• 20 min. – Overview Summary for students from *Shakespeare for Beginners.*

• 30 min. – Synopsis of characters in play, mimicry of characters' dialogue, discussion of basic function of each character. One possible activity for *Dream* is the Name Game: Have students draw names out of a hat and decide which social group in the play that they fall into just based on the type of name that they have. Place three circles on the board and fill in the circles as the students play the game. Discuss the reasons for Shakespeare's having chosen these names.

• 5 min. – Assign Homework: Students receive a list describing characters and choose one that they like. They will then find a contemporary person who fits the same basic personality/social characteristics, and write a brief summary describing why they chose to make that comparison.

Day 4: Introduction to Movement

• 10 min. – Place students in small groups to discuss homework. Students choose one summary which best fits the assignment to share with the class.

• 35 min. – Demonstrate for students the importance of movement in performance of a character's traits and qualities. *Dream:* light, quick steps on tiptoes for fairies; clumsy, labored steps for the rustics; precise, grounded steps for the nobles; precise, light steps for the lovers. *Tempest:* light and swift for Ariel; clumsy and heavy for Caliban, Trinculo, and Stephano; precise and grounded for the nobles: precise and light for the lovers. (If at all possible, invite a representative from a local ballet company to be a guest leader in movement.) As students practice the movements, play music which will enhance the understanding of the characters' actions in the play (i.e., music from a score created for one of the plays or teacher-chosen selections if the former is unavailable).

• 5 min. – Reflection with the students: "Did movement increase your understanding of your character? How?"

Day 5: Picture Perfect

• 10 min. – Discussion: "Do you have the same visual image as you did on day 3? Having had more opportunity to know your character, do you think that the character in your homework assignment would be different? Why or why not?"

• 40 min. – Classroom Activity (materials needed: magazines, newspapers, scraps of material, all sorts of textured odds and ends, glue, scissors, markers, paints, crayons and construction paper): Using the materials, or by freehand, students will create a picture of the character they chose on day 3.

Week 2–Week 4: *A MIDSUMMER NIGHT'S DREAM*
Week 2
Day 1: The Elements of Story

•10 min. – Mini-lesson: Give students the definition of story and let them discuss examples and non-examples. Give them the following journal topic: What makes a good story?

•40 min. – Show video of Acts I and II: Read to the class and discuss.

•5 min. – Give Homework: A writing assignment on "First Impressions" (This exercise is adapted from Stephen Kresky's *Write Away*.)

Write down your first impression of the following characters based on what you know about them up to this point: Theseus, Hippolyta, Oberon, Titania.

Day 2: On with the Show

• 10 min. – Mini-lesson: Give the students the definition of setting and discuss examples. Give the students the following journal topic: What is the setting for *Dream* and how can you tell?

• 40 min. – Act III: Show video and Act IV - Read to the class and discuss.

Day 3: Themes
- 10 min. – Mini-lesson: Give the students the definition of theme. Discuss some examples and have them give the themes in Dream (e.g., love, friendship, magic, traditions, family, honor).
- 20 min. – Classroom Activity: Illustrate a theme in one of the scenes. (Materials needed: construction paper, markers, colored pencils, and crayons) Choose one of the scenes and draw a picture to illustrate the theme. On the back of your picture, write a brief explanation.
- 20 min. – Act V–Show video and discuss.

Day 4: How Do Actors Do What They Do?
- 50 min. – Guest speaker–Ask a member of a theater group, your school's drama instructor, or a graduate student studying theater to discuss with the students how an actor gets into character. Have him/her explain what is involved in memorizing lines.

Day 5: Writing for Fun: "What Shakespeare left out . . . "
- 50 min. – Have the students choose one of the following to write, edit, rewrite, and publish:
    1. A wedding announcement
    2. Puck's Rap
    3. A police report filed by Demetrius against Helena on charges of stalking
    4. A song sung by the rustics
    5. A poem written by Lysander to Helena
    6. A poem written by Demetrius to Helena
    7. A poem written by Lysander to Hermia
    8. A letter to Ann Landers from Helena

Week 3

Day 1: Returning to the Text
- 15 min. – Review setting, characterization, and theme. Discuss with the students what they think was the strongest element used by Shakespeare to create his story.
- 20 min. – Present a lesson on writing to respond to literature. Give notes and read an example.
- 15 min.– Have students begin writing their responses to *Dream* using the strategies you have introduced to them.

Day 2: Writing to Respond to Literature Continued
- 50 min.– Have students continue with responses, edit, rewrite, and publish.

Day 3: Grammar in Context

•20 min. – Then and Now Mini-lesson: Review pronouns. For practice, have students rewrite Act II, scene 2, lines 134-143, changing the pronouns where necessary.

•20 min. – Mini-lesson: Punctuating dialogue. Review quotation marks and how and when they are used. For practice, have students rewrite Act 1, scene 1, lines 193–202 as if Puck were telling the story. (i.e., So then Hermia said, ". . ."

•10 min. – Give students their assigned group number and scene. Give them the rest of the period to review the scene, characters involved, and the situation.

Day 4: From Students to Actors

•50 min. – Rehearsals: Have students rehearse the reading and prepare for presentations.

Day 5: Opening Night

•45 min. – Set the mood for the students' presentations by coming in costume, creating Athens, and bringing in Greek cuisine. Groups will share their interpretations of their assigned scene through a performance.

•5 min. – Reflection: "Did you gain more understanding from your acting debut?"

Week 4

Day 1: Completing Your Experience

•10 min. – Have your students choose a partner or form a group of three. Give them a created rubric to use as guide to know how the projects are evaluated, and select one of the following projects:

    1. Write a plot for a 90s television sitcom

    2. Write a script for a soap opera

    3. Choreograph and videotape a music video for the fairy lullaby

    4. Write a skit for Saturday Night Live

Projects must use characters and a central theme from *Dream*, but dialogue must be original unless the group chooses #3.

Day 2–4: Work on Projects and Toward Completion

•50 min. – Have students work in their groups to complete projects. Give them some directions reminding them of the elements of story, characterization, and theme. Suggest to them to use one of the following:

    1. Power Point or Other Multimedia Presentation Program

    2. Videos

3. Word Processing Programs or Web Sites

4. Puppet Shows

Play music to create a background conducive to learning (i.e., reintroduce the score from *Dream.*) Encourage students to use music in their presentation to increase the audience's understanding of the play.

Day 5: The Finale

•40 min. – Have students present their projects. Give a rubric for students to use to score their peer's projects.

•10 min. – Final Reflection: "What have you learned from this unit? What is the most memorable activity for you?"

Week 2–Week 4: *THE TEMPEST*

Week 2

Day 1

•10 min. – Give students the definition of story and plot. Talk about Shakespeare's plot devices in *Tempest.*

•40 min. – Show video of Act I: Discuss the storm and the reasons why Prospero starts the story with a controlled storm. Discuss the storm's importance to the plot.

•5 min. – Give homework. Give students a handout with Act 1, scene ii, 190-237 on it. Have them write a story reporting the storm for a newspaper where they, as omniscient overseers, describe where everyone landed on the island and what shape they were in.

Day 2

•10 min. – Read news stories in small groups and have students choose one that seems most interesting. Have them discuss what ingredients hold their interest.

•10 min. – Mini-lesson on latitude and longitude. Use an overhead, a map and a globe to explain latitude and longitude. Discuss the place where the ship might have landed based on textual clues.

•20 min. – Have students look at globes in small groups and talk about what countries are close by the pinpointed spot on the globe. Discuss influences, sounds, dialects, weather, and seasons that one might find at that particular spot because of its location.

•10 min. – Journal Assignment: Have students write their thoughts about the setting and atmosphere up to this time.

Day 3–The Island

•5 min. – Discuss the journal assignment from the previous day. Have students reread their entries.

•30 min. – Choose one of the following two classroom activities or create another similar one. (Materials needed: construction paper, glue, markers, scissors, paints, and any other odds and ends that you have for creating pictures).

> 1. Draw your island showing where it is in relation to the other countries around it. Use the classroom maps and globes to ensure that your drawing is accurate. Label the countries surrounding your island.
>
> 2. Draw the island from an overhead view where you label certain places on the island that show where all the passengers on the ship landed. Use the lines in Act 1.ii.190-237 for that information.

Day 4–The First Time Ever I Saw Your Face

•10 min. – Mini-lesson: Discuss themes in *Tempest*. Ask students to brainstorm possible themes in the story up to this point such as magic, power, and love.

•5 min. – Re-read I.ii.406-503 and discuss how the students would feel in Miranda's shoes, seeing a man for the first time. Discuss the themes surrounding this idea.

•5 min. – Journal Activity:"Write about how you would feel if you were in Miranda's shoes and seeing someone from the opposite sex (your age) for the first time."

•30 min. – Show video of Act 2 and discuss it.

Day 5–Laughter Is the Best Medicine

•10 min. – Discuss humor and characterization in Shakespeare's plays. Discuss the video piece from the day before.

•20 min. – Pick out certain scenes from Act 2 and call up students to act them out before the class. Have them imagine what Caliban must have looked like to Trinculo and how the two must have looked when Stephano found them.

•10 min. – Journal Writing: Write a descriptive paragraph showing in your own words the scene with Caliban, Trinculo, and Stephano in lines 1-107.

Week 3

Day 1–How Do Actors Do What They Do?

•50 min. – Guest Speaker: Ask a member of an acting company, your school's drama instructor, a local theater director, or a graduate student in theater to discuss with the students how an actor gets into character. Ask him/her to talk about memorizing lines.

Day 2–Moving Along
- 25 min. – Read Act III together as a class.
- 25 min. – Watch Act IV.

Day 3–Language and Meaning
- 10 min. – Mini-lesson: Discuss Shakespeare's choice of language for various characters.
- 10 min. – Choose some dialogue from each of the characters in Act IV and discuss the differences in how Shakespeare has them speak. Do characters each use a distinctly personal vocabulary? Do some use longer words? Rhymes?
- 15 min. – Ask three students to come up and act out lines 194-255 in Act IV.
- 5 min. – After reading the above lines, ask students if Caliban still seems like a monster. Discuss their varying responses.

Day 4–"All the World's a Stage"
- 30 min. – Watch Act V.
- 10 min. – Discuss Prospero's role in the last act and the idea that this is where he sums everything up, frees everyone, gives up his magical powers and forgives his wrongdoers.
- 10 min. – Journal Writing: "Write in your journal what you might have chosen to do with everyone had you been Prospero. Think about who deserved to be freed or forgiven, rewarded or punished, and who did not."

Day 5–Respond to the Play
- 15 min. – Mini-lesson: Review all the previously viewed concepts. Ask students about Prospero's possible motives in this play. Discuss whether and when his motives change.
- 20 min. – Ask students to compare and contrast Prospero and Caliban.
- 15 min. – Now ask students to write an essay emphasizing either the characters' similarities or differences.

Week 4–Rounding It Out
Day 1
- 50 min. – Students continue with responses, editing, rewriting, and publishing.

Day 2–Divide, Act and Conquer!
- 5 min. – Divide students into groups and have them choose out of a hat some possible pieces of the play to act out. Fifty

lines should be your maximum length.

•10 min. – Small groups discuss their scenes and begin to work out who will play what. Ask students to incorporate found costumes, movement, music, and artwork into their production.

•35 min. – Allow students time to work on their production while being available yourself as an advisor only. Try not to control their interpretations.

Day 3–Rehearsal

•50 min. – Rehearsals: Have students rehearse the reading and prepare for presentations.

Day 4–Curtains Up!

•45 min. – Set the mood for the students' presentations by coming in costume, creating a Mediterranean Island, and bringing in Island cuisine. Groups will share their interpretations of their assigned scene through a performance. Videotape their performances.

•5 min. – Reflection: Did you gain more understanding from your acting debut?

Day 5–Finale

• 40 min. – Show video of students' performances.

• 10 min. – Reflect on the experience gained from this unit.

V. Conclusion

By giving these students a thorough study of Shakespeare, we as teachers help to create potential life-long admirers of the theater and strengthen their literary connections. We hope that you and your students will have as much fun using our plans as we had creating them. We truly believe that you will gain many great teaching moments as your students make connections.

Resources

Krensky, Stephen. *Write Away*. New York: Scholastic, 1998.

Wolfe, Denny, Chair, National Council of Teachers of English Standing Committee on Teacher Preparation and Certification. *Guidelines for the Preparation of Teachers of English Language Arts*. Urbana, IL: NCTE, 1986.

The Young Company
A Shakespearean Story of Transformation

—☙

Judith Rubinger

Judith Rubinger describes the success of Orlando Shakespeare Festival's Young Company working with at-risk students.

—☙

THE YOUNG COMPANY IS A STORY OF TRANSFORMATION—of small miracles the likes of which I was privileged not only to bear witness to but to help bring about. While the young people who participated are the stars of this story, the process is one that can be universally applied. Before I move to methods, however, I want to describe three of the many instances of transformation that I witnessed in the seven years' duration of working with the singular and thrilling project formerly known as The Orlando Shakespeare Festival: The Young Company. I have selected these three cases not because they are unique, but rather because they are typical. I have also chosen them because they reflect something of the diversity of our student actors. Some of the names have been altered to respect the privacy of the individuals involved.

Carlos

Carlos was a tall handsome young man of Puerto Rican descent. At 19 he auditioned for our Shakespeare ensemble for the second year in a row. Carlos and his high school were constant combatants: he was as eager to be done with them as they with him. No one really knew where he stood academically at the time of his first audition; he seemed probably somewhere in his junior year. Our only certainty was his cockiness and consistently smug expression. That first year we ended up selecting a talented, but intensely shy, young man over Carlos.

When he reappeared at our audition the following season, Carlos arrived carrying a wooden cane. We learned that he had been involved in a battle with a vending machine that summer. Having flown into a rage over the loss of his change without receiving the requisite soft drink, Carlos had attacked the soda machine. With his exceptional strength, he had managed to knock it over; unfortunately, the unwieldy machine fell on his leg, crippling him. Once so very strong and arrogant, Carlos, at 19, would walk for the rest of his life with the aid of a cane. We selected the tall and strikingly handsome Carlos that next season for the role of King Alonso in our production of *The Tempest*. While retaining the superficial arrogance of an aspiring con-artist, Carlos now possessed a new, unwanted vulnerability.

As with the other participants in our ensemble, Carlos was assigned a mentor—one of a core of dedicated university students who opted to work with our ensemble, serving as big brothers and sisters, chauffeurs, academic tutors, line coaches, friends, advisors, and generally performing any additional supportive functions mutually deemed necessary and helpful.

Throughout *The Tempest,* King Alonso struggles with his conscience. He has betrayed Prospero, former Duke of Milan, and spends the play in a tempest of misadventures, leading to deep soul-searching remorse, genuine contrition, reconciliation with the man he has betrayed, and a final rediscovery of his personal integrity. While the king's transformation occurs in the final act of *The Tempest*, Carlos's transformation occurred two thirds of the way through our rehearsal period. I remember arriving at our rehearsal that day and being unexpectedly greeted by Carlos, who, together with his mentor, Samantha, nervously pulled me aside. As we headed towards one of the empty classrooms in the church building where we rehearsed, I wondered what this latest crisis would be about. I was accustomed to crises with these youngsters; in fact, there were only two certainties in the work we had undertaken: first, we could be sure that there would be more crises along the way than any of us would be prepared for, and secondly, we knew we would inevitably meet with the unexpected. Had someone gotten arrested, expelled from school, thrown out of his house, or possibly just decided to "quit" the company?

Samantha's words were startling. "Carlos called me at three this morning," she began. "He couldn't sleep." She then nudged Carlos, who hesitantly launched into his confession. He had phoned her in the middle of the night so consumed by guilt that he had been unable to sleep. Like the other members of the ensemble, he had signed a written contract with The Young Company, promising, among other things, to remain in school, maintain a certain academic standard, and graduate. Unbeknownst to any of us, he had been expelled from school several weeks earlier. Fearful of being dismissed for his breach of contract, Carlos had opted to keep this from all staff members. This time, however, instead of lying and manipulating, Carlos found that for the first time in his life, his conscience was bothering him—bothering him so badly, in fact, that he was compelled to confess—first to his mentor; later, to me.

Carlos expected to be dismissed from the production. Overwhelmed by his courage and newfound integrity, I came to an understanding with him and added an amendment to his contract. He would complete his studies in night school and take the high school equivalency exam to get his GED. With Samantha's assistance, I monitored his progress and he received his GED several months later. He also finished the season with The Young Company, presenting one of the most truly felt performances in the history of our ensemble. In recognition of his remarkable turnaround, I presented him with his King Alonso crown as a keepsake. Never was a king's crown more truly deserved.

Leora

Leora first appeared at one of our auditions upon the recommendation of a particularly perceptive history teacher. She was a fighter, he warned us, on the verge of being expelled from high school. Her problem seemed to be, in his opinion, that while she was enormously intelligent, she had become repeatedly frustrated in being insufficiently challenged by her school; moreover, she had patience neither for wasted classroom time nor for repeated academic "spoon feeding." Leora, her teacher informed us, desperately needed a positive creative channel for her overwhelming physical energy as well as for her mind.

The role of Titania, the fairy queen in *A Midsummer Night's Dream*, seemed ideal. Not only did Titania's words offer Leora an entrée into majestic poetry, the fantasy of the fairy world offered her an almost unlimited turf for her imagination. We found out as well, that Leora was a natural dancer—the explosive energy that she had formerly expended in fighting was almost limitless; willing to take exceptional risks, she undertook to explore and invent unique ways to move and vocalize. But her frustration and anger remained. Working with Leora was like a roller coaster ride; in the end, however, the discipline required by the production fueled by Leora's infatuation with the role of the fairy queen, prevailed. While much of her aggressive impulsiveness was rechanneled, an unresolved restlessness still seethed within her.

Much to my surprise, Leora applied and returned the following season as an alumni volunteer to work as a role model and support new members of the ensemble. I was, at first, skeptical at the prospect, for it would require a great deal of patience and tolerance, qualities which had not been her strong points. I also wondered whether Leora was Jewish (as her Hebrew-sounding name seemed to indicate) and whether this brilliant, but often private young woman had been driven by a desire to investigate her Jewish roots, for our production that season was to be an original adaptation of *The Merchant of Venice* set in the Buchenwald concentration camp of Nazi Germany. When asked about her name the previous season, she had responded that her name was not Hebrew but Italian.

Aware of the pervasive ignorance of our general student population regarding the holocaust, we asked the local Holocaust Memorial Resource and Education Center of Central Florida to help us with educational resource material and assistance. As their materials and advice were absorbed by our sensitive, racially diverse group of young people, I noted their growing awareness of the very real horrors of prejudice and intolerance—and of the terrible atrocities perpetrated against the Jewish people by the Nazi regime in their attempt and near success in annihilating an entire people. Genocide and respect for our various individual backgrounds became more than vocabulary words and casual clichés. And "political correctness" took on a deeper meaning.

Leora that season understudied the role of Jessica, the self-hating daughter to Shylock, the Jew. As in the case of Carlos, we were approximately four months into the rehearsal period when her transformation became manifest. Appearing at rehearsal one day, Leora declared that she had brought with her a precious personal possession—a silver Star of David. She had brought it, apparently, in connection with a discussion during the previous rehearsal, a discussion that centered around Jessica's decision to discard her Jewish faith, family, and community so as to ingratiate herself with the dominant Christian community. At a critical moment in the play, Jessica chooses not only to secretly elope with the morally bankrupt Lorenzo, but to betray her father as well, stealing most of his worldly possessions, including a priceless turquoise ring, a gift to Shylock from Leah, his beloved deceased wife and Jessica's mother. Our discussion ended with Leora's suggestion that perhaps at the moment of her momentous decision, she could remove a Star of David which she might be wearing about her neck, in order to symbolize her personal rejection of her faith and community.

Leora arrived at our rehearsal prepared to test out the symbolically powerful act of removing the Star of David during the critical scene in the play. That impressive moment became a crucial part of our production. Later that day, props were collected to be held for future rehearsals. Leora grabbed her Star of David. "I can't leave it here," she told me, "it was a gift from my grandparents, and I couldn't stand for anything to happen to it. I'll bring it back myself next rehearsal."

Bits and pieces of Leora's Jewish identity cropped up in subsequent rehearsals. We learned details regarding Leora's family and their personal connection to the holocaust, along with the fact that her name was not Italian but Hebrew.

To the amazement of some of her high school peers, cohorts, and even former teachers, Leora, now a senior in high school, received a full scholarship to Princeton University. She majored in Near Eastern and Judaic Studies and decided to study at Hebrew University in Jerusalem for a year. Fascinated by Middle Eastern politics and tremendously stimulated by the intelligent, intellectual discussions surrounding her at Princeton, she wrote me that she had finally "found" herself and she thanked me and The Young Company for enabling her to accept and even embrace her true identity.

Alexi

My earliest memory of Alexi is as a shy, skinny teenager with stringy, waist-long hair and poor posture who never took his eyes off his feet. Several of his fellow actors referred to him only half-jokingly as "Jesus" because of his long hair, beard, and piercing dark eyes. We did not know it at the time, but Alexi's terribly low self-esteem came coupled with an inwardly suppressed anger.

Alexi joined our production of *Romeo and Juliet* as Tybalt, Juliet's angry young cousin. Consistent with our practice, we shifted the setting of the play from Verona, Italy of the 1500s to Sarajevo of 1993. In our production, Romeo and his family were Serbian, Juliet and hers Bosnian.

Because there was little we as American students and teachers could do to alleviate the suffering of the people of Sarajevo, we set the more modest goals of raising both the students' and the community's awarenesss of the timeless causes of genocide, now often referred to as "ethnic cleansing."

Alexi's character, Tybalt, was a Bosnian whose animosity against Romeo and his Serbian cohorts plays an important role in fueling, if not instigating, the unfortunate series of events leading to the play's catastrophic outcome: the tragically premature deaths of six of its young characters. Over and over again, we struggled with Alexi, reminding him to stand up straight so as to give outward expression to his anger, rather than directing it, inaudibly, towards his feet. In truth, Alexi created an expressive portrait of a deeply troubled young Tybalt. The carefully choreographed fight scene in which he kills Mercutio, and is subsequently murdered by Romeo, was moving and suspenseful. With each performance, Alexi's self-confidence seemed to grow; with each new audience, his voice became more and more assuredly audible, focused, and disturbing.

Like Leora, Alexi returned for a second and then a third season to serve as an alumni volunteer to our ensemble. After three seasons of work with The Young Company, his initial lack of self-confidence was hardly perceptible. Moreover, he had become our most constant "savior," entering the scene over and over again, to "rescue" the ensemble from some of the unexpected, as well as expected, crises that went along with working with "at-risk" youngsters. Serving as an emergency driver, prop man, publicist, or pizza deliverer, Alexi's concern for the success and overall cohesion of the company assumed a devotion that became a true model.

Upon graduating from high school, Alexi entered the local community college. Two years later, he attended a Young Company reunion, surprising all of us by appearing with his beautiful fiancée–a confident and intelligent young woman of color. With his head erect, neatly trimmed hair, and clean-shaven face, Alexi exuded self-confidence and warmth. He had run for and obtained an important position in the student government and now hoped to enter politics.

Carlos, Leora, and Alexi continue to amaze me because of the transformative power of what might have appeared, at first sight, to be little more than a mere theatrical venture. What was it that produced these and other similarly dramatic outcomes?

In retrospect, I believe that the changes arose from three basic ingredients: firstly, a structure of interwoven and mutually dependent principles–principles which are indeed the principles of all good ensemble work; secondly, a serious, but original probe into the profoundly rich material provided by William Shakespeare; and, finally, the participation of an extraordinarily devoted group of staff, volunteer associates, and university mentors.

How did we manage such transformations? Through ensemble. As in all meaningful teaching, these principles must be practiced, rather than merely preached, by the director as a model, and subsequently, by all connected with the project. The principles activate a process and environment which must be reinforced, safeguarded, and continually applied throughout the six-month rehearsal period. Concerns about the product must come second; the priority must be the ongoing nurturing of a love for and joy in the ensemble process and the providing of a safe, supportive environment that encourages creative risk taking, playfulness and honest exploration. It is only by the initial setting aside of the limitations created by expectations about outcome, that true discoveries—about self, others, and the play—become possible. In the end, these very discoveries paradoxically result in remarkable productions of impressive truthfulness and serve as a springboard for originality and human transformation.

The fostering of self-acceptance and embracing of the work begins, in our case, with an opening orientation, in which ensemble members are introduced to the staff, university mentors, alumni volunteers, one another, and to the goals of the project. The atmosphere of this opening meeting is critical: a tone of enthusiasm, friendly camaraderie, and commitment to the work and to each other must be established from the first moment of the group's coming together. The mere act of sharing a snack—even of a most simple nature (our financial resources were limited)—we found well worth the minimal expense and effort involved in terms of the payoff in group cohesiveness and bonding, and so we came to provide snacks regularly at all rehearsals and ensemble meetings.

The Young Company requires a contract signing to precede all work with the ensemble. This contract signing takes place at the opening meeting of the ensemble and must be regarded with the utmost seriousness and respect. Once this matter has been completed, basic theater games and exercises aimed at reinforcing some of the principles enumerated above are implemented. Decisions regarding the ultimate casting of the production are reserved for later in the rehearsal process. The early emphasis is on learning to work together with attentiveness, acceptance, and trust, and on experiencing the joy of creative play and true interaction among the ensemble members.

The second ingredient requisite to the success of The Young Company is a serious, yet jubilant, examination of the text of the play itself. In our case, the text was generally edited, and, often adapted, by the artistic and consulting directors prior to its being introduced to the students. The play itself is introduced, in fact, only after several weeks of preliminary ensemble building. It is then read out loud, with members of the ensemble assuming and rotating roles in a manner that is both attentive and playful. The improvisational ensemble games and exercises continue but begin to take shape in the context of some of the emerging themes and images of the particular play that we are reading and preparing to perform. Improvisation, musical effects, and movement games are interjected into the reading of the text. The study atmosphere is one of open-minded joint exploration as we attempt to elicit and build connections–both personal and social–between the world of Shakespeare's text and that of the participants.

While the artistic director of our ensemble maintains final authority as to the ultimate direction the production will take, honest suggestions and creative exploration by cast members must be welcomed and incorporated into the end product, which will be a compilation of the suggestions (often the framework) introduced by the director and original, honest, but respectful probing of the characters and situations by ensemble members, mentors, and participating alumni volunteers.

A few words will suffice here regarding the third necessary ingredient in The Young Company story–the participation of a devoted core of staff, mentors, and volunteers. There is very little guidance to be offered in this area that is not already self-evident. Finding those rare individuals who would work successfully with "at-risk" teenagers has more to do with finding people with compassion and a strong desire to make a difference in the lives of young people than with any other learned skill that it is possible to acquire.

With all three of the required ingredients in place, then, the rehearsal process continues and the play begins to take shape. While the ensemble members must usually be repeatedly reminded that the work they have undertaken must be seriously committed to with focus and self-sacrifice, the atmosphere of spontaneous playfulness must always be preserved. Characters and scenes are continuously open to development, reevaluation, and change. The combination of these apparent opposites–disciplined focus and free spontaneous play–can be challenging and frustrating; with perseverance and faith in the process, however, the shared struggle to realize an effective balance of opposites serves as a powerful unifying force in bonding the ensemble. Upon reflection, it occurs to me, in fact, that this is indeed a microcosm of the struggle that each one of us must do battle with as we grapple with challenging issues confronting the day-to-day living of our lives. Moreover, the notion that there may just possibly be a positive creative application to living life joyfully in the moment and relating to others honestly and without prejudgment of outcome, while maintaining our sense of discipline and focused perseverance–may be one of the most valuable lessons to be drawn from an experience such as The Young Company.

Are the unique personally transformative outcomes to be realized through the journey a matter of the miraculous or due merely to a common-sense process as simple as respecting our young people as human souls awaiting the opportunity to be heard, challenged to understand, think independently, and create with singular individuality? I leave this to your own determination. For me, however, as well as for those who have worked alongside of me, the visible results in human transformation continue to testify to the fact that the process inevitably works. And whether it is a matter of miracle, faith, or plain common sense, The Young Company's program is one whose replication might just serve that need for meaningful discovery of self that continues to be so painfully unmet for countless young people today. And let us remember that Shakespeare's favorite book was Ovid's *Metamorphosis*.

Epilogue
Shakespeare, Summer, and Kids

___୧

Sidney Homan

Sidney R. Homan, a professor of English at the University of Florida, offers an overview of a broad initiative to bring Shakespeare to Gainesville's youth. An award-winning actor, director, and producer, he has published influential books on Shakespeare and modern theater, produced and directed Samuel Beckett's Waiting for Godot in Florida prisons, and worked with teachers and students throughout Northern Florida.

___୧

SEVEN YEARS AGO, THE GAINESVILLE ASSOCIATION for the Creative Arts launched an ambitious program called "Shakespeare, Summer, and Kids." With a grant from Gainesville's Department of Cultural Affairs, it formed three companies of middle- and high-school students, fifteen to seventeen people to a company. Funds for scholarships allowed the GACA to include children from different economic and cultural backgrounds, and especially at-risk students. Each company staged one of Shakespeare's comedies. Rehearsals generally ran two to three hours a day, four days a week, for five weeks. Directors were chosen who had had experience working with young people, but who, no less, were accomplished artists in the theater. That is, the concern was not just "putting on a play" for the delight of the parents, though this surely was one goal, but even more, exposing the actors to the challenges, the demand, the rules, and professional etiquette of "real" theater. In the course of the rehearsals, the actors also gained experience in every aspect of the theater (from set design to preparing the program, from publicity to costuming, lighting to stage management).

At the end of the five weeks each company gave several performances in a variety of settings ranging from a local theater to retirement communities. Initially, "Shakespeare, Summer, and Kids" focused mostly on Shakespeare's early comedies: *The Comedy of Errors, Two Gentlemen of Verona, A Midsummer Night's Dream, Twelfth Night, The Merry Wives of Windsor,* and *The Tempest.* The reason for confining the repertoire to comedies was that these, we thought, would be most accessible to young people, By the fifth year, however, we felt confident enough to include *Macbeth* and to venture into Stoppard's serio-comic reworking of *Hamlet, Rosencrantz and Guildenstern Are Dead.*

What Happened and What It Cost

I am happy to report that in seven years, staging twenty-one plays and giving some sixty performances, we had no major problems. The kids quickly realized that they were members of a company, that they had a "product" to make within five short weeks, that they had to submerge their own personal needs and agendas to the good of the production. On their part, the parents just as quickly learned that rehearsals started promptly, and adjusted their drop-off and pick-up schedules accordingly. More than that, the parents pitched in by lending household items for the sets, sewing costumes, providing snacks, getting every aunt and uncle to attend the performance. There was, ultimately, no difference during rehearsals between "regular" (or whatever adjective will suffice here) and at-risk kids. Friendships were formed. Coming from all over the city, from different schools, strangers, representing a collage of races and economic and social backgrounds, the kids, without exception, became a cohesive company, and quickly.

There were numerous reasons for this. We were doing Shakespeare, the ultimate, the most radical, the coolest of playwrights. And we were doing him like professionals. The laws of the theater held sway. We had fun, but it was not shallow fun where putting on the play is the means not the end, where the end is little more than having an after-school activity or pleasing parents and grandparents. But taking Shakespeare, the theater seriously led to an "ensemble" spirit among the cast, the sense that they had shared a sacred task.

The program was also a success in terms of audiences. We received numerous compliments that affirmed the quality of the productions—even making allowances for those special critical dispensations given to younger performers, or for biased relatives. I've worked in the theater long enough to be able to separate the praise of well-wishers from the more sober judgments, pro and con, of audience members who take a production seriously.

An easier measure of success was the size of the audiences. Again, making allowances for the fact that we could count on parents and friends coming, the fact remains that our houses were uniformly full, indeed overflowing with audiences often showing up at 5:30 p.m. for a 7:00 p.m. curtain.

I should also add that we—the GACA staff, the kids themselves, and their parents—also did our part in building audiences. It was not unusual for an actor, at the suggestion of the director, to have twelve or so friends at a performance; posters were prominent in every business that the parents of our actors frequented. The very novelty of staging three productions of Shakespeare by three different companies within a one-week period and in a relatively small town appealed to the media, and so "Shakespeare, Summer, and Kids" got more than its share of publicity, both requested and volunteered.

Our costs were minimal. We paid each director (for preparation, five weeks of rehearsal, and performances). I received a similar amount as general director of the program, a job that involved cutting the texts, visiting each of the companies, coming in—on the director's invitation, of course—whenever they needed my help, and assisting with the publicity and general management of the program. We gave each production $50 for set, costumes, and other expenses. The GACA itself budgeted for expenses connected with running the program, including office items, publicity costs (such as posters), and postage. Rehearsal and performance space was donated by the city's Department of Cultural Affairs and the Alachua County School System. We charged the kids $95 for enrollment and used the GACA's scholarship funds for at-risk students and others for whom the fee could have been prohibitive. Rather cost-effective, I think, given the fact that 'Shakespeare, Summer, and Kids" involved almost fifty young people, four directors, five weeks of intense rehearsals, nine performances, and a total audience estimated, conservatively, at 1,800.

Cutting the Text

Along with the plays chosen, the other major decision was to cut the text. In general, I cut the text by 60%, so that the running time for each play is, roughly, 50 to 55 minutes, rarely over an hour. Now purists will raise an alarm here. Cut Shakespeare? Sure.

Professional companies cut all the time. *Hamlet* without cuts runs over four hours. My assumption was and remains that, for young actors, a cut text has several advantages. First of all, there is that much less to learn, so the play becomes "manageable" not only for the performers also for their large heterogeneous audience. Besides, different audiences make different demands, have different expectations about the theater. If the clipped dialogue of a Samuel Beckett play or the interchanges in Harold Pinter would be unthinkable in the Renaissance, the reverse is also true: Shakespeare's age relished metaphor, extended similes, rhetorical devices in a way that ours does not.

Now there are ways and ways to cut texts. I've seen a production of *Hamlet* where Fortinbras and his over-plot were eliminated. In the nineteenth century, *Much Ado About Nothing* was often billed as Beatrice and Benedict, a signal that their witty skirmishes were left intact, while the Claudio-Hero affair, Don John's villainous plot, and the roles of the other courtiers were vastly curtailed.

My principle has been to cut lines but never to eliminate any scenes. The one exception was the young William's scene (where Shakespeare parodies a Latin lesson) and the German visitor scenes (mostly a topical allusion to some real-life German visitors to England) in *The Merry Wives of Windsor*. Both have nothing to do with any aspect of the main plot, although cutting the latter reduces somewhat the Host's lines. The conspirators' scenes in *The Tempest* (including Gonzalo's long discourse on utopia) were included, but more economically. My experience has been that these scenes bore audiences eager to see more of Prospero, the lovers Ferdinand and Miranda, and the comic subplot of Caliban, Trinculo, and Stephano. You don't want to cut the scenes in *A Midsummer Night's Dream* involving Bottom and his company, but, once the argument between Titania and Oberon over the changeling boy is established, the long passage given to listing the disorders in nature that have resulted from their quarrel can, I think, be cut somewhat. On only one occasion have I seen an audience "get" that extended jest linking time, the loss of hair, and porridge between Dromio and Antipholus of Syracuse in *The Comedy of Errors*. In *Much Ado* Shakespeare gives Don John only one scene (1.iii) in which to explain the cause of his villainy, and so I preserved almost all of his dialogue with Conrade, who cautions him to be more rational and restrain his anger. But a lot of the dialogue earlier in the play can be cut even though it establishes the mood of that shallow court surrounding Beatrice and Benedict. Conversely, you wouldn't want to drop a line from the "Kill Claudio" scene where Beatrice asks Benedict to prove his love for her by murdering his best friend. No one would want to cut any of the three Viola/Olivia scenes in *Twelfth Night* which chart Olivia's misdirected passion and, no less, her emergence form her posture a mourner for her dead brother. Nor would you want to cut the scene where Malvolio stumbles upon a supposed love letter, for in an instant the dour Puritan turns ardent swain. Keep those, to be sure, but search for where cuts can be made.

The *Comedy of Errors* is, by good chance, a relatively short play, and yet Adriana's long speech on marital fidelity, after it reveals the deep love she bears for her erring husband, retards the action. Conversely, I cut very little from Egeon's long speech at the beginning of that play where he recounts the tragic events that have splintered his family. That scene, something of a somber induction to the wild events that follow, establishes a contrastive mood and needs to be there in (almost) its entirety.

I cut passages that are just too obscure for the average audience. And sometimes, when Shakespeare offers us a string of metaphors, all with the same "objective correlative" (as T.S. Eliot would call it), I sometimes chose not to include all five. Would four do just as well? Or three? At times I shaped my dialogue so it would move more quickly.

Cutting is never absolutely good. And it has consequences. But my concern here is that young actors like Shakespeare, be willing to give him a chance, find him "do-able," that the director, working with a young company, can mount a good production in four weeks of rehearsal, and that the varied audience for those productions feel comfortable, with both the running time and the text itself. In no instance did I reduce Shakespeare to the mere plot. And I always tested the abridgments in rehearsals and performances ready to reconsider in both directions.

Given the length, it is even possible to do two plays in a single evening, in effect, offering the audience the more customary two to two and a half hours of playing time. Putting, say, the middle-class world of the *Merry Wives of Windsor* (with Falstaff its sole aristocrat, and one in disfavor at that) alongside the aristocratic *Much Ado About Nothing* makes for a wonderful pairing, or the mad, accident-driven world of *The Comedy of Errors* against Prospero's controlled island.

I also printed Shakespeare's verse as prose, because I think that doing so makes the text appear more "user-friendly" to the young person. It also keeps them from delivering the dialogue as if it were blank verse in a non-dramatic poem. The fact is that the rhythms are still there, both within and between lines, as are the color of individual lines; printing verse as prose, I find, encourages the young actor to adopt a more natural speaking style.

Some Ideas: Old, Perhaps Redundant, Perhaps New, Hopefully Useful, All with the Best Intentions

Some of these suggestions will seem obvious; if you have had experience staging shows, particularly with young people, I will be telling you nothing new. If not, my remarks will be of some help. Nor is anything absolute here. What I propose below comes from my own long and varied experience in the theater. At the risk of boring you, I'd rather be inclusive than exclusive. Many of these suggestions come from working with adult companies, and, in one sense, will apply to casts that are more mature than those I've worked with in "Shakespeare, Summer, and Kids." But they are no less relevant. You may, for example, find yourself directing a full-scale production involving young actors, one that has a four-week run in regular theater. Still, even if you are working with very young actors, and with an abridged text or a nontraditional theater space, you will want to apply as many of the professional standards and techniques to their work as you would with an older cast, amateur or professional. A warning: my concern here is the topics themselves, rather than the strict chronology of events attending a production. And so at times some items are purposely out of order: that is, remarks on the read-through preceded those in auditions.

Before you meet with anyone else—designers, actors, technicians—take time to develop your director's concept by yourself. Ask yourself some basic questions. What is the play about? What mood do I want to create? What relation with the audience? How would I define the "world" of the play? In what period do I want to set it in? Shakespeare's day? The present? How realistic or surreal do I want it to be? Is, say, *A Midsummer Night's Dream* essentially a parody of lovers or a feminist statement? Is that forest real? Or surreal, a forest of the mind? Given the presence of Bottom and his acting company, how much does the play have to do with the theater? Where should my production fall between the extremes of, say, realism and metadrama? How light or how dark should the comedy be?

Your production needs to start with you, with that clear director's concept. One of our "Shakespeare, Summer, and Kids" directors saw the *Comedy of Errors* as a precursor of the Marx Brothers films, and her director's concept, accordingly, set the style for everything from costumes to blocking. Another took Shakespeare's one rural comedy, *The Merry Wives of Windsor*, and put it in a hillbilly setting, complete with Southern accents, jugs of moonshine, and overalls and suspenders for Falstaff.

Delegate Responsibility (As Long as the Delegates Are Responsible)

The Ideal is for you to focus on directing and not to have to attend to publicity, or new set constructions, or the myriad of tasks involved in a production. It would be nice, for example, to have a producer who would coordinate everything from publicity to being sure that parents dropped off their kids on time, from making arrangements with the various places where you will perform to securing rehearsal space, from ordering any material for costumes to checking out the lighting, from handling the books (if you charge students a fee for the program) to keeping tabs on what progress—or lack of progress—your set designer or props person is making.

Speaking of designers, it would be heaven to have a set designer, even if that means little more than rearranging some of the available furniture or borrowing items from parents to establish a living room set. And a lighting designer; again, even if that might mean simply refocusing track lighting at the retirement center where you will perform so that it is set on the stage area. While we are at it, throw in a props person and a sound person. Such designers might enlist the kids to help them and hence give your actors valuable experience in the technical side of production. The point is, however, that as a director you don't have to do these tasks, even though each designer should be responsible to you, working within your general concept of the play.

And by all means have a stage manager, someone who can be "on-book" during rehearsals so that he or she can give a line to an actor, if needed, while you focus your ears and eyes on what is happening onstage. That same stage manager should literally "manage the stage" during the performances, while you stand at the back of the house, or even sit with the audience, or get in the way of everyone by insisting on being backstage, being "gloriously irrelevant," as one of my actors once called me during a performance. Pick a stage manager who can be tough as nails, who can take the heat, who can come down, lovingly but firmly, on the actor who has not memorized lines by an agreed-on date, or the assistant who does not have those rehearsal props ready on time. (See S. Reese for additional suggestions.)

Publicity

I've seen actors give the same good performance at a matinee with just three people in the audience as they did the evening before to a full house. An audience is an audience, but surely a full house, not to mention an enthusiastic house, turns on actors. A funny line that draws a response from, say, twenty-five percent of the audience will go over that much better if that percentage comes from two-hundred spectators rather than twenty. I myself get neurotic if there is even one empty seat in the house: it sits there, silent and uninvolved.

So, however difficult, I'd make full houses for every performance your goal. At the very least, you'll feel better if you do everything within your power to get that full house. I'd mail out publicity and PSAs (public service announcements) four weeks before the opening and then send out two "reminder" notices (two weeks and then three weeks later) to make sure that your original announcement has been received and, equally important, will be appearing at the right time). If your show opens on Friday, it would be great if there were an announcement in the paper the Friday before, or at very least in the Sunday edition; you certainly don't want the first announcement to come out opening night! Those "reminders" need to be carefully phrased. Surely, you don't want to say, "Just checking to make sure you are planning to publicize our opening well ahead of time." Rather, you might want to "disguise" the reminder with something like, "I just thought you might like to know that we now plan to have a five-piece orchestra playing background music for that production of *The Comedy of Errors* we announced two weeks ago and that will open on Friday, March 21." The person in charge of events will see through this but will most likely understand and not be offended. We have a single newspaper in our town, and, as a consequence, every arts organization is almost totally dependent on it. If, even by accident, *The Gainesville Sun* neglects to mention the run of a show, it is a disaster. Hence, the reminder.

Announcements in the media are, I think, the best publicity. To appear on the local television channel, during their noon news show, chatting about your production, is a godsend. Yet equally effective is the listing of the show and its dates on the public service radio broadcast sponsored, in our case, by a local funeral home! Posters, I think, are a tricky proposition. If they are too attractive, people rip them off. If they share space with fifty other posters, that presents a problem, compounded when, say someone advertising a garage sale puts an announcement on top of your poster. Now, a poster in the front window of a popular local restaurant is perfect, safe and secure and visible behind the glass.

The one thing I would never rely on is your own estimate of why or how many people will attend. "It's such a good show, I know everyone will want to see it!" Don't bet on it. "It's Shakespeare; of course they'll come. We should have full houses for all six performances." Don't bet on it. "I've heard lots of people say they plan to come." Absolutely don't bet on it. Of course, if you have a good show, and if the attendance the first weekend is good, word-of-mouth will help build an audience for the second week; if they also like the show, there will be a cumulative growth for the next two weekends of the run. If you get a good review in the local paper in the two days after the first weekend of the run, that will probably hold attendance the second weekend.

Still, building audiences is an art and . . . wait . . . change that . . .

your responsibility. I feel no shame in telling my actors that I want each of them to be personally responsible for bringing thirty paying people to the performance, not comps (we give each actor two complimentary tickets for a run, including two for the director, and no more). And I ask the actors to give me a list of the names of those thirty people. If your actors and cast are proud of the show, if they feel an investment in it, they won't mind doing this.

For a production of *Hamlet*, I made a deal with all the local high-school English teachers. I would come into their classes, with my actors, both talking about the production and illustrating my points with scenes from the play, if in turn they would bring their students, as a group to a performance. We offered them a special rate, $4 a ticket (instead of the $5 that we usually charge for students). We would even hold additional matinees so that the teachers could use school buses to transport the students.

Auditions

If you do hold auditions, remember that this is a trying time, especially for young actors. Even if you tell them that auditions are just a chance for you to measure what strength each actor has, to become familiar with them, the actors will see auditions as a competition, a test of their worth as actors, maybe even as people. Who gets the lead? Who gets the biggest part? Why was she called back? Why wasn't I?

I think it best during the initial phase of auditions that actors wait outside the theater and come in one by one: that is, their only audience is the director and perhaps his or her stage manager. You may have asked them ahead of time to prepare a one-minute dialogue or, if music is involved, a monologue and a song to be accompanied by a rehearsal pianist. Make sure each actor fills out a form, giving necessary information: name, telephone number, height, previous experience in the theater, any potential conflicts with the rehearsal and performance schedule which you might print at the top of the form. I think it useful if you have the actors check a "yes" or "no" before an entry that reads: "I will, if selected for this show, take any part." If "no," then ask the actor what part he or she would consider; but don't hold this against them. Also, on the form ask the actor to list any other abilities, such as stage management or lighting or costuming experience, and ask if the actor would like to help in any of these areas, whether or not the actor is chosen for the cast.

I also like to include what I call an "ethical obligation" clause. Here you ask the actor to respond to a statement followed by a reminder: "I am willing to be cast in any role in the production, or if I am interested in only a certain part (or parts) I indicate here [followed by a space]." The reminder reads: "Please understand that if you are cast in the production, it is your ethical and artistic obligation to fulfill that commitment." One actor told me he was willing to take any role in Stoppard's *Rosencrantz and Guildernstern Are Dead,* but when I called him the next day, saying I had cast him as one of the Tragedians, he came up with some lame excuse for dropping out of the production. I will never work with him again.

You might also, giving due notice, have a call-back the next night, telling the actors this first night that you will post the call-back list by a certain time and in a certain place tomorrow morning. Callback will resemble the cold-reading, except that far fewer actors will participate, and it will become clear that you are thinking of certain actors for certain parts. Tell them that the next day, again at a specific hour and place, you will post the cast list.

I always phone all actors who come out for auditions, thanking them for doing so, commiserating with those who were not chosen, hoping "we'll have a chance to work together in the future," asking that actor, not chosen but who said he was interested in props, if he might like to assist the props person. I also like to keep that initial list of audition candidates just in case.

Read-Through and Table Work

I hold read-throughs about a week before the start of the rehearsals. If parts have already been assigned, then the good actor will be prepared for the read-through, will have highlighted his or her part, will have read the play several times, and will have given some preliminary thought to the character. An actor who stumbles through the lines or even pronunciations at a read-through is obviously not prepared. (See Stu Omans' essay, "Standup, Listen, Whisper, Whistle, and Shout Your Way to Shakespeare: An Approach to a Three-Dimensional Read Through.")

A read-through serves several purposes. First of all, everyone gets to hear the entire play, something that might not happen again until later in the rehearsal process when you start doing run-through of the acts. For the director, the read-through can also give some sense of the play's running time.

One word of advice if you do make cuts in the text. Let's say that the play uncut will run three and a half hours, and you know this will be too long for your audience. I'd make cuts before the read-through. If there are numerous cuts, I'd try to give the actors a clean copy of the revised play, rather than the printed text showing lines deleted. Actors like to have as many lines as possible. If they get a clean text from the start, they will tend to treat this as the "official" version.

In addition to timing the revised text, you can also listen for moments when a cut isn't working: perhaps you've deleted an essential piece of information; perhaps the scene is too abridged. You can always restore lines.

Besides letting cast members become familiar with each other, with the other voices they will be hearing onstage, the read-through can also be a time when the actors experiment, trying out different deliveries and accents, emphases. Sometimes read-throughs can be terrible since everyone is afraid to commit, afraid to appear foolish, and so they rein in their voices, that sense of experiment, and just plod through the lines. But read-throughs can be exciting: the attitude is that since it's only the read-through what does one have to lose.

Some directors will even spend the day or two days after the read-through doing table work. That is, the company sits around the table, rereads the play, discusses it, makes suggestions, perhaps even answers Socratic questions from the director to get a feel of the script.

If you are meeting your actors for the first time at the read-through, then you can use the occasion as something of an audition. Pass around the parts, let everyone read four or five characters, make sure the actors know—for they have tender egos—that no parts have been assigned yet, that you are just getting used to their voices and styles, that you won't put up a cast list until, say, the next day, or after formal auditions.

Schedules and Preparing for Rehearsals

I would set a good example for young actors by showing them that rehearsals will not just be "getting together"; I echo here that line from those Judy Garland/Mickey Rooney movies of the 1940s: "Hey kids, let's do a play to raise money for the football team so they can go to state!" Rather, rehearsals are formal, well-planned affairs—business. Therefore, I give them a rehearsal schedule before the first meeting, a calendar listing all rehearsal dates.

I would be even more specific. While the first date might simply say, "Read-through." and the second, "Blocking Act I," I would thereafter list for each date just what we are going to do. For example: "Monday, May 21, Rehearsal 2-5 p.m.: 2-3 p.m., Act I, scene i; 3-4 p.m., I.ii; 4-4:30 p.m., I.iii; 4:30-5 p.m., II.i." If an actor only appears in Act I, scene iii, then he or she will be ready to go onstage by 4:30 p.m., and know also that the scene work will be finished by 5 p.m. Precisely. I always stick to the schedule. In the midst of last-minute changes, bruised egos, anxieties about opening night, troubles with the set, an illness, or someone dropping out, the one thing everyone can count on is that from 4:30 to 5 p.m. on Monday, May 21, we will be rehearsing II.i. If you can rely on your actor to be on time and for parents to be on time, then that same actor doesn't need to come to rehearsals until 4:25 p.m. Actors appreciate directors sensitive to their schedules and to other demands on their time.

A ten-page scene generally gets double the rehearsal time of a four-page scene, and a scene involving ten characters might get more time than one, though of equal length, involving only two. In a four-week rehearsal period, make sure that each scene gets—this is my average—six individual rehearsal slots, slots in proportion to the length and complexity of the scene. In the third week you might have to say "Run act I," and all actors should be present at 2 p.m. Or you might list, "Spot work, TBA [to be announced]." I never know until we are in rehearsal what parts of the play might require special work.

Actors should also know on what date you will use real props, instead of rehearsal props; on what date you will work on the sound, or the lighting, or the costumes. These, by the way, should come as early as possible during the final week of rehearsal. Of course, changes will invariably be made in the schedule; things come up that no one could have anticipated. But even when changes are made, the announcement of the change should come as early as possible.

I think it is wise, with four weeks of rehearsal, to have the play in good shape by the end of the third week, because that final week may involve moving from a rehearsal hall to the actual stage and bring in lighting, props, costumes, and sound. During technical rehearsals, the actors need to get used to stopping a scene so that a lighting adjustment can be made or so that the set designer can change the position of a chair. One of those rehearsals will be a "dry tech" that moves from cue to cue for lighting and sound. (See Sandria Reese's essay, "The Soul of a Man Is His Clothes.")

Let me make a radical suggestion about another type of "scheduling." My actors laugh when I do this, dismissing me as an obsessive-compulsive. Some directors like to figure out the blocking during rehearsal; that is, they go into the play with a completely blank sheet. Others have a general idea of what they want, where exits and entrances are to be made, the basic stage pictures. Still others are very specific about certain important crosses and business involving stage movement. None of these approaches is necessarily right; the right way is the one that works best for the specific director and his or her actors, one that leads to the play's being ready by opening night, indeed by the dress rehearsal.

Since I, however, am terrified of vacuums, I figure out all of the blocking weeks before rehearsals start. My director's copy is filled with "John X [cross] SR [stage right] on this line." Or "Betty turn and face US [upstage] as he lifts his cocktail glass." Then, I send the blocking notes to my actors, asking that they write in pencil in their scripts all blocking notes for their character. If we spend the second and third night of rehearsals on blocking, we already have a head start. Lots of adjustments will be made on those two evenings. The actors have, up to this point, just pictured the movement in their minds whereas actually doing it onstage is another matter. A cross I wanted may not work because I forgot that the character to be confronted is standing downstage instead of near the upstage exit. The actors are free to offer alternatives. If an actor's revision is better, then I go with it. Such flexibility builds up confidence, the sense of having a hand in the play. As with the scheduling, giving out the blocking before rehearsals signals to the actors that since I am prepared, they will surely want to be equally prepared.

Talking with Actors before Rehearsals

I think it is a good idea to hold individual conferences with the actors before rehearsals begin, perhaps two or three weeks before the read-through (see below). This is a good time to chat about the character, to answer technical questions, and to give a sympathetic ear to any anxieties. Of course, at this early date you can't expect to have the character all figured out, although some actors, afraid of letting things sink in more gradually during the rehearsal process, may want to get a hold on the character this early. This is a good time to be alone with your actor, to be, as I called it recently in a note to one of my actors, a "fellow traveler, about to journey with your actor into the world of the play." Most certainly, you don't want to be prescriptive here, and so if the actor asks you, "How should I play him?" you will want to be noncommittal. This talk can be a delightfully free period where nothing needs to be settled, where nothing is absolute (See Sibyl Lines' essay, "Adventuring between the Lines.").

Working with the Actors

I have hinted above at what I want to say here. Indeed, these suggestions follow inevitably from what I have said in "Scheduling and

Preparing for Rehearsals." Our experience in the GACA's "Shakespeare, Summer, and Kids" program is that the kids are their most productive, learn the most, and—of no small importance—perform best when there are clear rules that are enforced.

Rehearsals must start on time. An actor arriving two seconds late, or two minutes late, or ten minutes late, is late—and this is inexcusable. When this happens with adult actors, my stage manager makes the actor apologize to the company. He or she has wasted the time of every member of the cast; the rehearsal was impoverished by the lateness. A good actor arrives ten to twenty minutes before the rehearsal and uses the extra time to warm up or to study lines. With an adult company, an actor who is late a second time would be dropped from the cast. I am always up-front about this. I do not want to hear excuses. Of course, there will be emergencies, but my experience has been that the bad actor, the mediocre actor, usually has a disproportionate share of such "excuses."

Now, you might want to be less strict with your actors; you might not want to have a late actor apologize before the company. Still, I think enforcing rules for prompt attendance at rehearsals does great service to those young actors, and I believe this is precisely what they want. With young actors, you can use rehearsal rules to teach responsibility and maturity.

Rehearsals are not social occasions. The only talking going on occurs onstage, between the director and the actors. Other actors, sitting in the house, waiting for their scene, should not talk. Rather, they memorize lines, or go outside and read lines together, being sure, by the way, to tell the stage manager where they are, perhaps even asking the stage manager to give them a specific time to return. In addition, I never allow an actor, during rehearsal, to criticize a fellow actor. The offended actor can speak to me in private, and I will consider what he or she says—it goes no further than that. I also do not allow eating in the theater.

The rehearsal is a wonderful time, a period of discovery, of bonding among actors, that exquisite moment when the director collaborates with the actor, when the play is shaped, when opinions are explored. It is all that and more. But it is not a social get-together.

If you choose to be more lenient with young actors, establish your guidelines early. Will "lenient" mean four rather than two unexcused latenesses? You may want to make allowance for the kid whose parents don't communicate as effectively as they should on the issue of transportation. The kid with no experience in theater, who has never been in a company before, will take some breaking in. Still, bearing down on the issue of promptness is not unreasonable. You may need to demonstrate how it can bear fruit throughout the rehearsal; being a member of a smooth-functioning, orderly team where personal needs take second place to the good of the show can lead to enhanced self-esteem and enhanced performance in that larger world offstage.

Actors should bring pencils, perhaps even notebooks to make changes or suggestions from the director in their script. This should be their responsibility. I worked with one professional stage manager who charged a dollar if they came without a pencil and tried to borrow one from her.

If you give adequate notice, telling the actors to be off-book—to have lines memorized—for a certain scene on a certain day, then there should be no excuse for an actor not being off-book. At that stage any actor still needing a script retards fellow actors and fouls up the rhythms and connections. An actor not off-book by an agreed-upon date penalizes fellow actors. If an actor is having trouble with lines, make provisions to help him or her. I know a director who refuses to let an actor not off-book into rehearsals; the stage manager, instead, reads the part until the actor is prepared.

If you cast the show before the first rehearsal, and if the actors have a script well in advance of that date, it is not unreasonable to ask that they be off-book by the first rehearsal or at least by the fourth one, after you have put in the blocking. Actors generally memorize lines best when they are actually moving about the stage, in the presence of fellow actors: they know that they say such and such a line as they cross downstage right, or that when this character appears upstage left, they are to deliver a welcome. So, nothing beats an actual rehearsal for getting off-book. But getting off-book early has tremendous advantages. As director, you can get to all those nuances, all the subtext, and all the physical subtlety only when actors are onstage without scripts, when their focus is not on remembering lines but exploring the character.

Good directors, the saying goes, never give an actor a line reading. They never tell them what to do. If you tell the actor to cross stage left on that line, the cross needs to make sense to the actor, needs to fit his or her own reading of what the character would do. If the actor questions one of your movement directions, be prepared to explain your reasoning.

Conversely, when an actor makes a suggestion, try it out; never look at a suggestion as a challenge to your authority. Assume that the suggestion grows out of his or her interest or involvement in the show. You will make the final judgment, to be sure, but ultimately it is not an issue of boss and worker, leader and follower.

Remember that the role is the actor's. You are only an additional pair of eyes and ears. The actor has the part; he or she will not, cannot, should not play the character exactly as you might, if positions were reversed. The actor should be glad to use suggestions you make, indeed, should always try them out, whatever misgivings he or she might have. And you should be no less glad to incorporate any suggestions from the actor that fall within the concept of the play. Both of you have the same final goal: to make the show as good as possible, to be the best possible translator of the author's intentions. Shakespeare, I like to remind my actors, is dead, and so we cannot ask him what he meant here or what his character's object was there. And even if the playwright were alive and ready for consultation, his voice, however important, would be just one of many influencing a production. When the author decides to express himself in a public medium such as theater, he or she gives up exclusive rights to the play.

Avoid speaking prescriptively, resist a limited sense of directing, however tempting, however an actor may beg for the answer. If an actor does something clearly wrong, like exiting before he should or upstaging other characters, then you should put your foot down. But such moments constitute only a tiny minority of the rehearsal process.

Phrases like "What if," "Do you think," and "I think" always work better than "You should" or "You need to." Actors want feedback; they want ideas; they want a strong director. But, like all of us, they rebel at dictators. They know that you have the final control over the production, that you can, if you wish, insist that they do this or not do that. But insisting almost never works. And remember, however central the director may be to the production, it is the actor who owns the part.

Some directors give notes at the end of the scene; others wait until the end of the rehearsal, and then, with the company gathered around, give notes. For me it is important to give notes efficiently and quickly. If we have one hour to rehearse the opening scene of a play for the initial time, I first have the actors run the scene, just to get used to things. Then I have them run it again. This time I give three or four minutes of notes immediately afterward, and let them run it a third time, trying to incorporate my suggestions.

Next, I do a "stop and go," which involves my standing onstage with the actors, keeping out of the way, and stopping the scene anytime I think something needs to be corrected or clarified or changed completely. I may spot something interesting or revealing we might want to discuss and experiment with. I always remind the actors that I'm on their side: I want to understand what they're doing. Because I am more familiar with the play than the audience will probably be, if I am having trouble, we clearly have a problem with clarity.

This stop-and-go can be a little disconcerting to actors. Sometimes they won't get more than a few lines into the scene before I stop them. After stopping and discussing, they need to get right back into character and continue where we left off. Remember that the actors may need to back up a bit in order to get back in the mood or they may need to start at a clear point in the scene (a beat, a distinctive bit of blocking). That's fine. But I might stop them again in just a few seconds, or perhaps in a minute. But stop I will, whenever I think that something needs to be examined: a delivery, a cross, a gesture, a motive, an actor's grasp of her character's object or subtext, even something mechanical. If an actor picks up a coffee cup, where does he put it down so that he can lift both hands in the air in frustration at the line on the next page?

Attending to issues on the spot rather than waiting until the end of the scene has several advantages. The moment will never be as fresh. Stop-and-go provides much more detailed coverage than later discussions. Recognize that it can be hard for an actor to break character constantly and go over the passage with the director. But if done properly, stop-and-go has the effect of that proverbial fine-tooth comb.

My approach to directing may reflect my view of audiences: they are all potential narcoleptics. You need to amuse, entertain, interest them second by second in the show. If an actor delivers the first line magnificently but the flops on the second one, the latter stays in the audience's mind. As actor, as director, we are always proving ourselves to them. Since a play happens moment by moment, an audience will turn off, tune out, and fall asleep as soon as the scene stops working or an actor fails to project or the energy level dips or a piece of stage action seems gratuitous. Of course, you can build up a bank account with the audience: if you were fantastic in the previous scene, they will greet you eagerly in your next appearance. But if that second appearance fails to live up to the promise generated by the first, watch out: they will nod off in an instant. Stop-and-go can capture those moments to make sure that the production works second by second, line by line, word by word.

Other methods can also work well. If your schedule permits, it's useful to have an improv night, where the actors, in character, are given situations and asked to play them the way their character might. This exercise helps firm up each actor's concept of his character's life outside the play. Once the actors are secure with their characters, I like to spend a night where each actor shares with the company his character's history from birth up to the present moment of the play. Here, the actor reveals to us the character's subtext, all those events and influences that made him or her the person we meet in the play.

If I have time, I like to have a rehearsal of the more immediate subtext, all those things the character says to himself or herself, thinks consciously, feels semiconsciously, all those unversed lines that never quite make their way into the text but influence the way the actor plays the text. When we devote a rehearsal to playing the subtext, the characters speak to each other directly from the heart, with that private voice otherwise known only to its owner, exposing themselves in a way that we do not when we observe the social limits of public language. If the hostess offers you another piece of her cake after the last one almost made you throw up, you generally follow social convention to avoid hurting her feelings, "I'd love another piece." During this rehearsal, you voice all those thoughts and feelings: "Oh, sure, I'd love another piece. Just to see if I can get it down without barfing. How can this idiot be so naïve about her cake? Does she have no taste? Still, except for being such a bad cook, she's a nice person, even lent me money when I was down and out, and I couldn't for the world upset her by refusing another piece."

One final word on working with actors. I would never begin a rehearsal without doing warm-up exercise. Stretch the parts of the body and the voice; emphasize physical and verbal exercises that underscore connections among actors, the sense of company, as well as those which let the actors focus on the business at hand and shut out the world offstage. Every director has his or her own exercises. Let me describe my typical warm-up schedule. If the call on performance night is, say, 7 p.m. and the actors take fifteen minutes to complete their physical preparation (e.g., costume, makeup), I will, typically, have the stage manager call them onstage at 7:15 for ten to fifteen minutes of warm-up before the house opens at 7:30. I might have a member of the company conduct these warm-ups, rotating the task among the actors. Sometimes, however, I like to conduct the warm-up myself, to remind the actors that I am one of them, just another person in the cast.

If you end the exercises by 7:25, the actors have time to finish their costuming and makeup. There is even five minutes left, before the house opens, to have a fight call. Fight choreographers always want a run-through, for reasons of both art and safety, of any fight sequence in the performance. Opening the house a half-hour before curtain allows the audience to settle in, to chat, to be "un-corked like a bottle of wine, to aerate, before being served," as I like to tell my house manager.

I would never, never let my actors go onstage without a warm-up. One of the reasons that many productions seem so stiff for the first ten minutes or so is, I think, because the actors are warming up during the play, rather than beforehand.

Just before curtain, I go backstage and give each of the actors a kiss.

The Run and After

Ideally, the stage manager will take over the play from opening night onward. You should stand at the back of the audience, or sit up in the booth with the techies, and watch the production, in particular your audience's reaction. If something is not working, if that funny bit you thought would have them laughing in the aisles, plays to dead silence, then rework it. Note those moments and tell the actors about them. How attentive is the audience? Does anyone leave before the play is over? Count any yawns. Does the audience focus on the production or do they chat?

You should always have a house manager, responsible not only for making sure everyone gets seated–before the curtain–but also alert for any problem in the audience: an unruly spectator here, a couple there more intent on kissing than watching the play. I once had an audience member answer a cell phone during a production, telling the caller in a loud voice that he was "watching a great play." Within seconds my house manager had the cell-phone man by the arm and escorted him, despite his praise, out of the theater.

Once the play starts, I don't think anyone should be seated. Some people, perhaps used to the more relaxed behavior of rock concerts, think they can stroll into the house five minutes late. I never allow this. Once the play starts–that is, once the house lights go off and stage lights come on–we lock the door to the theater, and the house manager stands outside to tell latecomers that not only can they not be admitted until intermission but that if they choose to leave–they usually do–we cannot refund their tickets. If you want to be more informal with your audience, that is certainly our choice. I believe, however, that audiences have obligations, as do actors and directors, and among those obligations are arriving on time and, once in the theater, focusing on the production.

My practice is to give notes about the performance the next day, usually in the form of individual letters taped to the dressing room mirrors. I give the actors compliments, make suggestions, ask them to reassess something which is not working, and, of course, invite them to talk at greater length with me if they wish. Some directors only come opening night; others watch selective performances. I am there at all performances and, as a consequence, give notes each day of the run. When the play is finished, the audience files out of the theater. My practice, again perhaps draconian, is not to let the audience wait in the theater to see the actors, let alone to go backstage. Rather, my house manager tells them politely–including parents and dates–that the actors are changing, will be told "you are waiting for them," and will come outside as soon as possible. Again, you might want to be less rigid. Keeping the audience outside might not be possible with certain playing spaces. For me, the theater is a special place where something important has just happened. The stage is only for the actors, not a waiting area for well-wishers. When the actors leave the stage, after taking curtain calls, the audience leaves the house: the theater is abandoned, only to come alive the following performance.

On one level, the production is complete. But it will always resonate with all those who participated. Since we all have a tendency to look back as well as forwards, I always wait about two weeks after the final performance and hold a post-play discussion with the entire company, including the designers and crew members. By that time we have gained some perspective on our successes and failures. That meeting always proves a good time to analyze what went well and what could have gone better. Equally important, it allows all of us to renew those friendships and that sense of a company which developed during rehearsal and run.

Index